English Elements
Refresher A2

10 units

with back-up material

including 1 CD

Sue Morris

Max Hueber Verlag

We would especially like to thank

- **Dr Gill Woodman** (Language Teacher and Tutor, Department for English and American Studies, Ludwig-Maximilians-University, Munich) for advice and feedback on English Elements – Refresher A2.

- **Olivia Rainsford** (English Teacher and Teacher Trainer, Erlangen) for writing the Revision Units in English Elements – Refresher A2.

4.	3.	2.		Die letzten Ziffern
2010	09	08	07	06	bezeichnen Zahl und Jahr des Druckes.

Alle Drucke dieser Auflage können, da unverändert, nebeneinander benutzt werden.
1. Auflage
© 2005 Max Hueber Verlag, 85737 Ismaning, Deutschland
Redaktion: Rebecka Howe, München
Druck: Druckerei Appl, Wemding
Printed in Germany
ISBN 3–19–202732–0

Introduction to English Elements – Refresher A2

This student's book is for you if:
– you learnt some English at school or in a course at the VHS, but this was a long time ago.
– you can understand more than you can say in English.
– you want to consolidate and re-activate your knowledge of English in a short time.

In this book you will find all you need to refresh your English. It doesn't start at a high level. The progression in the first units is a gentle one so that you get used to speaking English again using topics that are of interest to you. Look on the **contents pages** to see what these topics are and what you can find in each unit.

Students want to learn English for many different reasons. If you want to communicate in everyday situations, or to speak English on holiday and book hotels or rent cars on-line, there are activities in the book for you. If you want to learn English because you need it at work, the **job talk** sections in the units will help you.

There is a grammatical progression in the book because we hope you want to be accurate when you learn English again, but if you want to speak English, you need more than grammar.
In this book there are lots of activities to help you learn more vocabulary and to practise your speaking, listening, reading and writing. All the listening activities from the units and the revision units are on the **CD** so that you can hear different people speaking English and listen to English at home.

We hope you can come to your English course regularly, but if you can't, there is a **key** to all the exercises so that you can check the answers to the exercises that you missed. If you need more practice outside the classroom, the **back-up** section after each unit offers exercises you can do at home and there are three **revision units** that can help you, too.

You will learn not only about the students in your group, but from them as well. When the teacher asks questions from the **culture corner** section, we hope you will tell us about your country if you were not born in Germany.

Everyone learns in a different way. In the units you will also find **learning tips** which give you ideas about how your learning can be more effective.

When you finish this book you can take the English Language Certificate A2 to show how successful all your hard work was. If you don't want to take an examination, then you can learn more English in books 3 and 4 in the *English Elements* series.

Above all, we wish you lots of fun learning English with *English Elements – Refresher A2!*

Your English Elements team

Contents

Contents chart

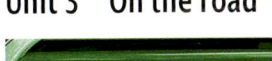

Contents chart

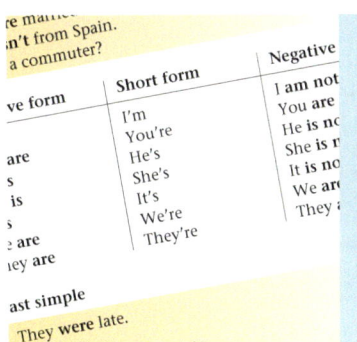

1   Names

> What's his first name?

> What's her surname?

a   Do you know the names of these famous people?
How do you spell his surname? How do you spell her first name?

 **b**   Listen to the dialogues and write down the names that you hear.

1. _____
2. _____
3. _____

c   Now think of a famous person. Spell his or her surname. Then ask your partner:
What is his/her first name?

2   Nice to meet you

 a   Listen to the dialogue first and fill in the missing information in the text below.

> Hello, my name's Robert.
> Nice to _____ you.

> _____ to meet you, too.
> My name's Ludmilla.

> And what's your _____?

> Taguieva.

> Can you _____ that, please, Ludmilla?

> _____. It's T-A-G-U-I-E-V-A.

> Thanks.

> You're _____.

b Over to you. Talk to your partner. Ask about his/her first name and surname. Look at dialogue **2a** on page 8 for help.

c Look at the list 'My class' in the back-up section on page 17. Fill in your first name and surname. Then ask your teacher to spell her/his first name and surname. Now stand up and ask the people in your class to spell their names and surnames.

Personal pronouns - Determiners		
I	–	**my** name
you	–	**your** name
he	–	**his** name
she	–	**her** name
we	–	**our** name
they	–	**their** names

 Check the grammar reference section on page 120 for more information on pronouns.

3 Where are you from?

a Paul Hogan's from Australia. Mel Gibson's from Australia, too. They're both from Australia.

- ● Where are you from?
- ■ I'm from Germany. And you?
- ● I'm from Poland.

Germany is a country. Poland is a country, too.

Look at this list. Can you find the names of the countries in this list?

asturai — *Austria*

rssiua

hnugray

stwzilrenda

iltya

cczhe rpebilcu

crioata

sinap

psriea

jpnaa

rmoanai

b Now stand in a circle. Your teacher will begin.

Example: I'm from _____ . Where are you from?

Now report back.

In our class there are students from _____ countries.

There are _____ students from Germany but there are also students from

_____ .

_____ is from _____

_____ and _____ are from _____ .

Plural of nouns	**The verb 'to be'**		
For plurals add -s: 1 student 2 students	*long form* I am … You are …	*short form* I'm … You're …	*question form* Am I …? Are you … ?
Be careful with spelling: 1 country 2 countries and pronunciation: 1 address 2 addresses	He is … She is … It is …	He's … She's … It's …	Is he …? Is she …? Is it …?
Some plurals are irregular: 1 child 2 children	We are … They are …	We're … They're …	Are we …? Are they …?

 Check the grammar reference section on pages 120 and 125 for more information.

4 I'm or I've got?

a Match the words below with **I'm** or **I've got**.

> married ▮ single ▮ a partner ▮ a son ▮ divorced ▮ a bicycle ▮
> a member of a fitness club ▮ over 20 ▮ interested in football ▮ three children ▮
> a dog ▮ under 40 ▮ a cat ▮ German ▮ a car

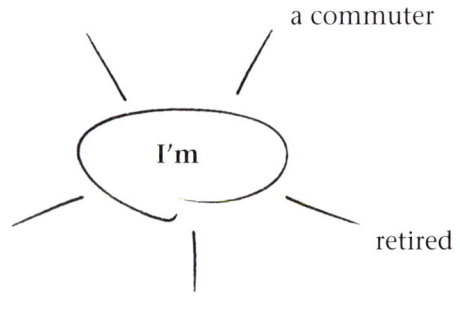

a commuter

I'm

retired

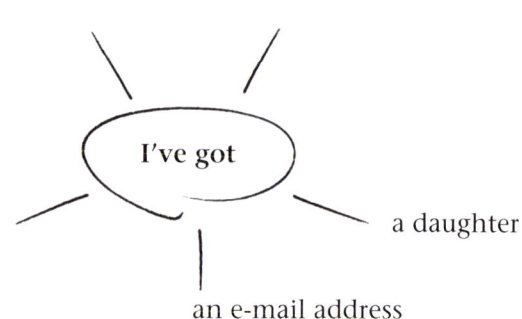

I've got

a daughter

an e-mail address

b   Look at the words from **4a** for one minute.
Then close your book.
Your teacher will say a word. Match it with **I'm** or **I've got**.

> ## Learning Tip – Vocabulary
> Word wheels can be a good way to remember vocabulary. It helps you remember words that can go together.
> Add more words when you find them.

c   More about you. Choose the information that is true for you. Add a little bit more, if you can.

Example: I'm not married. I'm over 20 and under 40. I've got a dog. His name's Snoopy.

Me   *My partner*

I'm married / single / divorced.   _____

I'm over 20/40 and under 40/60.   _____

I'm retired.   _____

I'm a member of a fitness / football / skiing / … / club.   _____

I've got one / two / three / four / child / children.   _____

I haven't got any children.   _____

I've got / I haven't got a dog / cat. His/her name is …   _____

I've got / I haven't got a garden.   _____

I've got / I haven't got a car.   _____

I've got / I haven't got a bicycle.   _____

I've got / I haven't got an e-mail address.   _____

I'm a commuter.   _____

I'm interested in …   _____

I'm from Germany / Austria / Switzerland / …   _____

d   Now tell your partner.
Then listen to your partner and write down what is true for her/him.

Have got		
short form	*negative form*	*question form*
I've got	I haven't got	
You've got	You haven't got	Have you got …?
He's got	He hasn't got	Has he got …?
She's got	She hasn't got	Has she got …?

➡ Look in the back-up section on page 14 for more practice with I'm and I've got.

e   Tell the group three things about your partner from **4d**.

5 My family

 3

a Listen to the CD and fill in the names on this family tree.

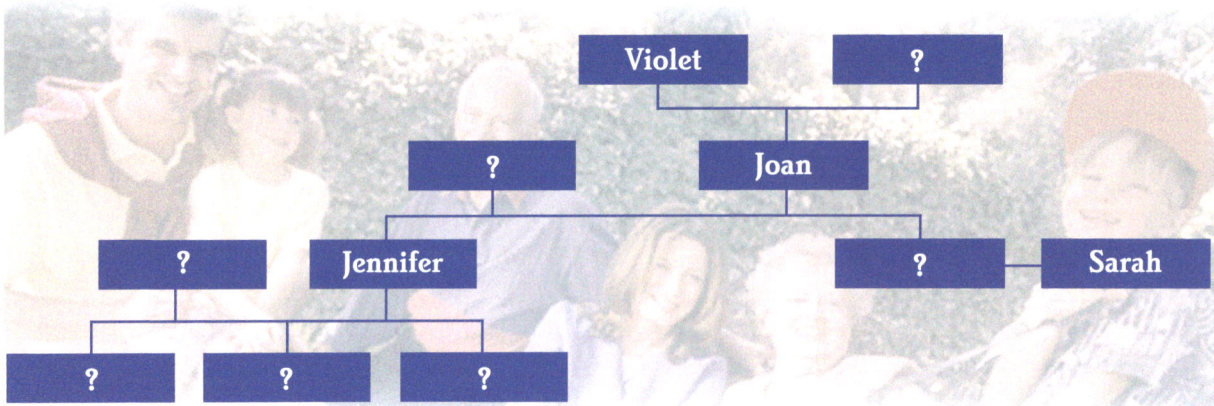

b Now write the first names of five people in your family.
Work with a partner. Show the names to your partner. Ask questions about the names.

Example: Who's Robert?

's	Can be short for 'is'.	's	Can be possessive.
	Example: He's from Germany.		*Example:* Klaus is Barbara's husband.
	(He is from Germany.)		(the husband of Barbara)

 Look in the back-up section on pages 15–16 for more work with 's and family words.

6 First name or family name?

Read these short stories and say if the statements are true or false.

My name is Lee Kwai Sin. Lee is my family name. In a Chinese name the first name is the family name. My husband's name is Lee See Chai. I live in a house with my husband, my son and daughter, my mother and father-in-law and my father's old grandmother. She is ninety. My husband has got two brothers. The brothers are both under forty but my husband is over forty. In a Chinese family the eldest son always lives with his mother and father.

	True	False
1. See Chai is Kwai Sin's wife.	☐	☐
2. Lee is a Chinese surname.	☐	☐
3. Lee See Chai lives with his mother and father-in-law.	☐	☐
4. Lee Kwai Sin's grandmother is ninety.	☐	☐
5. Lee Kwai Sin has got two brothers-in-law.	☐	☐

My name is Fatimah binti Din. Fatimah is my name and Din is my father's name. So my name is Fatimah, Din's daughter. My mother's name is Anizah binti Zainal because her father's name is Zainal. I live in a house in the country with my father, my mother, my two brothers and my sister. I haven't got a dog, because they are forbidden for a Muslim, but I've got a cat.

	True	False
1. Fatimah is a Malaysian surname.	☐	☐
2. Fatimah's mother's name is Anizah.	☐	☐
3. Fatimah's grandfather's name is Zainal.	☐	☐
4. Fatimah has got three brothers.	☐	☐
5. Fatimah hasn't got a cat.	☐	☐

What do you know about family names in other countries?

7 Look back at the unit

Here are some instructions in English from this unit. The words are in the wrong order.
Sort them out.

Example: the listen dialogues to → Listen to the dialogues.

1. down the that write you hear names _____
2. the information fill missing in _____
3. a work partner with _____
4. teacher ask your _____
5. partner tell your _____
6. in the look section back-up _____
7. them sort out _____
8. the partner names to show your _____
9. the three group things tell partner about your _____
10. the choose true you for words are that _____
11. in a stand circle _____
12. teacher will begin your _____

What is the German for these instructions?

Back-up

1 Plurals

a Write down the plural of the words below.

1. sister _____
2. student _____
3. country _____
4. family _____

5. daughter _____
6. child _____
7. address _____
8. dictionary _____

b Now put the words in these sentences.

1. There are ten _____ in my English class.
2. How many e-mail _____ have you got?
3. Mr and Mrs Mason have got three _____. One son and two _____.
4. I've got one brother and two _____.
5. I've got two _____. One is English-German and one is German-English.
6. Students in my English class are from five different _____.
7. Jones is a surname from Wales. Many _____ have this surname.

2 Sentences

Write sentences from these lists of words.

I	hasn't got	retired.
He	is	commuters.
They	has got	a daughter.
We	are	two sons.
	am	interested in food.
	have got	a dog and two cats.
	haven't got	divorced.
	isn't	over 30.
	aren't	under 40.
		a garden.
		single.
		a partner.
		two e-mail addresses.
		from Germany.
		a car.
		a bicycle.

Examples: He isn't from Germany.
They are divorced.

How many sentences can you write that are true for you?

3 'Are you' or 'have you got'?

Write five questions with 'Have you got ...?'

_____
_____
_____
_____
_____

Write two questions with 'Are you ...?'

_____
_____
_____
_____

Ask the questions in the next English lesson.

4 Families

a   Who is it? Choose from the list of words.

cousin ▪ niece ▪ sister-in-law ▪ granddaughter ▪ grandson ▪ aunt ▪ uncle ▪ grandmother ▪ nephew ▪ brother-in-law ▪ mother ▪ grandfather

1. My sister's husband is my _____ .
2. Your brother's wife is your _____ .
3. My father's wife is my _____ .
4. His mother's mother is his _____ .
5. My brother's son is my _____ .
6. Her grandmother's husband is her _____ .
7. My father's brother is my _____ .
8. Your mother's sister is your _____ .
9. Her sister's daughter is her _____ .
10. His uncle's son is his _____ .
11. My daughter's son is my _____ .
12. Her son's daughter is her _____ .

b In this little text change the words underlined. Choose from this list:

> they (x2) ▪ their (x2) ▪ she ▪ his ▪ her

Violet and Richard have got one daughter. <u>The daughter's</u> name is Joan. <u>Joan</u> is married to Joe. <u>Joan and Joe</u> have got two children. <u>The children's</u> names are Jennifer and Peter. Jennifer is married to Alan. <u>Jennifer and Alan</u> have got three children: one son – <u>the son's</u> name is Philip – and two daughters. <u>The daughters'</u> names are Melanie and Angela.

5 's

Underline the parts where 's is short for 'is' and circle where it is possessive.

Example: He's a commuter.   (He is …)
Ann's husband's retired.   (Ann's – possessive / … husband is …)

1. Peter's a member of a fitness club.   _____
2. Who's Barbara?   _____
3. He's retired.   _____
4. Jason's wife's a commuter.   _____
5. Her daughter's interested in books.   _____
6. His wife's name's Jane.   _____
7. His surname's Jackson.   _____
8. My sister's over fifty.   _____
9. Fatimah's a Malaysian surname.   _____

At the end of this unit I … :

- can say 'hello' and spell my name.
- can ask 'What's your name?' and 'Where are you from?'
- can ask questions with 'Are you …?' and 'Have you got …?'
- can read a short text about families in other countries.

✓✓ = I can do this easily.
✓ = I can do this.
✗ = I need to work on this.

Words and expressions from this unit for my personal **word bank** are:

_____

_____

Back-Up

My class

My first name:
_____

My surname:
_____

My teacher's first name:
_____

My teacher's surname:
_____

The students in my class

First name: **Surname:**

1. _____   _____
2. _____   _____
3. _____   _____
4. _____   _____
5. _____   _____
6. _____   _____
7. _____   _____
8. _____   _____
9. _____   _____
10. _____   _____
11. _____   _____
12. _____   _____
13. _____   _____
14. _____   _____
15. _____   _____

UNIT 2 In my free time

1   2   3   4

1 A dangerous hobby?

a Look at these pictures and match the numbers to the sentences below.

Number _____ is an energetic hobby.   Number _____ is a relaxing hobby.

Number _____ is an expensive hobby.   Number _____ is a creative hobby.

Number _____ is a dangerous hobby.   Number _____ is an exciting hobby.

b Work with a partner.

Partner A:
Think of a hobby. If you
don't know it in English ask: What's it called?

Partner B:
Ask your partner questions to find out
about this hobby.

Examples: Is it a dangerous hobby? (Yes, it is.)
               Is it an expensive hobby? (No, it isn't.)

> **Indefinite articles**
> **a**   dangerous hobby   **an**   expensive hobby
> **a**   creative hobby   **an**   exciting hobby
>
> You usually use **an** before the letters a/e/i/o/u.

➡ Look in the back-up section on page 26 for more work with 'a' and 'an'.

> **Note**
> **Questions with 'Is it …?' and short answers**
>
> Is it …?   – Yes, it is.
>   – No, it isn't.

c Now report back to the group.

2 Your free time

a Look at this list and then match the words to the words in the table below.

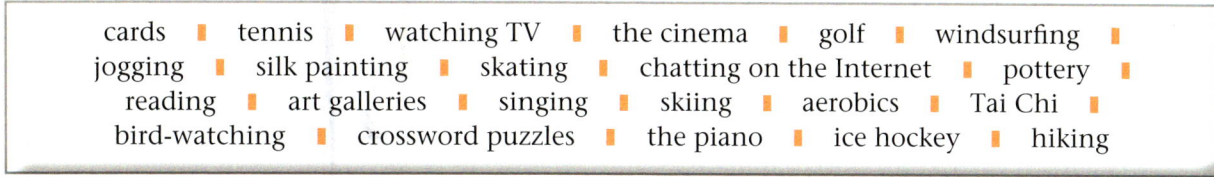

cards	tennis	watching TV	the cinema	golf	windsurfing
jogging	silk painting	skating	chatting on the Internet	pottery
reading	art galleries	singing	skiing	aerobics	Tai Chi
bird-watching	crossword puzzles	the piano	ice hockey	hiking

like	go	go to	play	do

Is your hobby on the list? Can you add your hobby?

b Now choose the words for your hobbies and write about them.

Example: I play ice hockey and go to the cinema in the winter and I go hiking and do a lot of photography in the summer.

> **Learning Tip – Vocabulary**
> It's useful to learn word partners – words that go together. Example: do aerobics, play golf etc.

3 In winter or in summer?

4

a Listen to four people talking about hobbies and fill in the missing information.

name	in the summer/dry season	in the winter/wet season
Bob		ice hockey
Jan		
Doug		
Shashi		

b Listen again and say if these sentences are true or false.

Jan

	True	False
Jan goes surfing along the coast in the summer.	☐	☐
He goes skiing in the winter.	☐	☐
He does a lot of photography in the summer.	☐	☐

Bob

	True	False
Bob is from Canada.	☐	☐
He plays ice hockey in the winter.	☐	☐
He goes hunting in the winter.	☐	☐
He plays in an ice hockey team.	☐	☐

Doug

Doug plays soccer and American football.	☐	☐
He goes swimming in the summer.	☐	☐

Shashi

Shashi plays cricket in the wet season.	☐	☐
He likes reading.	☐	☐

Check your answers with your partner.

C Look at your answers in **2b** and the information about Bob, Jan, Doug and Shashi.

I play ice hockey in the winter.

Bob _____ ice hockey in the winter.

I do photography in the summer.

Jan _____ a lot of photography in the winter.

> **Note**
> **What do we add to the verb for 'he/she'?**
> I play   He/she plays
> I do   He/she does

➡ Look in the back-up section on page 26 for some writing practice with this 's'.

4 Sounds /z/ and /s/

5 **a** Look at these two lists of words. Listen and decide which word you hear.

1. pens ☐ – pence ☐
2. bus ☐ – buzz ☐
3. Sue ☐ – zoo ☐
4. place ☐ – plays ☐
5. said ☐ – zed ☐
6. lose ☐ – loose ☐
7. Jews ☐ – juice ☐

b Work with a partner. Choose one word from each pair of words and dictate it to your partner. He or she writes it down. Compare notes.

5 Guess the hobbies

a Your teacher will give you the names of two students in your class. What are their hobbies? What do you think? Write the names and the hobbies on cards like this.

Astrid
skiing (yes/~~no~~)
the cinema (yes/~~no~~)
karate (~~yes~~/no)

b Now stand up and ask the two people questions.
Examples: Astrid, do you go skiing? – Yes, I do.
Do you go to the cinema? – Yes, I do.
Do you do karate? – No, I don't.

c How many correct guesses have you got?
Example: I've got two correct guesses:
Astrid goes skiing and she goes to the cinema.

d Our class profile. – Help your teacher make a list of hobbies and sports on the board.
Then listen to your teacher and answer her/his questions.

sports & hobbies	Astrid	Thomas	...	...
skiing	✓	✗		
cinema	✓			
karate				
reading		✓		
...				
...				
...				

Does Astrid go skiing? – Yes, she does.
Does Thomas go skiing? – No, he doesn't.

e Now talk about the students in your class.
Example: Thomas likes reading but he doesn't go skiing.

The present simple	Questions and answers in present simple
I play	Do you play tennis? – Yes, I do./No, I don't.
You play	Does Tatiana go skiing? – Yes, she does./No, she doesn't.
Thomas (he) plays	Do they do judo? – Yes, they do./No, they don't.
Tatiana (she) plays	
We play	
Thomas and Tatiana (they) play	

 Look in the grammar reference section for more information about verbs in the present tense.
Look in the back-up section on pages 26–27 for some practice.

6 Why not?

6 **a** Read and listen to these little dialogues. Listen for the different sounds in 'can' and 'can't'.

Which sound do you hear in 'can/can't'? [kən], [kæn] or [kɑ:nt] ?

1 ● Do you like chatting on the Internet?
■ No, I don't.
● Why not?
■ Well, I <u>can</u> type but I <u>can't</u> type fast and I don't understand all text messages.

2 ▲ <u>Can</u> YOU text?
◆ Yes, I <u>can</u>. It's easy!

b Do you use your mobile phone to send text messages? Can you understand these text messages?

2nite _____
HaPEBday _____
HaPEHolidAz _____
THNQ _____
URGr8 _____
CU _____
MunE$$$£££MunE _____
RUOK _____

Look in the key for the answers.

c A questionnaire: Answer the questions and then ask your partner the questions. Remember the correct sound for 'Can you …? – Yes, I can./No, I can't.' from **6a**.

Can you …	Me	Partner	Name
speak Russian?	Yes, I can./ No, I can't.	Yes, he/she can./ No, he/she can't.	
swim?			
operate a DVD player?			
order a beer in four languages?			
change the oil in your car engine?			
eat with chopsticks?			

d Tell the group about your partner.

Example: Peter can speak Russian.

Questions with 'Can …?' and short answers		
Can you …?	–	Yes, I can.
	–	No, I can't.

7 Games in different countries

a Work in two groups. Group A reads the text on this page about the game 'Sepak Takraw' and Group B reads the text about 'Kudoda' on page 106.

First look at these questions:

Is it an energetic game?

Is it a dangerous game?

Is it an expensive game?

Is it a team game or can you play alone?

How many people can play?

Do you need a lot of equipment to play this game?

Do you play this game inside or outside?

Can you have a winner? Who wins?

Group A

Sepak takraw
This is a sport for two teams. The name comes from two languages – 'sepak' means to kick in Malay and 'takraw' means ball in Thai. There are three players in each team. It's like volleyball but players can't hit the ball with their arms or hands. It's an energetic and entertaining sport. It isn't exactly dangerous but you can hurt yourself when you kick the ball and fall. It's not a very expensive sport because you only need a net 5 feet high and a ball made of rattan or plastic. You can play this outside or inside on a court that is like a badminton court. A player serves the ball and players on the team can only hit the ball three times before they send it over the net. If the other team doesn't send the ball back then the first team scores a point. The first team that wins 2 sets of 15 points wins the match.

Ask the people in your group or your teacher if you don't understand all the words.

b Your teacher will give you a number. Find the person with your number from group B and answer his/her questions about 'Sepak Takraw'.

c If you have access to the Internet you can find more information about 'Sepak Takraw' from: http://www.takrawworld.com

Games in different countries can help you to learn about different cultures and increase your knowledge of this new culture. What kind of games do you know?

8 Office talk

a Here are four everyday English conversations in the office. The lines are in the wrong order. Sort them out.

That's no problem. Would you like to play on Saturday?
That would be very nice.
Yes, I do. My handicap is not very good, though. It's 18.
Do you play golf?
Good. See you on Saturday.
Fine. I look forward to it.

Yes, I am. The local team in Canada is very good.
Are you interested in ice hockey?
I'm sorry, I can't this weekend.
Yes, that would be fine.
Would you like to go to a game on Saturday? I can get tickets from a friend.
And next week?
Fine. See you on Saturday then.

Would you like to go on a tour of Ludwig's castles?
Oh, yes. I'd like that very much.
Is this your first visit to Munich?
Yes, it is.
Good. I can book the tour for Saturday. See you then.
See you then. I look forward to it.

With milk and sugar?
Black with no sugar.
Sorry, I don't drink coffee, but tea would be nice.
Good morning. Can I help you?
Good morning. I've got an appointment with Mr. Harris.
I'm sorry, Mr Harris is still in a meeting.
That's OK. I'm early.
Do sit down. Would you like a coffee?

> **Note**
> Do you like …? *(every day, in general)*
> Would you like …? *(now, on one occasion)*

b Now practise conversations with a partner.

Would you like | a coffee?
a cup of tea?
a glass of water?

Would you like to | play golf?
go on a tour of the castles?

 Yes

That would be very nice
That would be fine.

No

I'm sorry, I can't.
Sorry, I don't drink/like …

c How many different ways can you say 'See you …'?

See you | later.
on Saturday.
…
…
…

 Everyday English

a Read this dialogue.

● Excuse me, does this bus go to Oxford Circus?
■ No, it doesn't. You want the number 7.
● Thanks very much.
■ You're welcome.

Now match the questions 1, 2, 3 to the answers a, b, c.

1. Excuse me, does this train stop in <u>Birmingham</u>?
2. Excuse me, does this bus go to <u>Heathrow</u>?
3. Excuse me, does the coach to <u>Bath</u> leave from here?

a. Yes, it does. It goes to all four <u>London airports</u>:
   Heathrow, Gatwick, Stansted and Luton.
b. No, it doesn't. You need stop number <u>4</u>. Over there
   where there's a queue.
c. No, it doesn't. You want the one from platform <u>9</u>.

 Listen to check your answers.

b Now practise the dialogues with a partner. You can
change the underlined words to make new dialogues.

➡ Look at the tapescript on page 134. Can you find
different ways of saying 'Thank you'?

Back-up

1 'a' or 'an'?

Put 'a' or 'an' in the blanks in these sentences.

1. He's _____ retired businessman.
2. He's _____ American football player.
3. Bungee jumping is _____ dangerous sport.
4. Her name's Ludmilla. That's _____ Russian name.
5. His name's Robert. That's _____ English name.
6. My father plays golf. It's _____ expensive hobby.
7. He's a commuter so he catches _____ early train every weekday morning.
8. Yoga is good for you because it's _____ relaxing hobby.
9. I don't think cricket is _____ interesting sport. I think it's very boring.
10. In the winter he goes swimming in _____ indoor swimming pool.
11. He's got _____ unusual hobby. He collects beer bottles.
12. Baseball is _____ typical American sport.
13. He's _____ energetic person and he plays golf and goes swimming in the summer and he plays football in the winter.
14. She has got _____ very creative hobby. She does silk painting.

2 About people

a Look at the information about these people. Write some sentences about them.

name	country	town	job	hobby
Sandra	England	Chester	an accountant	Tai Chi
Cameron	New Zealand	Christchurch	a lorry driver	rugby
Aznan	Malaysia	Penang	a doctor	badminton
Janet	Wales	Cardiff	an artist	bird-watching
Gary	Northern Ireland	Belfast	an airline pilot	fishing

Example: Sandra comes from England and lives in Chester. She works as an accountant. In her free time she does Tai Chi.

> **Note**
> Remember the third person **s** in 'she liv**es**' and 'she do**es**'.

b Choose the correct form. The first one has been done for you.

Andy and Denise *live/~~lives~~* in Glasgow. *He/they* have got two children, Fraser and Olivia. Denise *work/works* as an accountant for a big company in Glasgow. She *gets/get* to work by bus. Andy is a writer so he *don't travel/doesn't travel* to his office every morning, he *works/work* at home. He *get/gets* up early and *starts/start* work at six o'clock because he *collect/collects* the children from school when they *finish/finishes* at 4 o'clock. He *make/makes* supper for them and then he and Denise *has/have* dinner together when she *come/comes* home at 6.30 or 7.00 in the evening. Fraser and Andy *like/likes* skating. They *go/goes* skating on the lake in the park when it is frozen in the winter. Denise *don't like/doesn't like* skating. She and Olivia *go/goes* swimming in the summer and in the winter. In the summer they *swim/swims* outside and in the winter they *swim/swims* in the big indoor swimming pool. "I really *love/loves* life in Glasgow," *say/says* Andy. "The people *are/is* friendly and we *enjoy/enjoys* our free time."

3 'Do you ...?' or 'Can you ...?'

Make questions with these words and then answer them.

Do you ...? / Can you ...?

	get to work by train?
	drive to work?
	drive a BMW?
	drink tea for breakfast?
	live near Berlin?
	eat with chopsticks?
	swim?
	ride a bicycle?
	drive a tractor?
	play football in a team?
	watch TV in the evening?
	play chess?
	speak Italian?
	like chocolate?
	play tennis in the summer and in the winter?

Example: Can you play chess? – No, I can't.
Do you travel to work by train? – No, I don't.

4 Vowels and hidden words

Take out the extra vowels to find the missing word. All the words are from this unit.

eiceuhockeey   *ice hockey*   oopeeriate   _____

pootteeray   _____   ewinenoer   _____

piianoa   _____   eequipomient   _____

iceinoemoa   _____   exciitoieng   _____

ophotoogereaphey   _____   idaangerouis   _____

✓ At the end of this unit I ... :

	✓✓	✓	✗
• can ask people about their hobbies and talk about my hobbies.	☐	☐	☐
• can understand text messages.	☐	☐	☐
• can read and understand a short text about games in different cultures.	☐	☐	☐
• can ask and answer questions with 'Do you ...?' and 'Would you ...?'	☐	☐	☐
• can understand people asking for information about trains etc.	☐	☐	☐

✓✓ = I can do this easily.
✓ = I can do this.
✗ = I need to work on this.

Words from this unit for my personal **word bank** are:

_____

_____

On the road

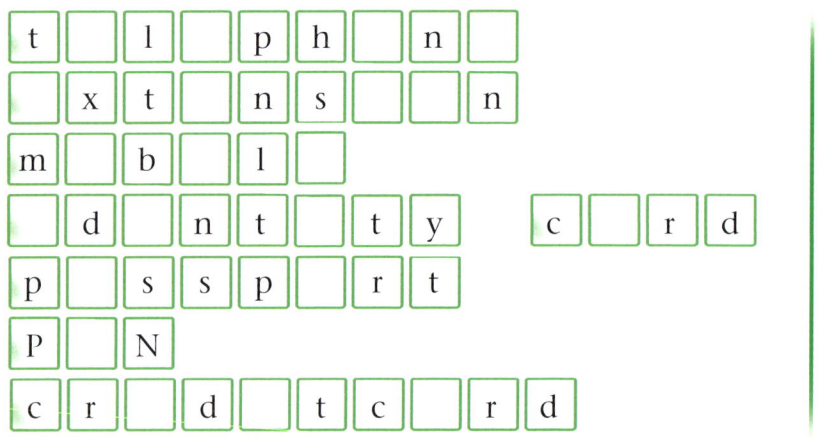

---

1 **What's his car registration number?**

a Look at the photos and match the numbers to the sentences below.

1. Kornelia comes from Gdańsk. What's her car registration number? ___
2. José drives a Volkswagen. What's his car registration number? ___
3. Klaus lives in Vienna. What's his car registration number? ___
4. Kim comes from the Netherlands. What's her car registration number? ___

b Have you got a car? What's your car registration number?

---

2 **Numbers**

a What other words can you put together with 'number'? Can you guess from these prompts? The vowels are missing.

t _ l _ p h _ n _
_ x t _ n s _ _ n
m _ b _ l _
_ d _ n t _ t y   c _ r d   **number**
p _ s s p _ r t
P _ N
c r _ d _ t c _ r d
...
...

Can you add any more?

What colour are registration numbers in your country? Can you see where a car comes from when you look at the registration number?

b Can you guess what is missing? Listen and write in the missing word.

A: What's your _____ number?
B: It's 0044 1729830468.

A: What's your _____ number?
B: 3920.

A: What's your _____ number?
B: 3750 30123822006.

A: What's your _____ number?
B: It's a secret!

A: What's your _____ number?
B: O177 456 4540.

c Work with a partner and dictate some telephone numbers to him or her.
Partner A looks at the file section on page 106 and partner B looks on page 109.

Numbers

1.

2.

3.

4.

Guess what country these numbers are from.

_____

_____

_____

_____

Now check your answers.

What do you say when you answer the phone in Italy? In Britain? In America? In a country you know? What is the international dialling code for your country? What is the area code for the town or city where you live?

d Over to you.
Now stand in a circle. Ask and answer some questions about numbers. Your teacher will begin.

What's your phone number?
What's your ...?

3 Questions and answers

a The questions in exercise **2b** all begin with the question word 'What ...?'. Here are some more question words. Choose from the list which goes in the blanks in the sentences below.

why ∎ how ∎ when ∎ who ∎ where

1. _____ do you play tennis? – At the weekend.
2. _____ do you live? – Near Zurich.
3. _____ do you meet in the pub every Friday? – My brother-in-law.
4. _____ do they get to work? – By car.
5. _____ does he work with? – John and Bill.
6. _____ do you like skiing? – Because it's wonderful to be in the fresh air.
7. _____ does he go skiing? – In Stubai.
8. _____ do they go to bed so early? – Because they get up at five o'clock.

b Match the following question words with possible answers.

When? _____

Where? _____

What? _____

Why? _____

How? _____

Who? _____

| coffee ▮ in London ▮ in Italy ▮ on foot ▮ at Christmas ▮ my brother ▮ |
| two colleagues ▮ by plane ▮ at six o'clock ▮ in the city ▮ toast ▮ squash ▮ |
| because it helps me sleep ▮ in the winter ▮ by car ▮ because it's good exercise ▮ |
| my boss ▮ because it's cheap ▮ by bus ▮ on my birthday ▮ in the summer |

c Over to you. Now make up your own questions with these question words.

What do you …?   Why do you …?   How do you …?
When do you …?   Where do you …?   Who do you …?

Now stand up and ask three people in your group these questions. Write down the answers.
Report back.

Wh-questions in the present tense

Where		you	live?	– In Berlin.
When	do	they	go on holiday?	– In August.
How			get to work?	– By tram.
Why	does	he	like his job?	– Because the pay is good!
When		she	start work?	– At half past six.

➡ Look in the back-up section on page 34 for more work with these question words.

4 ## Excuse me, have you got the time?

a Match the sentences with the picture numbers.

1. He gets up at six o'clock. ____
2. He catches the train at twenty to seven. ____
3. He starts work at half past seven. ____
4. He finishes work at quarter past five. ____

b Have you got the time? – Listen to these dialogues and write down the times that you hear.

1. _____   3. _____

2. _____   4. _____

c Over to you.

Work with a partner. In the top row draw four times on the clocks. Tell your partner the times on your clocks. Your partner listens and draws the times on the bottom row of clocks.
Then compare the clocks!

I get up at …   I go to bed at …   I have lunch at …   …
_____   _____   _____   _____

Note
Half past six or six-thirty in the morning.   6.30 a.m. (6.30)
Half past six or six-thirty in the evening.   6.30 p.m. (18.30)

➡ Look in the back-up section on page 34 for more work with times.

What time do people start and finish work in your country?

3

5 Prepositions

a Look at these sentences and underline 'at', 'on' and 'in'.

1. He finishes work at four o'clock on Friday.
2. His birthday is in July and it's on a Monday this year.
3. He goes on holiday to Tuscany in the summer.
4. He visits his mother at Easter.
5. In 2004 the 29th February was on a Sunday.
6. Children get presents on Christmas Day, that is on 25th December, in the UK.

Note
at the weekend (GB)
on the weekend (US)

Now match the prepositions with the correct explanation.

You can use	**at**	for days of the week and dates.
	on	for months, seasons and years.
	in	for times and festivals.

Learning Tip – Vocabulary

Try to collect expressions with these prepositions in your **word bank**. Have a page with 'at', a page with 'on' and a page with 'in'.

b Decide which preposition to use in the following sentences.

1. We go on holiday _____ August.
2. He starts work _____ six o'clock and finishes _____ 3.30.
3. My meeting is _____ 10 o'clock _____ Monday.
4. Australians celebrate Christmas _____ the summer not _____ the winter.
5. What do you do _____ the weekend?
6. Children get their presents _____ Christmas Day and not _____ Christmas Eve in England.
7. She was born _____ 29th February 1996. She was born _____ a leap year.

➡ Look in the back-up section on page 35 for more work with prepositions.

6 Rent a car

a Look at the details of cars you can rent and then decide which car is a good one for the people on page 33.

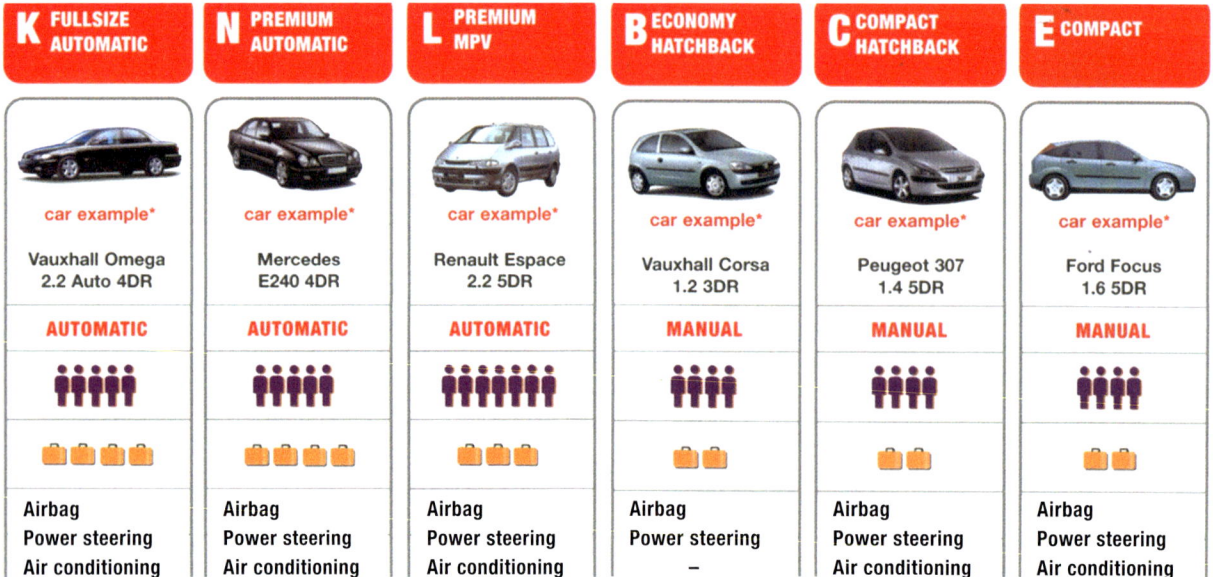

K FULLSIZE AUTOMATIC	N PREMIUM AUTOMATIC	L PREMIUM MPV	B ECONOMY HATCHBACK	C COMPACT HATCHBACK	E COMPACT
car example*	car example*	car example*	car example*	car example*	car example*
Vauxhall Omega 2.2 Auto 4DR	Mercedes E240 4DR	Renault Espace 2.2 5DR	Vauxhall Corsa 1.2 3DR	Peugeot 307 1.4 5DR	Ford Focus 1.6 5DR
AUTOMATIC	AUTOMATIC	AUTOMATIC	MANUAL	MANUAL	MANUAL
Airbag Power steering Air conditioning	Airbag Power steering Air conditioning	Airbag Power steering Air conditioning	Airbag Power steering –	Airbag Power steering Air conditioning	Airbag Power steering Air conditioning

1. Tom and Lisa have got four children. They take three suitcases with them when they go away. Tom likes automatic cars. _____

2. Jana and her husband Alex have got two children but they always take a lot of luggage with them when they go away for a weekend. Jana likes driving automatic cars but she doesn't like Mercedes cars. _____

3. Sarah is on a business trip to London. She is a freelance journalist so she doesn't have a company which pays for her car. She wants a small cheap car but she doesn't like Ford cars and she doesn't think that air conditioning is necessary in England. _____

4. Ranjit and Romy are on a business trip to Manchester. They want to rent a small car. Ranjit wants air conditioning and Romy doesn't like French cars. _____

b You want to book a rental car for your business trip to London. You want to pick it up at Heathrow airport in London at half past nine in the morning next Wednesday and you want to give it back at Heathrow airport on the following Friday at six o'clock in the evening.
Your flight number is LH 2345. Choose a car from the list in **6a** and fill in your details in the form below.

Driver details

Please provide the following information in order for us to process your reservation.

Title:	Mr ▾
First name / Surname:		
Address Line:	
Postcode / Town:		
Country of Residence:	▾
Telephone:	
Mobile phone:	
e-mail:	
Flight number:	

Rental requirements

Please enter your rental requirements

Country of rental:	United Kingdom Mainland ▾
Rental office:	– Please select a rental office – ▾ ➡ Search
Return office:	– Please select a rental office – ▾ ➡ Search
Car group:	Group C (e.g. Peugeot 307 1.4) ▾ ➡ Search
Pick up:	04 ▾ December ▾ 2003 ▾ 📅 09 ▾ 00 ▾
Return:	06 ▾ December ▾ 2003 ▾ 📅 09 ▾ 00 ▾

Back-up

1 'Who' or 'where'?

Choose the correct question word.

1. _____ does Camilla love? – Charles.
2. _____ does Harry Potter go to school? – At Hogwarts.
3. _____ is Beijing? – In China.
4. _____ is Mr Bean? – Rowan Atkinson.
5. _____ does the president of the United States live? – In the White House.
6. _____ does Richard Gere love in the film Pretty Woman? – Julia Roberts.

2 Questions and answers

Sort out the questions and then answer them.

Example: do / parents / your / where / live?
Where do your parents live? – In Geneva.

1. when / week / get / you / do / up / during / the?

_____

2. for / eat / you / do / what / breakfast?

_____

3. get / work / how / do / to / you ?

_____

4. does / start / your / work / boss / when?

_____

5. do / what / do / you / are / when / holiday / you / on?

_____

6. do / your / colleagues / what / do / on holiday?

_____

3 What time is it?

Write these times.

1. It's `4.15` *a quarter past four* _____ .
2. It's `5.45` _____ .
3. It's `7.10` _____ .
4. It's `11.20` _____ .
5. It's `12.25` _____ .

6. It's `2.35` _____ .
7. It's `8.40` _____ .
8. It's `4.50` _____ .
9. It's `9.55` _____ .
10. It's `1.05` _____ .

Back-up

4 Prepositions

1. My birthday is _____ November. I can't celebrate in a beer garden because the weather is too cold _____ the winter.
2. The train leaves from platform seven _____ quarter past eleven.
3. The film starts _____ four o'clock _____ Saturday.
4. What time do you get up _____ Sunday?
5. The plane leaves at 2 o'clock _____ the afternoon.

5 A crossword puzzle

Fill in the words in this puzzle.

Across
3. In Britain you wait for a bus in a …
5. Siemens is a big German …
8. A person who works with you is a …
9. My office … number is 2345.

Down
1. On holiday you put your clothes in a …
2. The Times is a …
4. I … my car from Sixt.
6. Not expensive – …
7. My … number is BA 9846.
8. Where do you … your birthday?

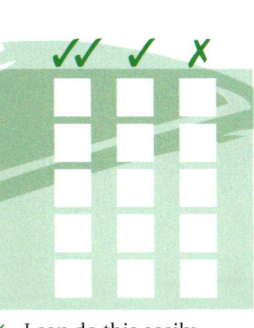

✓ At the end of this unit I … :

- can ask for a telephone number.
- can give someone my telephone number.
- can ask questions with 'who', 'where', 'how', 'what' and 'when'.
- can fill in personal details in a form.
- can ask about and give the time.

✓✓ = I can do this easily.
✓ = I can do this.
✗ = I need to work on this.

Words and expressions from this unit for my personal **word bank** are:

_____

_____

Reading

a Anja is talking to her friend Liam from Dublin. Read the dialogue first and then fill in the questions.

Anja: **you/what/in/free/your/time/do/do?** _____

Liam: I play hurling. Do you know it? It's a traditional Irish game, a little bit like hockey, but it's faster and more skilful!

Anja: **play/how/you/do/it?** _____

Liam: You play it with a stick, called a hurley, and a small leather ball, called a sliotar. There are two teams and the game lasts 70 minutes – there's a break in the middle, of course!

Anja: **rules/what/the/are?** _____

Liam: You can run with the ball, the sliotar, on the hurley or you can run a maximum of four steps with the ball in your hand. You can try to catch the ball when it is in the air, with your hand or with the hurley. You can try to get some points by hitting the ball into the goal. If it goes over the bar, you get a point, if it goes under the bar you score a goal, that's three points!

Anja: **does/win/how/a team?** _____

Liam: The team with the most points wins the game.

Anja: **practise/how often/you/do?** _____

Liam: I practise once a week. We meet on Saturday afternoon for practice.

Anja: **dangerous/it/is?** _____

Liam: No ... not really! I always wear a helmet, just in case!

b Read the dialogue again and then complete the sentences below.

1. Hurling is …
   a. … a game for two people. ☐
   b. … a game where each team needs two leather balls. ☐
   c. … a traditional game people like to play in Ireland. ☐

2. The team …
   a. … that scores the first goal wins. ☐
   b. … with the most points at the end wins. ☐
   c. … that scores points and goals wins. ☐

3. Liam wears a helmet …
   a. … because the game is very dangerous. ☐
   b. … because everyone wears a helmet. ☐
   c. … because the game can be dangerous. ☐

Listening

10 **a** Listen to the woman on the phone. She wants to book a room at the Black Swan Hotel. Unfortunately, the receptionist made some mistakes when he took down the information. Can you correct the hotel reservation form?

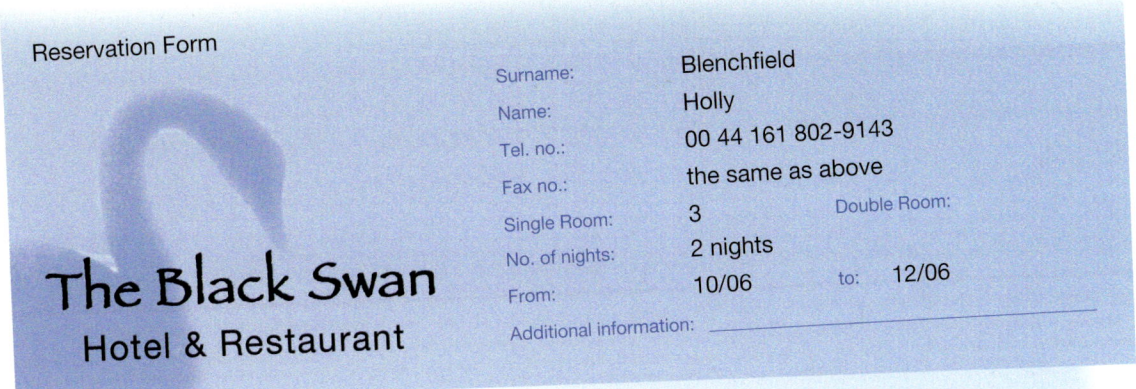

Reservation Form

The Black Swan
Hotel & Restaurant

Surname:	Blenchfield
Name:	Holly
Tel. no.:	00 44 161 802-9143
Fax no.:	the same as above
Single Room:	3 Double Room:
No. of nights:	2 nights
From:	10/06 to: 12/06
Additional information:	

b Listen again to check your corrections.

Speaking

Who is it?
Student A looks at this page. Student B looks at page 107.

Student A
Look at this family tree. Some of the names are missing – where do these names belong?

> Patricia   Emma   Jane   Susan

Ask your partner. Use the words you learned in Unit 1. For example:

A: Who is Evelyn?
B: She's Steven's wife. She's Tom and Emma's mother, and Sebastian's grandmother!
A: Ok, thanks. Who is …?

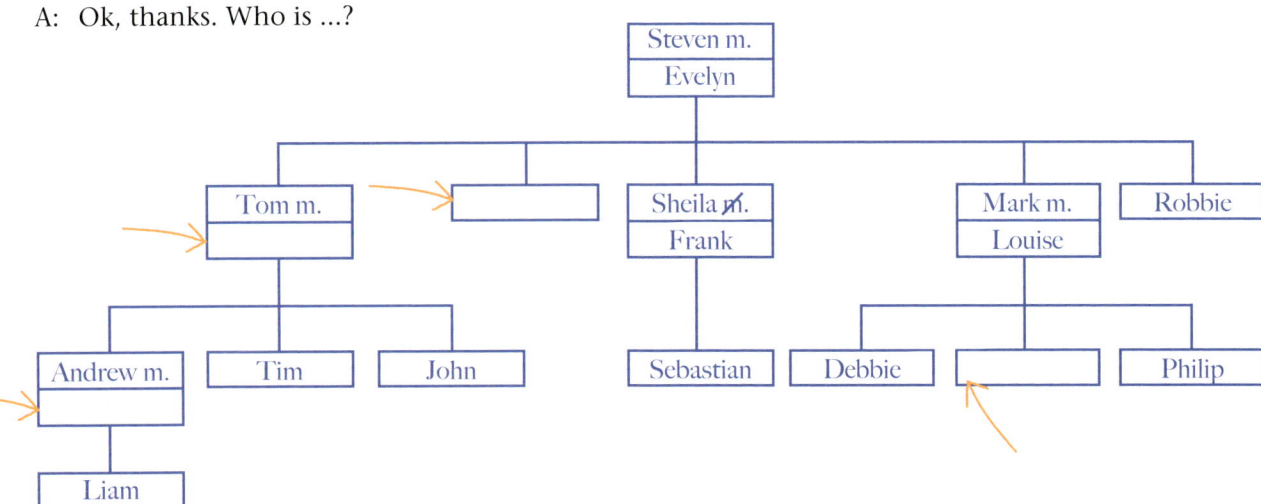

UNIT 4   No time

1 Routines

a You can answer questions with "how often …?" using the words from the list below. Can you fill in the missing words?

once a day
twice a _____
three times a month
_____ times a _____

c Now report back to the people in the group.

Examples: Robert goes shopping once a week.
Jessica looks at her e-mails three times a day.

b Ask your partner questions with "how often …?" using the prompts below.

Example: How often do you read a newspaper? – Once a week.

– look at your e-mails
– work overtime
– use the Internet
– go shopping for food
– listen to music
– read a newspaper
– go on holiday
– go skiing

2 Routines in Maria's life

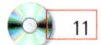 11

a Now listen to Maria and answer these questions.

How often does she work overtime? – _____
How often does she answer her e-mails? – _____
How often does she book flights/hotels online? – _____
How often does she read trade journals? – _____
How often does she go shopping for food? – _____
How often do the children go swimming? – _____
How often does she go to yoga classes? – _____
How often does she go on holiday with her family? – _____

Maria goes on holiday twice a year. Is that normal in your country? How many days holiday a year do people have in your country? And in the US and the UK?

b What do you think? Are office routines today different from routines in the 1990s?

> **Yes**
> Yes, I think so.
> I send e-mails. I don't write faxes or letters.

> **No**
> No, I don't think so.
> My routine's just the same.

c How often? Match the sentences in column A with the sentences in column B.

A
1. I go jogging twice a year.
2. I go jogging before breakfast but not on Sunday.
3. She doesn't have time to read the newspaper.
4. She reads trade journals every day after lunch.
5. I work overtime two or three times a week.
6. I work overtime once a month.

B
a. I often work overtime.
b. I seldom work overtime.
c. I seldom go jogging.
d. I usually go jogging before breakfast.
e. She never reads the newspaper.
f. She always reads trade journals.

d Decide which word fits in the sentences below.

| always | ▮ | usually | ▮ | often | ▮ | sometimes | ▮ | seldom | ▮ | never |

1. He reads a newspaper once a month. – He _____ reads a newspaper.
2. They go to the cinema every Saturday or Sunday. – They _____ go to the cinema at the weekend.
3. We go skiing every weekend in the winter. – We _____ go skiing.
4. I get up at half past six but not on Sundays. – I _____ get up at half past six.
5. Every year we go on holiday to Italy, either Tuscany or Umbria. – We _____ go on holiday to Italy. We _____ go to Tuscany and we _____ go to Umbria.
6. I don't like the smell of coffee. I _____ drink coffee.

Check your answers with a partner.

I **never** read a newspaper.
She **always** goes shopping on Sunday.

These **adverbs of frequency** come before the main verb in a sentence.

Be careful! The order of the words is different with the verb 'to be'.
He is **sometimes** late for work.
I am **often** tired.

 Look in the grammar reference section on page 123 for more information about these adverbs of frequency. Look in the back-up section on page 46 for more work with them.

e Complete the following sentences on a piece of paper.

I seldom eat _____ .
I never _____ on Sunday.
I sometimes _____ on Saturday.
I always _____ before I go to bed.
I often _____ .

Give the piece of paper to your teacher. He/she will give the paper to someone else.
Your teacher will also give you a new piece of paper. Who is it from?

3 Work and stress

a Do you have a lot of stress at work?

Match a word from column A with one from column B.

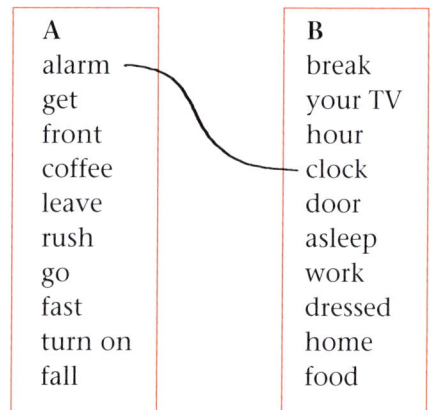

A	B
alarm	break
get	your TV
front	hour
coffee	clock
leave	door
rush	asleep
go	work
fast	dressed
turn on	home
fall	food

Check your answers with a partner.

c Listen again. Your teacher will sometimes stop the CD.
Say what the next word will be.

What do you think? What's this person's routine? Does she like her job?

b Now work with your partner and decide which words from **3a** go in the song.

(Come out of the darkness)
Get up, alarm _____, lip gloss, what a shock
Get _____, front _____, more stress, what for?
Trapped in your world
You know you're trapped in your world
Lunch hour, fast _____, telephone, more abuse
V.U. headache, cigarettes, coffee _____
Trapped in your world
You know you're trapped in your world.
(Come out of the darkness)
Come out of the darkness, over the tower blocks
Into the Light
Go into the rush _____, out of the factory
Leave it behind
(Come out of the darkness)
Turn _____ your _____, back to suburbia, every night
Come out of the darkness, over the offices , into the light
(Come out of the darkness)
Leave _____, happy hour, too drunk by far
Bus full, Waterloo, _____ asleep on the tube
Trapped in your world
You know you're trapped in your world.

Vodka, lemonade, ashtrays, what a shame
Poor cow, sits alone, pubs close, go _____
Trapped in your world
You know you're trapped in your world.
(Come out of the darkness)

Come Out Of the Darkness

 12 Listen to see if you were right.

Learning Tip – Listening
Find the words of a song you know and like (and have the CD!) from the website www.purelyrics.com
Choose ten words that you don't know from the song and write them down. Then close your eyes and listen to the song. How many words from your list did you hear? Now look them up in a dictionary.

4 Stress managenent

a The person in the song has a lot of stress in her job. Your friend has a lot of stress in his/her job, too, and asks you for some advice about how to relax.

You give him/her some suggestions:

– Why don't you have a massage?
– You could listen to music on the way home.
– How about buying a pet?

b Look at this list of ideas for stress management and decide which five you think are good ideas.

– work in the garden
– have a massage
– listen to music
– smile
– drink two litres of water a day
– think of a beautiful place you know

– write down your worries
– go for a walk
– buy a pet
– go to a museum or art gallery
– wear something green or blue

c Work with a partner. Give him/her some suggestions.
Listen to your partner. Do you think the suggestions are good?

> *Yes*
> Yes, that's a great idea.
> Yes, I like that idea.

> *NO*
> Thanks, but I'm not very keen on that idea because I'd rather …
> Well, I'm sorry I don't think that's a very good idea because …

d Now look at the list in **4b** and choose *one* that you *and* your partner think is a good idea.
Why do you think so?

5 Pronunciation

 13

a How do you pronounce the word 'management'?
Listen and repeat these words.

1. men ☐ – man ☐
2. ten ☐ – tan ☐
3. bend ☐ – band ☐
4. send ☐ – sand ☐
5. pet ☐ – Pat ☐
6. lend ☐ – land ☐

Learning Tip – Pronunciation
Listen to the pairs of words from **5a**. Listen again and again. Can you hear the difference?

15 **c** Listen to six sentences and write down the words from the list in **5a** that you hear in the sentences.

1. _____
2. _____
3. _____
4. _____
5. _____
6. _____

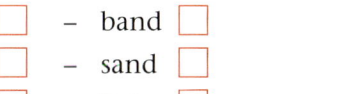 **14**

b Listen and decide if you hear a word from column A or one from column B.

4

6 Sleep

a You can count 'hours of sleep' but you can't count 'one sleep', 'two sleeps'.
'Sleep' is an uncountable noun and 'hour' is a countable noun.
In questions with countable nouns you ask: 'How _____ ?' and in
questions with uncountable nouns you ask 'How _____ ?'

Can you count 'wine' or 'glasses of wine'?
Can you count 'gin' or 'bottles of gin'?
Can you count 'water' or 'litres of water'?

b Make questions from this table.

How	much many	gin bottles of wine water cups of coffee herbal tea	do you	buy a week? drink a day?

Examples: How much water do you drink a day? – 1 litre.
How many cups of herbal tea do you drink a day. – 2.

c Now stand up and ask three people in the group the questions from **6b**. Write the answers in
this table.

name	herbal tea	cups of coffee	bottles of wine	gin	water

Report back to the class.

7 **Food and your job**

a Tim is someone who has a stressful job. Look at Tim's answers to a questionnaire on what he eats.

Tim

1. Do you eat brown bread?   No, I prefer white bread.
2. Do you eat nuts?   No, I don't eat nuts. I'm allergic to them.
3. Do you eat oranges?   Yes, two or three a week.
4. Do you eat fish?   No, I don't eat fish because I'm a vegetarian.
5. Do you eat chips?   Sometimes yes! But only maybe once a month.
6. Do you eat eggs late at night?   Well, I eat eggs but what's late? Sometimes I have my dinner at 8.30 or 9 p.m.

What about you?
How would you
answer
these questions?

b Do you think Tim eats things that are good for him in his job?
Read the short text in the file section on page 108 to find out.

c So in Tim's kitchen there aren't any nuts and there isn't any meat
or fish because he's allergic to nuts and he's a vegetarian.

The food you have in the kitchen can tell us a lot about you! Are you a good food detective?
Work with a partner and find out. Partner A looks on page 44 and partner B looks
at the file on page 110.

Countable and uncountable nouns
Countable nouns are things you can count: nuts, an orange.
Uncountable nouns are things you can't count. They are usually only singular: water, wine.

You ask questions with **How many ...?** for countable nouns.
Example: How many litres of wine do you buy a week?

You use questions with **How much ...?** for uncountable nouns.
Example: How much coffee do you drink a day?

In questions and negatives you use **any** for countable and uncountable nouns.
Examples: Is there any fish in the fridge?
            Are there any nuts in the cupboard?

            There isn't any water in the fridge.
            There aren't any eggs in the fridge.

 If you don't know the answer to "how much" or "how many", you can say "some". Look in the
back-up section on page 46 for some work with "some", "any", "how much" and "how many".

7 **Partner A**

C This is Paula's kitchen.

Give your partner the information he or she asks for:

Example: Your partner asks: You answer:

Is there any coffee in her kitchen? No, there isn't.
Is there any tea in her kitchen? Yes, there is.

Ask your partner about Brian's kitchen.

Example: Is there any coffee?

Mark your answers here:

	Yes	*No*
coffee	☐	☐
herbal tea	☐	☐
nuts	☐	☐
oranges	☐	☐
chocolate	☐	☐
eggs	☐	☐
meat	☐	☐
gin	☐	☐
water	☐	☐
beer	☐	☐

So does Brian eat things that are good for his brain? –
I think so … / I don't think so because …

d Now tell us what there is in your kitchen cupboard or in your fridge and tell us why as in 7a.

8 Making a booking

Maria works for a small textile company. She often makes phone calls for her boss Mr Sutcliffe. In the short conversations below some information is missing.

Choose from this list and fill in the information in dialogues 1 and 2 below.

a. Six.
b. The table is for Mr. Sutcliffe. That's S-U-T-C-L-I-F-F-E.
c. I'd like to book a table for six for Friday 13th February at 1 p.m., please.
d. No, I really need a small one for the morning but thanks anyway.
e. Fifteen.
f. About fifteen.
g. I'd like to book a small conference room for the morning of the 4th July.

1.

● Lotus restaurant. Can I help you?

■ _____

● Sorry, for how many people?

■ _____

● Er – let me see. Yes, that's fine.
  Can I have your name, please?

■ _____

● Fine. That's a table for six on Friday
  13th February at 1p.m.

■ Thanks very much.

● Not at all. Goodbye.

2.

● Hilton Hotel Heathrow Airport.
  Can I help you?

■ _____

● For how many people?

■ _____

● Sorry, was that fifty or fifteen?

■ _____

● I'm sorry, madam, but the small conference rooms are not available then.
  One small one is free in the afternoon or there's one that seats fifty that's free
  in the morning.

■ _____

● Not at all. Goodbye.

■ Goodbye.

16-17   Now listen to check your answers.

Note

Sorry? =	Can you repeat that?
	I didn't understand.
I'm sorry, but ... =	a way of saying 'no'

1 Adverbs of frequency

Put the adverbs of frequency in these sentences in the normal place.

1. I look at my e-mails after seven o'clock in the evening. (never)
2. She is relaxed because she always does yoga on Friday evening. (usually).
3. She plays the piano in the evening. (sometimes)
4. He goes on business trips to Dubai. (often)
5. I go jogging in the morning. (never)
6. I work overtime. (seldom)
7. We play tennis on Saturday morning. (usually)
8. He hires his car from Sixt. (always)
9. I have a stressful job so I am tired. (often)
10. We go to art galleries. (sometimes)

2 Visitor to Britain

You can get special offers on travel cards in London and Heritage passes to visit interesting places in Britain. You can't buy some of these passes in Britain. You can only buy them before you leave home. Visit the web-site: www.britaindirect.com to find out the answers. If you can't visit the web-site ask a friend if he/she can help you!

1. How _____ days can you buy a London travel card for?
2. How _____ does a three-day travel card for zones 1-6 cost?
3. How _____ zones are there in the London underground system?
4. How _____ does a Historic Scotland Explorer Pass cost for a child for 7 days?
5. How _____ Euro does a Great British Heritage Pass cost for 4 days?
6. How _____ money can you save if you buy a London Pass when you visit London?
7. How _____ interesting places can you visit with a London Pass?

Why don't you look at some of the links from this web-site. How much useful information can you find? Tell the class in the next lesson.
www.visitbritain.com......................www.visitscotland.com......................www.visitwales.com............
www.discovernorthernireland.com

3 much / many / some / any

Put the correct word in the blanks in these sentences.

1. How _____ wine do you drink a day? – One glass of red wine.
2. I'm sorry, we don't have _____ information about the London Eye here. Try asking at the next window.
3. There isn't _____ wine in the house.
4. How _____ eggs do you eat a week? – I have one every morning for breakfast.
5. We don't have _____ fish or meat in the house because we're vegetarians.
6. Is there _____ coffee in the cupboard? – Sorry, I don't drink coffee, only tea.
7. How _____ water do you drink a day? – About 2 litres.
8. How _____ glasses of beer do you drink at the weekend?
9. You should eat _____ brown bread every day. It is good for your memory.
10. How _____ hours do you spend in front of the computer screen? – Too _____! Seven or eight.
11. Do you eat nuts? – Yes, I eat _____ in my muesli every morning.
12. Where are the oranges? There aren't _____ in the fruit bowl.

4 Vocabulary

Answer the questions and find the words by using the letters in the word squares.

1.

You write with this. – _____
You cook with this. – _____
Your male child is your .... – _____
A flower. – _____
You smell with this. – _____
Have you got a PC or a ... top? – _____
How old are you? – That's a ... question! – _____

2.

A colour. – _____
A woman sometimes wears this. – _____
... me an e-mail. – _____
Children play in this on the beach. – _____
Not happy. – _____
I always ... a newspaper on Sunday morning. – _____
There is ... in the night. – _____

3.

How many words can you find in this square?

_____
_____
_____

At the end of this unit I ... :

✓✓ ✓ ✗

- can understand the words 'always', 'usually', 'sometimes', 'seldom', 'never' and use them to talk about routines.
- know how to give someone some advice.
- know how to accept or refuse advice.
- understand when to ask a question with 'How much ...?' and when to ask a question with 'How many ...?'
- can ask and answer questions using 'any'.
- can understand a simple telephone conversation.

✓✓ = I can do this easily.
✓ = I can do this.
✗ = I need to work on this.

Words and expressions from this unit for my personal **word bank** are:

_____
_____

UNIT 5 Communication

1 Modern communication

a How often do you send e-mails when you are on holiday?
How often do you send a text message to a friend?

Read this text to find out about Keith's opinion on modern communication before you tick the statements below.

Today, it is very usual for people to communicate by mobile phone, either speaking or by text message. This is made possible by modern technology, including satellites in space and tall aerials on top of buildings and on hills.

The phone is an important fashion accessory. You can buy it in different colours and you can change the covers: Monday green, Tuesday red, and so on. You can also change the ringing tone or even record your own tone.

Have you ever listened to the phone call of another passenger on a tram or bus? A lot of phone calls made in public are not really important. They replace doing nothing. They help pass the time. But what happens when there is suddenly no connection? Panic! Because a lot of small, unimportant, decisions are now made when travelling. So I do not know what time or where I will meet my friend. What do I know, however, is that there are other people on the tram or bus in the same situation. Perhaps this is the chance to communicate and make some new friends!

	True	*False*	*Possible*
1. More and more people are communicating by text messaging.	☐	☐	☐
2. You can change the colour of your phone.	☐	☐	☐
3. You change the ringing tone of the phone in a shop.	☐	☐	☐
4. A lot of phone calls made in public are very important.	☐	☐	☐
5. People panic when there is no connection.	☐	☐	☐
6. It is easy to find friends on the tram or bus.	☐	☐	☐

b What do you think about Keith's opinion? Do you talk to people on the tram or bus?

2 Family photos

a How often do you send digital pictures to a friend's computer? How often do you look at old family photos in an album? Listen to Rachel and Clare talking about people dressed up for a wedding. As you listen write the names below the pictures.

b Who is it?

She's wearing a turquoise hat. – _____

He's living in Windsor with his new wife. – _____

He's travelling round the world. – _____

She's training to be a nurse. – _____

c Over to you.

Find out how many people in your course are …
– … reading a good book
– … trying to lose weight/get fit
– … studying in the evening for an examination   at the moment.
– … learning to drive/swim
– … decorating/renovating the house/flat
– … learning to use a laptop/a digital camera

Report back.

Example: Two people are reading a book at the moment.

> **Note**
> one person, two people (GB)
> one person, two persons (US)

> **The present progressive**
> You use the present progressive:
> – for descriptions of things you can see in a photo/picture.
> *Example:* She**'s wearing** a pink hat.
>
> – to talk about what is happening now, at the time of speaking.
> *Example:* Thousands of people **are singing**.
>
> – to talk about non-permanent situations.
> *Example:* He**'s travelling** round the world in his gap year.

 Look on page 57 in the back-up section for work on the present progressive and the present simple.

3 You've got an e-mail

a Roger (from exercise 2) is travelling round the world with his friend Alan and he communicates by e-mail when he is travelling.
How do you communicate with your friends when you are on holiday?

b Read this e-mail and answer the questions: What's happening? What event is taking place?

sender:	Smelly12@yahoo.com
to:	natalie@ntlworld.co.uk
	¡Hola, my love

Well, here we are in South America. All is well. Business first. Can you transfer £500 to the American Express office in Rio? I think you've got the details with all my other emergency contacts. Thanks.

It's hot and humid here. We had some problems with the heat at first but we are getting used to it now. I'm sending this from an e-mail café near Praça General Osório where the Banda de Ispanema is playing. According to the guide book it's the most popular band here. I can believe it. The atmosphere

is great. Thousands of people are singing and cheering enthusiastically and dancing wildly to the hot samba rhythms. I'm glad I'm not trying to phone you! The music is very loud. The drag queen procession is about to leave and we want to march behind with the crowds – so only a short mail this time. Some of the costumes are unbelievable. The drag queens dress outrageously for this procession every year. Pink is in this year and some are wearing long pink ball dresses and pink wigs with platform shoes, some are wearing lots of old jewellery and long pink feathers in their

hair. Some taxis can't move forwards because of the mass of people in the streets, but the passengers are just laughing and enjoying the entertainment. No-one is shouting or complaining loudly about how they can't get home from work or back to their hotel. Don't worry about us – the police are warning everyone to be careful of pick-pockets and people are drinking A LOT of beer but there aren't any fights, not around here anyway.

I must go. Do you like the digital photos?
Love,
Roger:-)))

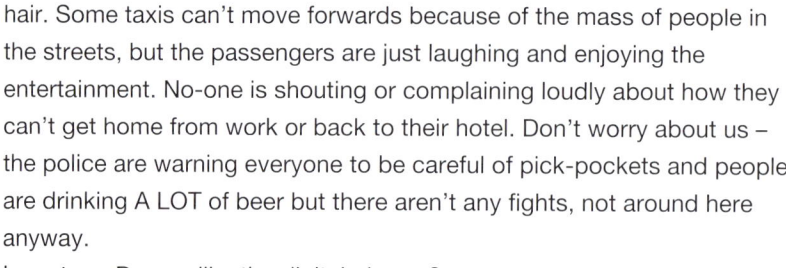

What do you know about carnival in Rio?
What happens every year at carnival time in your area?

c Now look again at the e-mail and underline all the words that end in -ly.

> **Adverbs and adjectives**
> The music is very loud.   'loud' is an adjective.
> No-one is complaining loudly.   'loud**ly**' is an adverb.
>
> Adverbs describe verbs. They can answer the question 'how'.
> *Example:* How do the drag queens dress? – Outrageously.

 Look in the grammar reference section on page 123 for more information about adverbs and on page 57 in the back-up section for some practice.

d Match suitable adverbs with the verbs on the left. More than one answer is possible.

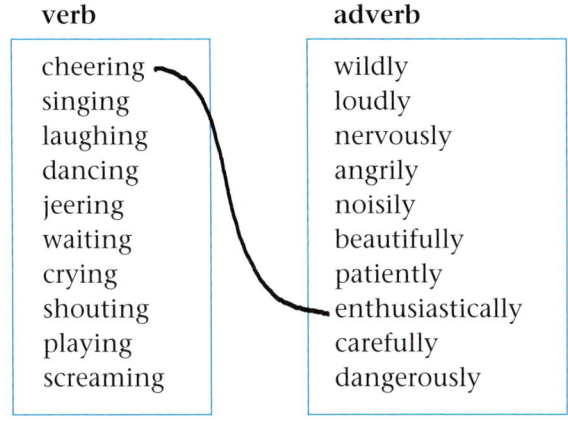

verb	adverb
cheering	wildly
singing	loudly
laughing	nervously
dancing	angrily
jeering	noisily
waiting	beautifully
crying	patiently
shouting	enthusiastically
playing	carefully
screaming	dangerously

> **Note**
> careful – careful**ly**
> enthusiastic – enthusiastic**ally**
> angry – ang**ri**ly

Can you add more adverbs to the list?

4   An exciting event

Work in small groups. Your teacher will give your group a letter. You are going to send a text message to your friends. Use some adverbs and verbs from **3d**.

Group A look on page 113.   Group C look on page 114.
Group B look on page 107.   Group D look on page 108.

5   Are they cheering or jeering?

 a Look at these two lists of words. Listen and repeat them.

 **b** Then listen again and decide if you hear a word from column A or one from column B.

	[tʃ]	A	[dʒ]	B
1.	cherry	☐	Jerry	☐
2.	cheap	☐	jeep	☐
3.	choke	☐	joke	☐
4.	chill	☐	Gill	☐
5.	chest	☐	jest	☐
6.	chin	☐	gin	☐
7.	choose	☐	Jews	☐
8.	cheer	☐	jeer	☐

 **c** Listen to four sentences and answer these questions.

Where is Gill? – _____

What is Jerry doing? – _____

Is the jeep expensive? – _____

What are the Turin fans doing? – _____

6 Shopping and the Internet

a Which statement is true?

		True	False
Our class uses the Internet	mainly to send e-mails.	☐	☐
	mainly to find information.	☐	☐
	mainly for shopping.	☐	☐

b Work in groups of three and say what you think about these statements.

– I think it's dangerous to do shopping via the Internet.
– It's quick and easy and not dangerous to buy books via the Internet.
– I don't think it's a good idea to buy clothes via the Internet because you can't try them on.

Yes — Yes, I think so, too.

No — I'm afraid I don't think so. I feel that …

c In the well-known British high street shop Marks and Spencer's assistants are trained not to ask "Can I help you?" because the customer's natural reaction is "I'm just looking. Thank you."

These two sales assistants are well-trained!
In the first dialogue the customer is buying a pullover and in the second one the customer is buying a shirt. Sort them out.

	dialogue 1		*dialogue 2*
_1_	Can you find the colour you want, madam?	____	
____	Yes, please.	____	
____	The fitting rooms are over there.	____	
____	They are a bit small. Have you got a bigger size?	____	
____	Are you looking for a shirt to go with those trousers, sir?	_1_	
____	Yes, it's nice. Can I try it on?	____	
____	Certainly. The fitting rooms are over there.	____	
____	How about this one?	____	
____	Fine, I'll take it.	____	
____	No, I'm sorry, we haven't.	____	
____	Oh, well, I'll leave it then.	____	
____	Do you have these pullovers in red?	____	
____	Yes, we do. Here you are. Would you like to try them on?	____	
____	Yes, it fits very well. How much is it?	____	
____	£23.	____	
____	Yes, I am.	____	
____	Any particular colour?	____	
____	Have you got anything in green?	____	

 22 Now listen to see if you were right.
Practise the dialogues with a partner.
The tapescript is on page 136–137.

7 I'm sorry, we haven't

a The sales assistant in the conversation in Marks and Spencer's said 'no' politely! The rhythm of the sentences is:

A   ○   ●○   ○   ●○   ○
   I'm sorry, we haven't.

B   ○   ●○   ○   ●
   I'm sorry, I don't.

b Here are some more ways of saying 'no' politely. What is the rhythm – A or B?

1. I'm sorry, we haven't. __A__
2. I'm sorry, I don't. __B__
3. I'm sorry, I can't. _____
4. I'm sorry, I'm not. _____
5. I'm sorry, there isn't. _____
6. I'm sorry, it doesn't. _____
7. I'm sorry, you can't. _____
8. I'm sorry, it isn't. _____

c Now match the answers from **7b** above with these questions.

1. Do you know his phone number? – _I'm sorry, I don't._
2. Are you free on Sunday? – _____
3. Is the rental car insured for my wife? _____
4. Can I smoke in here? – _____
5. Excuse me, is there an Internet café near here? – _____
6. Excuse me, does this bus stop at the main station? – _____
7. Can you give me a lift to the airport? – _____
8. Have you got a double room free for tonight? – _____

 23 Listen to check if you were right.

8 Telephone expressions

a Look at the following telephone conversations. Can you fill in the missing expressions?

1.
- ● _____ Michael Grundy. Can I speak to Mr. Sutton, please?
- ■ I'm sorry, <u>he's having lunch</u> at the moment. Can I _____?
- ● It's OK. It's not urgent. I'll _____ later.
- ■ Fine.

2.
- ◆ _____ Charles Morton. Can I speak to Mr Archer, please?
- ▲ I'm sorry, <u>he's attending a conference in Rome</u> at the moment. Can I _____?
- ◆ It's rather urgent. Can I have his mobile number?
- ▲ Of course. It's <u>01717 480567</u>.
- ◆ Thank you for your help.
- ▲ Not at all. Goodbye.

 **24** Then listen to check if you were right.

b Now practise the dialogues with a partner. You can change the names and words that are underlined.

9 What's in the news?

a Do you read a newspaper regularly or do you watch the news on TV to find out what is happening in the world? Do you subscribe to a magazine? Do you have a print version or do you subscribe to one on-line?
Can you name some foreign newspapers? What foreign language newspapers or magazines can you buy where you live?

Look at these sections of a newspaper. Decide which sections the people below read and then fill in the missing words in the statements 1.–8.

> home news ▮ sport ▮ world news ▮ entertainment pages ▮ gossip columns ▮
> science and technology ▮ business and the economy ▮ human interest

1. I read the _____ pages first because I'm a Bayern Munich fan.
2. I'm interested in what famous people are doing so I read the _____.
3. I'm interested in what is happening in my country so I read the _____ section.
4. I read the _____ because I am interested in what is happening in the world of cinema and theatre.
5. I like to know what ordinary people are doing so I read the _____ stories.
6. I work in banking so I read the section on _____.
7. I read the _____ section because I want to know what new developments there are in the world of computers.
8. I am not only interested in what is going on in my own country so I read the _____.

What about you? What do you read first?

Note
Why do you read the sports pages? – **Because** I'm a Spurs fan.
I like to know what ordinary people are doing **so** I read the human interest stories.

b Here is a newspaper story. The headline is:

You CAN do

something about junk mail!

What section of the newspaper does it come from?
What is junk mail?
How much junk mail do you get every week?
What do you do with junk mail?
What can you do to stop junk mail?

c Look at the text and answer the questions.

1. What is Christopher trying to do?
2. What do people do when they visit his web-site?
3. What sort of companies write to Thelma's mother regularly?
4. Where does Peter live?
5. Where does Sarah Jones live now?

6. What does Christopher do?
7. Which web-site can help Thelma?
8. Which web-site can help Peter?
9. Which web-site can help Robert and Alison Simmonds?
10. Does Peter read the catalogues he gets through the post?

"Enough is enough," says Christopher Moreton from Bovingdon, Hertfordshire. "No more junk mail!" It all started when he came back from a _____-holiday and couldn't open the front door because of all the junk mail. Most people get irritated by junk mail but Christopher is trying to do something about it and he is collecting a lot of junk mail horror stories on his web-site.

Stories from people like Thelma Roberts from Bourne End. She gets regular junk mail from companies that are trying to sell trekking holidays to her mother _____. Or Peter Moran who still gets catalogues for _____ clothes for Sarah Jones who moved from the address in Tring to Reading five years ago.

There can be serious problems with junk mail. Robert and Alison Simmonds are suing a supermarket because their dog broke its leg when it jumped up and pulled junk mail out of the letterbox. John Adamson is very angry about all the junk mail he gets every week and so he sends it all back in envelopes with screws inside them. The post office is suing him for sending dangerous packages through the post because workers thought the envelopes were bombs.

Mr Moreton is very surprised by the interest in his web-site. "I'm spending about two hours a day on this project at the moment," says the _____ computer programmer. "Every evening I write letters to companies in the area, answer e-mails and give information about helpful web-sites."

He can't help the Simmonds or John Adamson with legal problems but he is helping people like Thelma. So, for example, people who don't want their names and addresses on company mailing lists can register online with the Mailing Preference Service (www.mpsonline.org.uk or telephone 0207 291 3310). When companies update their mailing lists they can check this register. Companies can also check who is living at a certain address if they buy software from the REaD group www.readgroup.co.uk . Christopher hopes that companies who know about the REaD web-site will send less junk mail to people like Peter. "And save money, of course," he adds. "They won't send _____ catalogues through the post that Peter throws straight into the dustbin." Let's hope Christopher is right.

(freely adapted from articles in the Daily Telegraph)

Check your answers to the questions with a partner.

d Now look at the text again and put the missing words in the correct place in the text.

four-week
32-year-old
expensive
children's
who is 95

Learning Tip – Reading

Why don't you buy an English newspaper once a month! Choose one story. Look at the pictures and then look at the headline. What do you think the story is about? What words do you think will be in the story? (You could think of words in German and then look them up in a dictionary). If you think first it will help you when you read.

Back-up

1 Vocabulary revision

Newspapers often contain misprints. Can you correct the mistakes in these sentences?
Be careful, in some sentences there is more than one!

1. The dog is eleven ears old.
2. At the moment they are loving in a flat in Oxford.
3. He's wearing a dark grey sit.
4. She's wearing a back skirt.
5. Her son is travelling round the word in his gap year.
6. The football fans are jeering enthusiastically.
7. The people in the crowd are cheering nosily.
8. Jim and Hanna are renovating their holiday fat.
9. Companies bend a lot of punk mail.
10. She is preparing a big weeding party for her daughter.
11. It is hit and humid in Rio and a lot of tourists are having problems with the meat.
12. The phone is an impotent fashion accessory.
13. The dog tried to pull junk mail from the litterbox.
14. I red the science and technology section of the newspaper because I am interested in developments in the world of commuters.
15. There is a bog crowd watching the football match.

2 Clothes

a Match the words with the pictures.

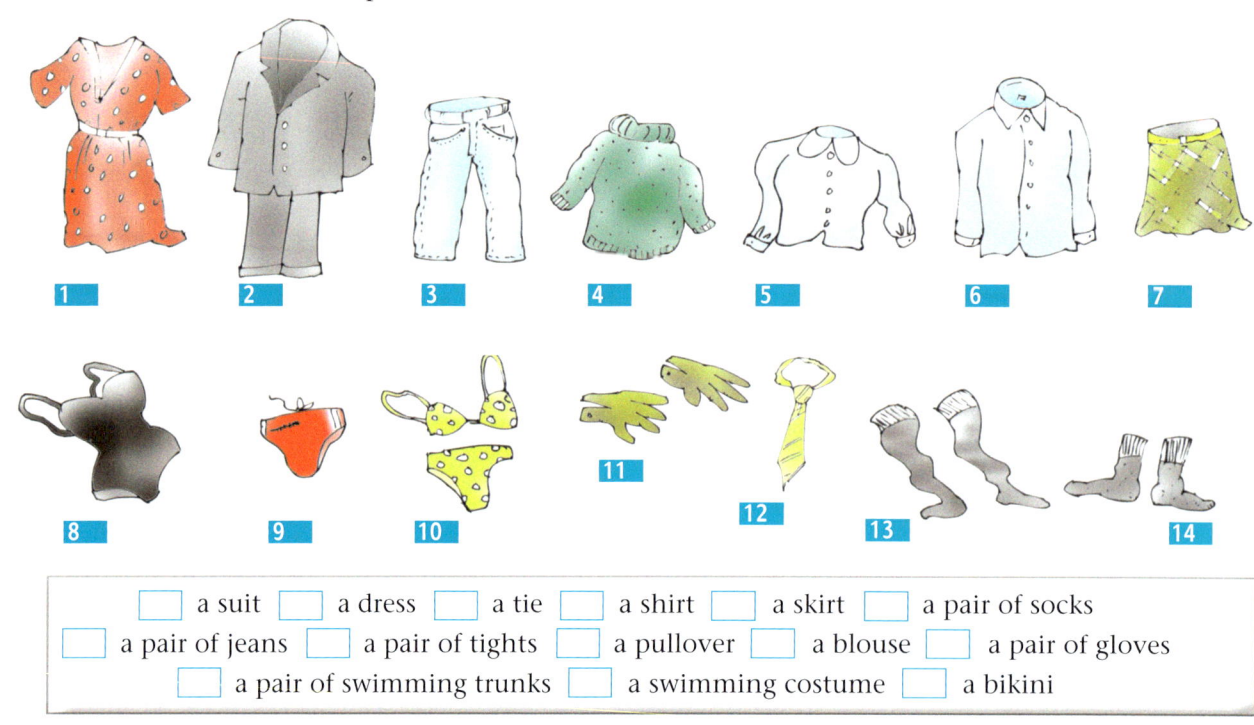

	a suit		a dress		a tie		a shirt		a skirt		a pair of socks
	a pair of jeans		a pair of tights		a pullover		a blouse		a pair of gloves
	a pair of swimming trunks		a swimming costume		a bikini

b What do you wear | at work?
at the weekend?
when you come to your English lesson every week?

What are you wearing now?

Back-up

3 Adverb or adjective?

Choose the right word in these sentences.

1. I don't think it is *dangerous / dangerously* to buy things from the Internet.
2. She speaks very *quiet / quietly* so it is sometimes difficult to hear her when she is speaking on her mobile phone.
3. I don't like driving with my grandfather because he drives very very *slow / slowly*.
4. At carnival time everyone wears *outrageously / outrageous* costumes.
5. The fans are singing *loud / loudly*, but there aren't any fights.
6. When you are watching an event in a big crowd be *careful / carefully* of pick-pockets.
7. What's that noise? The couple in the flat next door are having a *wild / wildly* party.
8. Her examination results were *superb / superbly* because she worked very *hard / hardly*.
9. Look! The passengers are waiting *patient / patiently* for the bus. It's a British queue.
10. I don't want to rent a car when I am on holiday because I'm a *nervous / nervously* driver and everyone drives so *dangerous / dangerously*.

4 Present simple or progressive?

Write the verbs in this short text in the correct form – present simple or present progressive.

Good afternoon ladies and gentlemen. Welcome to Wimbledon. The tournament _____ (start) every year six weeks before the first Monday in August and _____ (last) for a fortnight. Players from over 60 countries regularly _____ (compete). 6,000 people _____ (work) here during the two weeks of the Championships every year. This year the Wimbledon All England Lawn Tennis Club _____ _____ (employ) over 250 temporary workers. They have very different jobs, some of them _____ _____ (sell) programmes, some _____ (prepare) all the strawberries that are so famous, and so expensive. Don't forget the ball boys and girls of course who _____ (wear) a purple shirt and green shorts. They _____ (come) from schools in the area and training for these pupils _____ (begin) in February.

It is 9.30 now and I _____ (speak) to you from in front of the Millennium building, opened in the year

2000 for the press and media representatives. Journalists from over fifty countries _____ (come) here to report on this Grand Slam tournament every year. This year The United States _____ (send) 55 journalists and Germany _____ (send) 42.

Play _____ (start) at 12 o'clock every day on courts 2-19 and at 1 p.m. on court number one and centre court. And now the no. 1 tennis player in the world _____ (arrive) by limousine. For the public the grounds _____ (open) at 10.30. I can see a long queue of tennis enthusiasts who _____ _____ (wait) patiently. Over 500,000 people _____ (attend) every year and millions more _____ (watch) the matches on TV or through the Internet.

Ok, so let's go to our camera on the practice courts and see who we can find.

At the end of this unit I ... :

* can understand the description of a person.
* can understand an e-mail from a friend.
* can understand a short dialogue in a shop.
* can write a short and simple text message.
* can express my opinion in a short and simple way.
* can say 'no' politely.

✓✓ = I can do this easily.
✓ = I can do this.
✗ = I need to work on this.

Words and expressions from this unit for my personal **word bank** are:

1 Where to stay

a   When you go on holiday you can stay in | a hotel.

b   Leading hotels of the world.

Work in three groups A, B and C.
Group A reads about the Madison Hotel, Washington DC, on page 112.
Group B reads about the Banyan Tree in the Maldives on page 116.
Group C reads about the Rambagh Palace Hotel in Jaipur, India, on page 111.

As you read fill in this table.

	The Madison	The Rambagh Palace	Banyan Tree
how many rooms?			
how far from the airport?			
how many restaurants?			
price per room per night?			
shopping? no			
health and recreation facilities?			

c   Now work in a group of three and tell the group about your hotel. Fill in the information in the table above.

Which hotel would you like to stay in? Money is not a problem!

d   All these hotels are expensive.

The Madison is expensive.
The Rambagh Palace is more expensive than the Madison.
The Banyan Tree is the most expensive.

Now make some more comparisons of the three hotels.

Comparative and superlative of adjectives
For short adjectives add **-er** and **-est** to the basic adjective: cheap, cheaper, (the) cheapest.
Example: Hotel A is **cheaper than** hotel B, but hotel C is **the cheapest**.

Longer adjectives put 'more' or (the) 'most' in front of the basic adjective: comfortable, more comfortable, the most comfortable.
Example: Are the beds in hotel B **more comfortable than** the beds in hotel A?

Two-syllable adjectives ending in 'y', e.g. noisy, happy, etc., change the 'y' to 'i' and add -er or -est to the basic adjective.
Example: The streets of Hong Kong are **noisier than** those in London.

Irregular forms:
good – better – (the) best
far – further – (the) furthest
Example: Which hotel is furthest from the airport?

 Look in the grammar reference section on page 122 for more explanations of comparative and superlative adjectives.

2 Can you recommend a hotel?

a Some friends from the US are coming to your area and need your advice about where to stay. In your groups think about these questions: How many restaurants and hotels are there in your area? Are they cheap or expensive, quiet or noisy? Is the food good? What do your friends like in a good hotel?

Now write your suggestions on a piece of paper.

Examples: There are … hotels in the area. Hotel X is quieter than hotel Y but it's more expensive.
The food in hotel X is better than the food in hotel Y.
We would recommend the … hotel because …

b Put your recommendations on the wall. Stand up and look at all the suggestions. Do you agree with them?

3 Honeymoon in Hong Kong

a What do you know about Hong Kong? Anna and James stayed in the very expensive Peninsular Hotel in Hong Kong on their honeymoon. It was more expensive than the Madison Hotel but cheaper than the Banyan Tree Hotel. She rings her friend Pat when they get back.

Listen for the answers to these questions:

1. Where was the room? – _____
2. What was the view like? – _____
3. What were the people in the hotel like? – _____
4. What was the return flight like? – _____

You use the question "What was … like?" for singular and uncountable nouns.
You use the question "What were … like?" for _____.

b Match these adjectives with the nouns below. Some of the adjectives can go with more than one noun.

> windy ▮ spicy ▮ very comfortable ▮ expensive ▮ sandy ▮ noisy ▮ cold ▮
> helpful ▮ friendly ▮ quiet ▮ good ▮ beautiful ▮ international ▮ hot ▮
> humid ▮ boring ▮ dirty ▮ clean ▮ spectacular ▮ boring

hotel: _____

beach: _____

people: _____

food: _____

rooms: _____

weather: _____

view: _____

Learning Tip – Vocabulary

How can you increase and practise your vocabulary? – Think of one word a day and 'talk to yourself'. Think of all the adjectives you can think of to describe that word, like you did in this exercise, and say them quietly to yourself.

c Now think of some questions and answers using these nouns and adjectives.
What was the hotel like? – It was expensive but very good.
What were the people like? – Not very friendly.

d Some market research: Stand up and ask questions to find out where people in the group were on holiday last year. Find out what it was like and fill in the answers in the table below.

Where did you spend your holiday last year? – In Tuscany.

name	place of holiday	hotel	food	people	...
Peter	in Tuscany	expensive	good	OK	...
...					
...					
...					
...					

Report back.
So what was the most popular holiday destination for people in your class last year and which country was the best value for money for a holiday?

The past simple of the verb 'to be'

I **was**	I wasn't	
You **were**	You weren't	
He/she/it **was**	He wasn't	
We **were**	We weren't	*Examples:* The view **was** wonderful.
They **were**	They weren't	We **were** tired after the journey.

⇨ Look in the grammar reference section page 125 for more details about the verb 'to be' in the past simple.

4 The postcard

a Anna's postcard to Pat arrived two days after she got back from Hong Kong.
Read it and answer these questions.

How did they get from the airport to the hotel?   What did they do on Tuesday?
Where did they relax for the first two days?   When did they watch the laser show?

Dear Pat,
   We are having the best holiday ever! We can see Victoria Harbour from our suite in the hotel. We arrived safely on Monday night. Of course, we were very tired after the long flight, but a courtesy limousine picked us up from the airport – at first I didn't believe it really was for us!
   For the first two days we just relaxed by the swimming pool – it's indoor and outdoor. Then on Tuesday we walked round the flower market, the bird market and the jade market. I bought some jade. It's much cheaper than back home but I didn't buy any big pieces because I'm not an expert and James isn't either. Then at 8 o'clock in the evening we watched the Symphony of Lights. It was a laser show and laser beams lit up a lot of the tall buildings. It was really spectacular. We're going on a 'flight-seeing tour' by helicopter tomorrow and we hope to go into China too before we leave.
   Lots of love, Anna and James

b What word was in every question in **4a** above? – _____

In the answers to the questions find the last two letters of each verb. – _____

Can you find two negative sentences in Anna's postcard? – _____

The past simple of full verbs - regular
You use the past simple to talk about something completed in the past.

Positive
Form: add **-ed** or **-d** to the infinitive.
Examples: We walk**ed** round the flower market.
      We arrive**d** safely on Monday night.

Questions (yes/no and wh)
Form : **did** *and* another **verb** in the infinitive.

Yes/no questions
Example: **Did** you **have** a good time? – Yes, we did.

Wh-questions
Example: What **did** they **do** for the first two days? – They **relaxed** and **walked** round the markets.

Negative
Form: **did** + **not** and another **verb** in the infinitive.
Example: I **didn't buy** any big pieces.

6

5 Over to you

a Complete these sentences so that they are true for you.

On my last holiday I stayed with _____ in a _____
in _____ for _____ days/weeks.
We travelled by _____ and the journey was _____
When I'm on holiday I like to try the local food. One evening we had a terrible/very expensive/
romantic/cheap meal. The restaurant was _____.
We ordered _____.
We enjoyed/didn't enjoy the food because _____.
We liked/didn't like the wine because _____.
The service in the restaurant was _____ and the waiters were very
_____. We started our meal at _____ and we finished
it at _____.
We paid _____ for the meal.
I would/wouldn't recommend the food in _____ because
_____.

b Work with a partner. First ask him/her questions to find out where he/she was on holiday.

Examples: Did you have a holiday in Turkey? – No, I didn't.
Did you have a holiday in Italy? – No, I didn't
Did you have a holiday in Egypt? – Yes, I did.

Then ask your partner some questions about the
meal using these prompts:
How long / stay …?
How / travel …?
What / order in the restaurant …?
Did / enjoy / food …?
Did / like / wine …?
When / start the meal …?
When / finish the meal …?
How much / pay …?

Tell the class who had a good meal and who had a
bad meal on holiday.

Note
When you listen and you hear about something
bad you are sympathetic:
– Oh dear. I'm sorry about that.
When you listen and you hear about something
good you are enthusiastic:
– Oh, that sounds wonderful.

Listen and try to be sympathetic or enthusiastic.

6 Your reservation

a In which city are hotels the most expensive: Munich, Paris, New York or London?

b Mr Dixon inherited some money from his aunt so he booked a short break in the very expensive Dorchester Hotel in London. He booked on-line. Look at the details of his reservation and then say if the statements below are true, false or possible.

> Booking details
> Arrival date   10 August
> Departure date   12 August
> Number of rooms   1
> guests   2
> GO
> Sorry, we regret that there are no rooms available on the dates you selected. Please try alternative dates.

> Booking details
> Arrival date   28 August
> Departure date   30 August
> Number of rooms   1
> guests   2
> GO

> Reservation details
> Arrival date   28 August
> Departure date   30 August
> Number of rooms   1
> Number of guests   2
> Description   Superior King room, 24m², high speed Internet access, quiet location, lobby, marble bathroom
> Room rate   £325 including use of spa facilities and service charge

	true	false	possible
1. He booked the hotel for four nights.	☐	☐	☐
2. He stayed in the hotel with his wife. (or lover!)	☐	☐	☐
3. He and his wife arrived on the 30th August.	☐	☐	☐
4. The hotel was full on the 12th August.	☐	☐	☐
5. There were two single beds in the room.	☐	☐	☐
6. The room was noisy.	☐	☐	☐
7. He and his wife enjoyed the facilities in the spa.	☐	☐	☐
8. He paid £650 pounds for himself and £650 for his wife.	☐	☐	☐
9. He and his wife watched a musical in one of London's theatres.	☐	☐	☐
10. They travelled home after breakfast on the 12th August.	☐	☐	☐

Back-up

1 and / but / so / because

Fill in the gaps in these sentences with 'and', 'but', 'because' or 'so'.

1. We booked a trip to China _____ a cruise round the harbour.
2. It rained a lot on our holiday _____ we enjoyed it.
3. The weather was hot _____ humid.
4. The people were friendly _____ helpful.
5. The hotel was cheap _____ dirty.
6. The beach was sandy _____ clean.
7. The flight was long _____ not boring.
8. We didn't have a lot of money _____ we didn't stay in a five-star hotel.
9. We didn't stay in a five-star hotel _____ we didn't have a lot of money.
10. We didn't stay in the five-star hotel _____ we enjoyed afternoon tea in the lobby of one!
11. Their daughter was very ill in hospital _____ they cancelled their holiday.
12. The room in our hotel was small _____ cold, _____ my husband complained.
13. It was an expensive hotel _____ it was worth it _____ there was a lot of good entertainment for the children.
14. The beach was clean _____ rocky _____ the children couldn't build any sand castles.
15. We didn't go on a cruise round the harbour _____ it was very expensive.

2 Change these sentences into the negative or into the positive

Examples: We **enjoyed** our holiday very much. / We **didn't enjoy** our holiday very much.

We **didn't miss** the train. / We **missed** the train.

1. He didn't start his holiday in Rio. _____
2. We booked the hotel in advance. _____
3. She didn't visit the famous museum. _____
4. He didn't pay more than $100 a night for this hotel. _____
5. I didn't walk along the harbour promenade. _____
6. We watched a big laser show in the evening. _____
7. They wanted to buy some jade in the market. (be careful with this one!) _____
8. We stayed in a five-star hotel. _____
9. We didn't enjoy the holiday. _____
10. We didn't book the hotel on-line. _____
11. She arrived at the hotel after midnight. _____
12. They played tennis every morning. _____
13. I didn't reserve a seat on the train. _____
14. The children tried the local food. _____
15. The parents didn't relax by the swimming pool. _____

Back-up

3 Comparisons

a Your friend wants your advice. Help him or her and compare the following.

> I want to have a weekend break in a European city. **Which do you recommend?**
> Zurich, Vienna, Berlin, Paris, London

> I want to buy a car. Which do you recommend?
> Fiat Punto, Renault Clio, Toyota Yaris

> I want to start a new hobby. Which do you recommend?
> golf, hang-gliding, scuba-diving

b Complete these sentences and then find the answers.

1. What is the _____ building in your area? (high)
2. What is the _____ restaurant in your town or city? (expensive)
3. What is the _____ city in your area? (cosmopolitan)
4. What is the name of the _____ international airport? (near)
5. What is the _____ way to get from the city or town centre to the airport? (quick)

4 Vocabulary

Find the missing word in this acrostic by finding the words 1–10.

1. Hugh Grant is a … actor.
2. You can see a lot of boats if you go down to the …
3. Is this a good hotel? Would you … it?
4. In India the food is hot and …
5. Majorca is a … holiday island.
6. The room wasn't quiet it was very …
7. She was ill but her friend wasn't very …
8. There is a good … from the hotel room.
9. The … from Moscow to Vladivostok was very exciting.
10. We were on holiday in Crete last year. Where did you … ?

1.
2.
3.
4.
5.
6.
7.
8.
9.
10.

At the end of this unit I … :

- can compare things.
- can ask and talk about what a holiday was like.
- can ask and answer questions in the past simple.
- can express interest and sympathy when I am listening to someone.
- can understand an on-line booking form for a hotel.

✓✓ = I can do this easily.
✓ = I can do this.
✗ = I need to work on this.

Words and expressions from this unit for my personal **word bank** are:

_____

_____

UNIT 7 Too much waste?

1 Recycle it

a "In the twenty-first century we produce too much waste."
How do you feel about this statement?

A group of people who are dumpster divers feel strongly that this statement is true. Look at the picture. What do you think this person is doing?

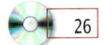 26 **b** You are going to hear an interview with Heather Steele, who is a dumpster diver. Number the things she talks about as you hear them.

a Why she became interested in dumpster diving. _1_

b. The furniture store dumpster. ___

c. The dumpster behind the apartment block where she finds clothes. ___

d. Why she likes this hobby. ___

e. The supermarket dumpster dive. ___

f. The toy store dumpster and the animals. ___

g. Her three favourite dumpsters. _3_

 26 **c** Now listen again and complete these statements.

1. She first read about this hobby _____.

2. Before she began dumpster diving she went to _____ and checked that it was legal in her area.

3. In her first dumpster dive she took _____ from a supermarket dumpster and put them in _____.

4. She began dumpster diving _____.

5. She sent _____ items of clothing to a hostel for the homeless last year.

6. She found a _____ in the furniture store dumpster, her husband repaired it and they gave it to their _____.

7. The best thing she found so far is _____.

8. She and her partner spent a wonderful day at Christmas at _____.

d In the sentences in **1c** find the past tenses of these verbs:

begin – _____	go – _____	spend – _____
find – _____	read – _____	take – _____
give – _____	send – _____	put – _____

These past tenses are irregular. You have to learn them! Let's practise them.

2 Are you a good detective?

a Heather's neighbour throws a lot of things in the garbage. Look carefully.
What did this person do last week?

Example: He or she ate some donuts.

Do you think the person who threw these things away is a man or a woman? Why?
What else can you say about this person?

b Over to you. – What you didn't throw away can also tell us a lot about you.
Your teacher will show you some things from his/her pocket/wallet/handbag and help
you with the words. Then tell him/her what he/she did last week.

Examples: You bought some wine yesterday because there is a receipt in your handbag.
You came here by car, because you've got some car keys in your handbag.

c Now show your partner some things from your pocket/wallet/handbag so that he or she can guess
what you did yesterday or last week.

The past simple of full verbs – irregular

Positive
You have to learn the past simple of irregular verbs. Look on page 133 for a list of verbs.
Examples: She **sent** clothes to a hostel.
She **found** a TV in the dumpster.

Negatives and questions are formed in the same way as for regular verbs.
Examples: **Did** you **find** the TV behind the apartment block? – No, I didn't.
Where **did** they **find** the soft toy animals?
She **didn't buy** the TV; she found it.

Learning Tip – Grammar
When you learn a new verb look at the list on page 133 or in a good grammar book
and see if it is regular or irregular. If it is irregular, learn the past tense, too.

3 That's not right

a Look back at the text on dumpster diving in the tapescripts on page 137 (1b) and correct the information in the sentences below.

Example: Heather **went** dumpster diving for the first time in the furniture store dumpster. –
Heather **didn't go** dumpster diving for the first time in the <u>furniture store dumpster</u>.
She **went** dumpster diving for the first time behind a <u>supermarket</u>.

1. Heather began this hobby four years ago.
2. She gave the TV to a children's home.
3. She sent 5,000 items of clothing to a hostel for homeless people.
4. She read about this hobby in a newspaper.
5. Heather and her partner took the toys to a school.

 **27** **b** Say it right!

Listen to the corrected sentences in **3a**. Which words are stressed? Write them down.

1. _____
2. _____
3. _____
4. _____
5. _____

 When you correct information you stress both the wrong and the correct information.
See page 73 in the back-up for an exercise to practise this.

> **Learning Tip – Pronunciation**
> Listen to the sentences in 3b at home. Stop the CD and repeat the sentences. Remember the stress.

4 Five verbs and five questions

a On five pieces of paper write down five verbs in the past tense about last week.

Example: I bought, I saw, I went, I drank, I ate

b Now work with a partner and show him or her the verbs. Ask and answer questions to find out what your partner did last week. You can only ask five questions! Then your partner gives you the answer.

Example: Did you buy a new car? – No, I didn't.
Did you buy a pair of jeans. – No, I didn't.
Did you buy a present for your partner? – Yes, I did.

Did you guess the answers with five questions?

5 British or American?

Heather, the dumpster diver, is from America and 'dumpster' is American English.

What is the British English for these words?
- garbage – _____
- trunk – _____
- store – _____
- apartment block – _____

Work with a partner. Partner A looks at the list of British words on page 112 and partner B looks at the list of American words on page 115.

> **Learning Tip – Vocabulary**
> When you go on holiday or on a business trip to a country where most people speak English, take a notebook with you. Make a note of words you see in the hotel or on the street or in the restaurant that are different from the words in your English coursebook!

6 Can you lend it to me?

a You are on a business trip. You left some things from the lists in **5** in your hotel room so you have to ask your business partner for some help.

28 Listen to these short dialogues and answer the questions below.

What did he/she leave in the hotel?

1. _____   3. _____
2. _____   4. _____

b Now listen again and write down how the person asked politely for help.
The first one has been done for you.

polite request	reply
1. Could you ...?	Sure.
2. _____	_____
3. _____	_____
4. _____	_____

How do you give a positive or negative answer to the question 'Could you ...?'

c Work with a partner and practise the dialogues. They are on page 138.
You can ask for different things.

7 Rules

a As with any hobby there are rules that you should follow. Match columns A and B to prepare a list with dos and don'ts of dumpster diving.

A	B
Don't take more	in your area.
Check if this is legal	cleaner than you found it.
Don't make a lot of	aid kit.
Wear	to reach a dumpster.
Wash your hands	than you need
Leave the area	gloves.
Don't climb over a fence	when you finish.
Don't forget a first	noise.

> **Positive commands**
> Form: infinitive
> *Example:* **Wash** your hands when you finish.
>
> **Negative commands**
> Form: Don't + infinitive
> *Example:* **Don't make** a lot of noise.

 Look in the grammar reference section on page 131 for more information on commands.

 b Now listen to Karen who finds out about the rules. Check your list in **7a**.

c Heather goes dumpster diving to save money and help the environment.
Work in small groups. Complete the following sentences with some dos and don'ts if you want to be environmentally friendly.

Examples: If you want to save water, **don't leave** the tap running when you clean your teeth.
  If you want to reduce your electricity bills, **switch off** all lights when you leave a room.

If you want to save trees, ...
If you want to reduce waste, ...
If you want to save money, ...
If you want to ...

> **'if' sentences type 1**
> You use a sentence with **if** to talk about a possible situation that may happen. You use the present simple in the 'if' clause and an imperative (or command) in the main clause.
>
> *Examples:* **If** you **want** to save money, **buy** your clothes in the sales. *(you must WANT to save money first; that is the condition)*
>   **If** you **want** to save trees, **don't use** your car for very short journeys.

 See page 132 in the grammar section for more information about 'if' sentences.

8 ## Don't throw it away, recycle it! Give it to charity!

a When did you last buy a new car? What did you do with the old one? What can you do if your car fails its inspection?

b You are going to read about someone who didn't sell his old car, he donated it to charity when it failed its inspection. The paragraphs are in the wrong order. Sort them out. Put the correct number in the boxes.

The Teddy Bear
Cops Car Donation Charity

____ a. "I was on patrol duty one Saturday evening when I saw a car that was driving along the highway at 80 miles an hour. I stopped the driver and wrote out a speeding ticket. Suddenly he began to scream and shout at me. His small daughter who was in the back seat began to cry but when I gave her a teddy bear she gave me a big smile. Your car donation made this possible. Thank you."

____ b. So I found out some information about this charity and then I filled out a car donation form online and a few days later a very friendly team came and took the car away. The charity sold it to a dealer. It was simple and in this system everyone is happy. I got a certificate to say that I donated a car to charity and so I got a tax reduction. The dealer got a car that he could repair or sell for spare parts. The charity got the money.

_1_ c. It all happened last year when my car failed its inspection because of rust. It was thirteen years old – an unlucky number for a car – I suppose. I bought it with my first pay check and I drove over 200,000 miles in those thirteen years. It was very hard to say goodbye to the car, but I didn't want to spend a lot of money on repairs. Then I read an advertisement in the local paper that gave details of a charity called 'The Teddy Bear Cops Car Donation Charity'. It sounded interesting.

____ d. Sometimes the stories of children in shock don't sound very dramatic, but if you can help just one child then it is worth it. I read one story on the charity's web-site after I donated the car. It was from a traffic patrolman and it went like this.

____ e. The charity uses the money it raises through the sale of cars to buy lots and lots of teddy bears and other soft toys. Ambulance drivers or police officers or men and women from the fire department give these to children in shock after a trauma – when there is an accident or a fire or a crime.

____ f. I knew then that it was a good idea to say goodbye to my old car. Why don't you think about doing the same?

Compare your answers with a partner.

c Now read the text again and decide if these statements are true or false.

	True	False
1. The car failed its inspection because it was thirteen years old.	☐	☐
2. A car dealer came and took his car away.	☐	☐
3. He paid extra tax because he donated his car to charity.	☐	☐
4. The charity sells the cars and buys teddy bears with the money.	☐	☐
5. The emergency services give these teddy bears to children in shock.	☐	☐
6. The traffic patrolman started to scream and shout at the car driver.	☐	☐

d Do you sometimes donate money to charity? Which one and why? Is there a charity you would never give money to? Why not? What is the name of the most popular charity in your country? Are there a lot of charities for animals in your country?

Back-up

1 The environment and money

Your partner wants to help the environment and save money. Complete these sentences with an 'if' clause to give her some suggestions.

Example: If you want to save oil, don't buy fruit packed in plastic.

If _____, join a toy library.

If _____, don't send paper cards for birthdays, send e-mail ones.

If _____, put kitchen waste on a compost heap.

If _____, buy second-hand electrical goods.

If _____, send old clothes to the Red Cross.

If _____, donate your old mobile phone to charity.

If _____, don't buy fruit packed in plastic.

If _____, don't throw away your old computer, sell it through eBay.

If _____, give cinema tickets as birthday presents.

2 What did she do?

Kate Hamilton decided to take some of this advice to reduce the things she throws away. So what did she do last year and what didn't she do? Complete the sentences with a verb in the past tense. Be careful, some are negative.

1. She _____ all her friends e-cards.

2. She _____ fruit from the supermarket packed in plastic, she _____ it from the market.

3. When she _____ a new computer she _____ her old one online through eBay.

4. She _____ a toy library because her children are now at university but she _____ a lot of their old toys to the local toy library.

5. She _____ her mother tickets to the cinema for her birthday. She isn't very interested in films, but she _____ her some theatre tickets.

6. She _____ all her printer ink cartridges.

7. When her old washing machine _____ down, she _____ it away, she _____ it to a recycling company, but she _____ a second-hand washing machine, she _____ a new one.

8. She _____ time to read a newspaper every day so she only _____ a newspaper on a Sunday.

3 I need your help

How would you ask for help in these situations? Write down your answers on a separate piece of paper.

1. You are staying in New York. You want to take a colleague to dinner in a restaurant that is very popular.
2. You ring a business partner. You need a hotel room for two nights.
3. You can't hear someone who is speaking very quietly on the phone.
4. There is a phone call for your boss at 10.00 a.m. He is in a meeting until 11.00 a.m.
5. You have a problem with your lap top and so you can't give the power point presentation. You need an overhead projector.

6. You are giving a presentation and there is no more water.
7. You want to go to the airport but there is no reply when you ring the taxi service.
8. You are on a business trip and it is your partner's birthday and you forgot.
9. You need copies of some important documents.
10. You are in a hotel and you forgot your very loud alarm clock. You want to get up at 6 a.m.
11. You are drinking a gin and tonic in the bar, but it isn't very cold.
12. You arrive at a very expensive hotel with some very heavy suitcases.

Look in the key to check your answers.

4 Sentence stress

Decide which words are stressed in these sentences. Then listen to check you were right.

1. I didn't buy the computer from Dixons, I bought it from Currys.
2. I didn't throw the TV away, I threw the radio away.
3. I didn't buy the new mobile phone for my son, I bought it for my daughter.
4. I didn't buy a computer last year, I threw one away.
5. I didn't recycle the shoes, I recycled the coat.

Learning Tip – Vocabulary and pronunciation
In a good dictionary the stress is marked like this: – 'salary, a'partment
or like this: – salary, apartment.
This will help you to say the new word correctly.

5 Vocabulary

a Look at this list of words from the unit. Put them into the categories below. There are two words for each category. ● indicates the stressed syllable.

Examples: garbage = ●○   furniture = ●○○

| salary ┃ dirty ┃ suddenly ┃ behind ┃ apartment ┃ nervous ┃ reduction ┃ ago |

●○   ○●○   ●○○   ○●

_____   _____   _____   _____

_____   _____   _____   _____

b Now listen to see if this helps you. Then look in the key.
Look back in this unit and see if you can find more words with the same stress patterns.

At the end of this unit I ... :

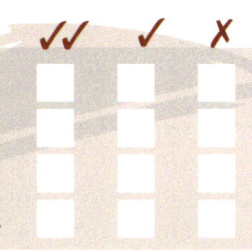

- can use irregular verbs to talk about what I did in the past.
- can understand negative and positive commands.
- can ask someone to help me.
- can understand how to say 'yes' or 'no' when someone asks me to help them.

✓✓ = I can do this easily.
✓ = I can do this.
✗ = I need to work on this.

Words and expressions from this unit for my personal **word bank** are:

_____

_____

Speaking

What's your dream holiday?

a You and your partner would like to go to England on holiday. What sort of hotel and holiday would you like? Can you agree on some points that are important for you both?

> city life   pubs and discos   a quiet village   good recreation facilities (e.g. a swimming pool or a gym)   a lot of shops   culture (e.g. museums or theatres)   people in my age group   luxury   a comfortable bed   no luxury – maybe a camping holiday   fresh air   peace and quiet   an activity schedule

… is/are important for me

… is/are important for my partner

b Look at these advertisements from an English language magazine. Can you decide together which hotel you want to visit?

New Tower Hotel
** Hotel in the middle of London's Bright and Busy City Centre!
Over 150 rooms on 14 floors!
Spectacular view of London's skyline from our Sky Restaurant!
Have a drink in The Tower Bar and dance the night away at our nightclub 'The Skyclub'
Rooms from £75 per night (single)

Orville Manor Hotel*****
Winner of Elegant Living's 'Best Hotel Award 2004'
Luxury Health and Fitness Centre, with indoor swimming pool and sauna
Award-winning restaurant 'Chez Louis'
All rooms with balcony and ensuite bathroom – 40 rooms in total – situated in the beautiful
Orville Manor Park, ten minutes on foot from Dollanbridge town centre
Only half an hour from London

- Three Star Hotel ***
- Only 2 hours from London!
- Fishing, horse-riding, walking opportunities in the area!
- 10 rooms, all with ensuite bathrooms
- Single room £50, double room £75

Riverdale Cottage Hotel and Restaurant
Highford

Riverdale Cottage
River End
Highford
MI5 E18
Tel.: 0555-55 55 55

Contact Mrs Ann Fingleton for more details or look at our website:
www. Riverdalecottage.com

Writing

What's your hotel like?

Now you know which hotel you would like to visit! Can you write 4-5 sentences about it, comparing it with the other hotels?
Use some of these adjectives. Add your own, if you want.

> comfortable   cheap   quiet   noisy   beautiful   expensive
> boring   exciting   near London

Example: We chose The Riverdale Cottage hotel because it is the cheapest. We think it is comfortable but we think the Orville Manor Hotel is the most comfortable hotel …

Reading

Bookcrossing

a Read this text about 'bookcrossing' to find the answers to the questions below.

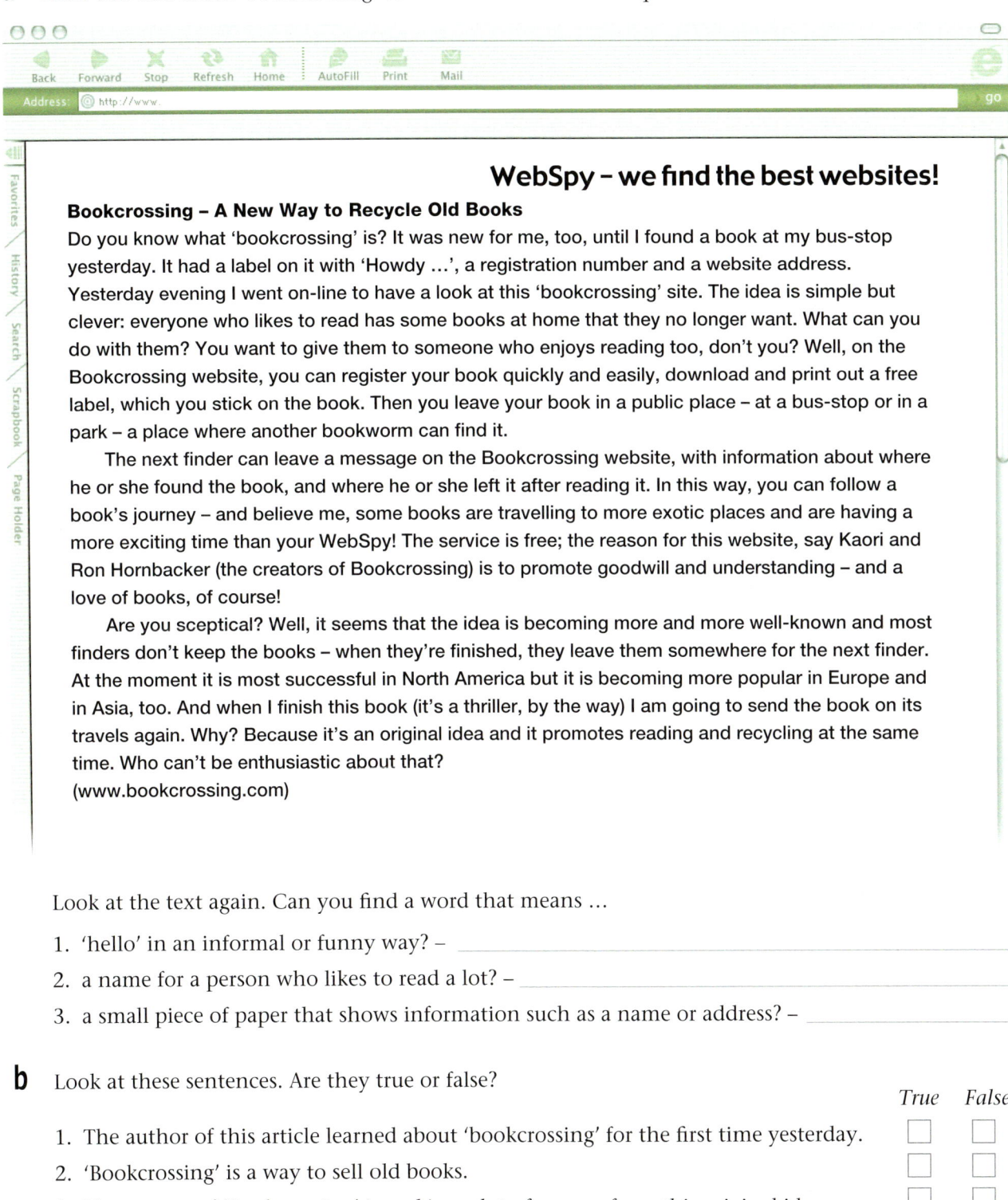

WebSpy – we find the best websites!

Bookcrossing – A New Way to Recycle Old Books

Do you know what 'bookcrossing' is? It was new for me, too, until I found a book at my bus-stop yesterday. It had a label on it with 'Howdy …', a registration number and a website address. Yesterday evening I went on-line to have a look at this 'bookcrossing' site. The idea is simple but clever: everyone who likes to read has some books at home that they no longer want. What can you do with them? You want to give them to someone who enjoys reading too, don't you? Well, on the Bookcrossing website, you can register your book quickly and easily, download and print out a free label, which you stick on the book. Then you leave your book in a public place – at a bus-stop or in a park – a place where another bookworm can find it.

The next finder can leave a message on the Bookcrossing website, with information about where he or she found the book, and where he or she left it after reading it. In this way, you can follow a book's journey – and believe me, some books are travelling to more exotic places and are having a more exciting time than your WebSpy! The service is free; the reason for this website, say Kaori and Ron Hornbacker (the creators of Bookcrossing) is to promote goodwill and understanding – and a love of books, of course!

Are you sceptical? Well, it seems that the idea is becoming more and more well-known and most finders don't keep the books – when they're finished, they leave them somewhere for the next finder. At the moment it is most successful in North America but it is becoming more popular in Europe and in Asia, too. And when I finish this book (it's a thriller, by the way) I am going to send the book on its travels again. Why? Because it's an original idea and it promotes reading and recycling at the same time. Who can't be enthusiastic about that?

(www.bookcrossing.com)

Look at the text again. Can you find a word that means …

1. 'hello' in an informal or funny way? – _____

2. a name for a person who likes to read a lot? – _____

3. a small piece of paper that shows information such as a name or address? – _____

b Look at these sentences. Are they true or false?

	True	False
1. The author of this article learned about 'bookcrossing' for the first time yesterday.	☐	☐
2. 'Bookcrossing' is a way to sell old books.	☐	☐
3. The creator of 'Bookcrossing' is making a lot of money from this original idea.	☐	☐
4. Most of the 'bookcrossing' takes place in the USA and Canada.	☐	☐
5. The author likes the idea of 'bookcrossing'.	☐	☐

Listening

A wild party

a Richard Cole's parents went away this weekend and left their 18-year-old son home alone. Of course, he used the opportunity to hold a big party! Now it's 11.30 a.m. the day after the party and he can't remember very much about the night before.
He remembers vaguely …
- that he danced
- that he sang
- that he chatted to Angela
- that he spoke to Mrs Leach, the next door neighbour
… but that's all.

32 Listen to the messages on his answering machine and put the callers in the correct order.

	Tom		Richard's mum		Katie
	James and Clare		Mrs Leach		Angela

b Listen to the messages on his answering machine again and answer these questions.

1. How did he dress yesterday evening? – _____

2. How did he dance? – _____

3. How did he sing? – _____

4. How did he chat to Angela? – _____

5. How did he speak to Mrs Leach? – _____

Speaking

New Year's resolutions

At the beginning of each year, we all promise to do things – and not to do things! – for example: stop smoking, eat less chocolate, go to bed early, etc.
Student A looks at page 113.

Student B looks at William's list of New Year's Resolutions. Did he do all the things he wanted to do? Ask your partner questions to fill in the missing information and answer his/her questions.
Example: Student A: Did he learn to drive?
            Student B: Yes, he did. He learned to drive in the summer.

Learn to drive before September.	Yes! Driving test in July!
Stop smoking.	
Lose 10 kg.	lost 5 kg!
Start going to the fitness centre.	NO.
Do an evening course – French? Karate?	
Remember my mum's birthday in February.	
Remember my dad's birthday in April.	Yes.
Bring all my old newspapers to the recycling centre every week.	
Learn to cook Thai food.	
Give money to charity.	Yes – to UNICEF.

Reading

Talking about your job history

Helen Smith is starting a new job as a marketing assistant tomorrow. Her new boss asked her to hold a short informal presentation to tell her colleagues a little bit about herself. She wrote some notes on cards.

a First read the notes and fill in the correct form of the verbs in past simple.

_____ a. When I _____ (hear) they needed a junior events manager in Simons' marketing department, I _____ (apply) for it – and I _____ (get) the job!

_____ b. While I was working as a personal assistant, I _____ (attend) a lot of workshops and seminars in the company and at the VHS. I _____ (do) computer courses and a marketing course, too, which I especially liked.

_____ c. I _____ (go) to school in Cardiff and _____ (do) my A-levels in modern languages. I originally _____ (want) to be a secondary school teacher but I _____ (change) my mind when I _____ (go) to college.

_____ d. After so many years at Simons, I wanted a change so I _____ (start) looking for a new job. I _____ (see) the advertisement for a marketing assistant at this company in the 'Süddeutsche Zeitung' and I _____ (apply). I _____ (be) very happy when I _____ (get) the job.

_____ e. So after I _____ (leave) college, I _____ (move) to Munich and _____ (find) a job in Simons' sales department as a personal assistant to one of the managers. I _____ (work) there for two years

_____ f. Then I _____ (start) college. I _____ (study) for four years in Birmingham – German and economics. I graduated in 1996.

_____ g. While I was studying in Birmingham, I _____ (do) an internship at Simons in Munich for 3 months and I really _____ (like) living in Germany.

_____ h. That's enough about me. I'm looking forward to working with you and I hope you will be patient with me in my first few days!

_____ i. My name is Helen Smith and I'm from Wales originally. I live in Munich now, and I love it. Let me tell you a little bit about myself …

_____ j. I _____ (discover) I loved working in this department. I _____ (work) on a lot of marketing projects. While I was working in this department I _____ (spend) 6 weeks in Los Angeles, working on a campaign for German beer. I _____ (stay) in this department till last April.

_____ k. After school I _____ (work) as an au-pair in Switzerland for a year.

b Unfortunately, the notes are in the wrong order. Read them again and put them in the correct order.

UNIT 8   What would you do?

1 Feelings

a Match the adjectives with the faces.

☐ angry   ☐ sad   ☐ happy   ☐ bored   ☐ cold   ☐ tired

How are you feeling at the moment? – I'm feeling …

b Look at this list and decide which three people make you feel the angriest.

A person who
– smokes in the underground.
– parks illegally.
– coughs during a concert.
– takes their dog for a walk and doesn't clear up the mess.
– plays loud music late at night.
– throws litter in the street.
– ignores you when you are shopping and want some help.
– holds long conversations on their mobile phone in a train.
– drives their car very slowly on the motorway.
– blows their car horn impatiently when there isn't any danger.

Tell your partner which three people make you feel the angriest and why.

Note
on their mobile phone = on his/her mobile phone

c Read these sentences and choose your answer.

If someone **threw** litter in the street, would you say anything?
If someone **lit** a cigarette in the underground, would you say anything?
If someone in your block of flats **played** loud music at night, would you phone the police?
If a shop assistant **ignored** you, would you report him or her to the manager?

 Yes | Yes, I would.

 No | No, I don't think I would. I'd (I would) …

78   UNIT 8

> **'if' sentences type 2**
> *Example:* If someone **lit** a cigarette in the underground, I **would ask** him/her to put it out.
>
> You are imagining this situation, it is not real now.
> When you talk about possible situations that you think *may not* happen, you use the following combination of tenses:
>
> | **'if' part** | **main part** |
> |---|---|
> | past simple | would(n't) + infinitive of verb |
>
> **Question form**
> *Example:* What **would** you **do** if your car **broke** down? – I'd (I would) use my mobile and phone my partner.

See the grammar reference section on page 132 for more information about conditionals and page 86 in the back-up for more work with this grammar point.

See the grammar reference section on page 132 ... and page 86 in the back-up

Learning Tip – Grammar
Remember this little rhyme to help you with tenses in if clauses:
'If' and 'would' –
it is no good.

d Look at the situations below and choose four. Put the verbs in brackets in the correct tense and make questions with "What would you do if ...?"
Be careful of the tenses. Look on page 133 to find irregular past tenses you don't know.

What would you do if ...?

- your car (break) down on the motorway
- you (lose) your voice
- you (lock) yourself out of the house
- someone (steal) your car/bicycle
- someone (steal) your handbag/wallet when you are on holiday
- your family pet (run) away
- you (need) a lot of money urgently
- you (break) your glasses / (lose) your contact lenses

Now work with a partner and ask him or her the questions.

2 This is serious

a Some people don't just complain when they feel angry, they go to court. They take legal action. Look at the headlines below. What is making people in America angry now? What is the missing word in every headline?

> Activists say .... restaurants should warn consumers about health risks

> .... chain relies on salads to improve its image

> More and more evidence that .... can be addictive

> Teenagers lose their fight with .... chain

b Now listen to this short news report to check (in **2a**) what is making people in America angry.

- If you went to a restaurant and you were sick the next morning, would you complain to the restaurant or would you just go to the doctor's?
- If you ate at some friends' house and you were sick the next morning, would you ring them and tell them or would you just go to the doctor's?

c A lot of people were interested in this news story and visited a chat room to post their ideas. Work in groups of three or four. Group A looks at the file below. Group B looks at file on page 114. Group C looks at the file on page 116 and group D looks at the file on page 109.
Follow the instructions in the file section.

Group A

Read the posting in the chat room and make sure you all understand the main point in it.

Then your teacher will give you a number. Find people who have got the same number as you and work with them in a new group. Tell them about your chat room posting.

Example: I read about Nga Tan. She thinks you should look at the menu carefully.

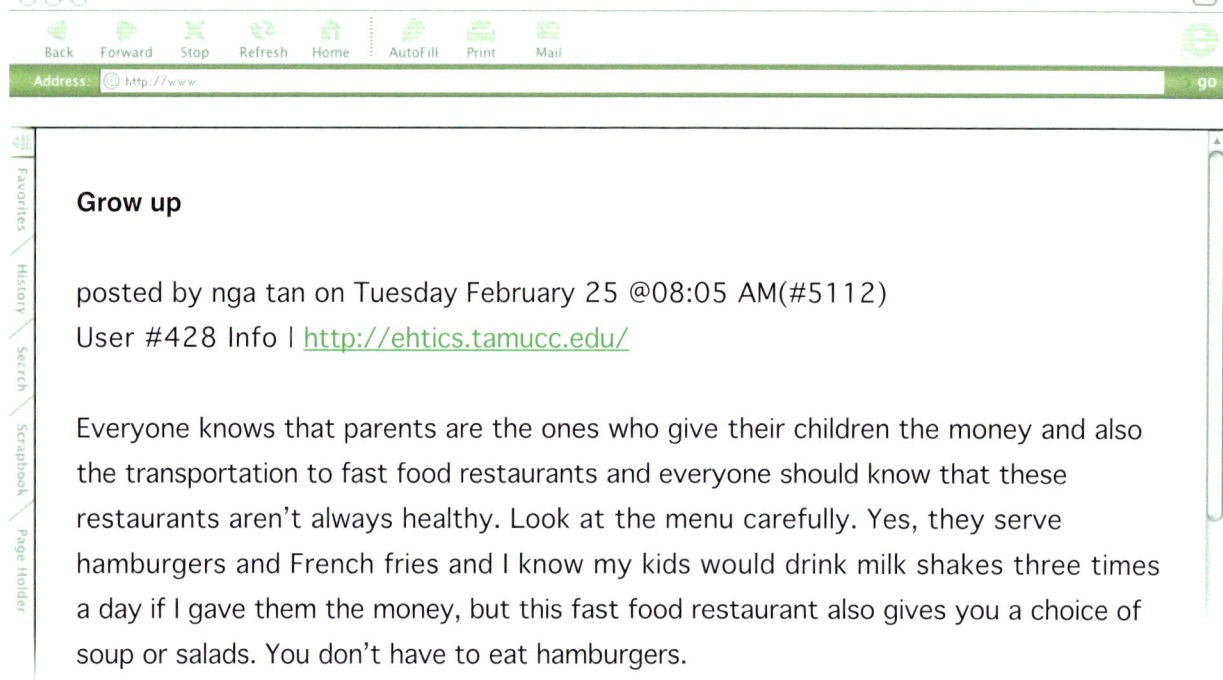

Grow up

posted by nga tan on Tuesday February 25 @08:05 AM(#5112)
User #428 Info | http://ehtics.tamucc.edu/

Everyone knows that parents are the ones who give their children the money and also the transportation to fast food restaurants and everyone should know that these restaurants aren't always healthy. Look at the menu carefully. Yes, they serve hamburgers and French fries and I know my kids would drink milk shakes three times a day if I gave them the money, but this fast food restaurant also gives you a choice of soup or salads. You don't have to eat hamburgers.

What do you think about fast food?

3 A healthy diet?

a A lot of doctors think that it is healthy to eat a 'Mediterranean diet'. This pyramid shows you what food is in this diet.

Look carefully at the pyramid and decide if the following statements are true or false.

	True	False
1. You should take some exercise every day.	☐	☐
2. You shouldn't eat pasta every day.	☐	☐
3. You should eat fruit and vegetables every day.	☐	☐
4. You should eat cheese or yoghurt once a week.	☐	☐
5. You shouldn't eat fish.	☐	☐
6. You shouldn't eat chicken every day.	☐	☐
7. You should eat some eggs every week.	☐	☐
8. You shouldn't eat meat every week.	☐	☐

Check with your partner.

b Look at the pyramid again and make some more statements about it using 'should' and 'shouldn't'. What should fast food companies do?

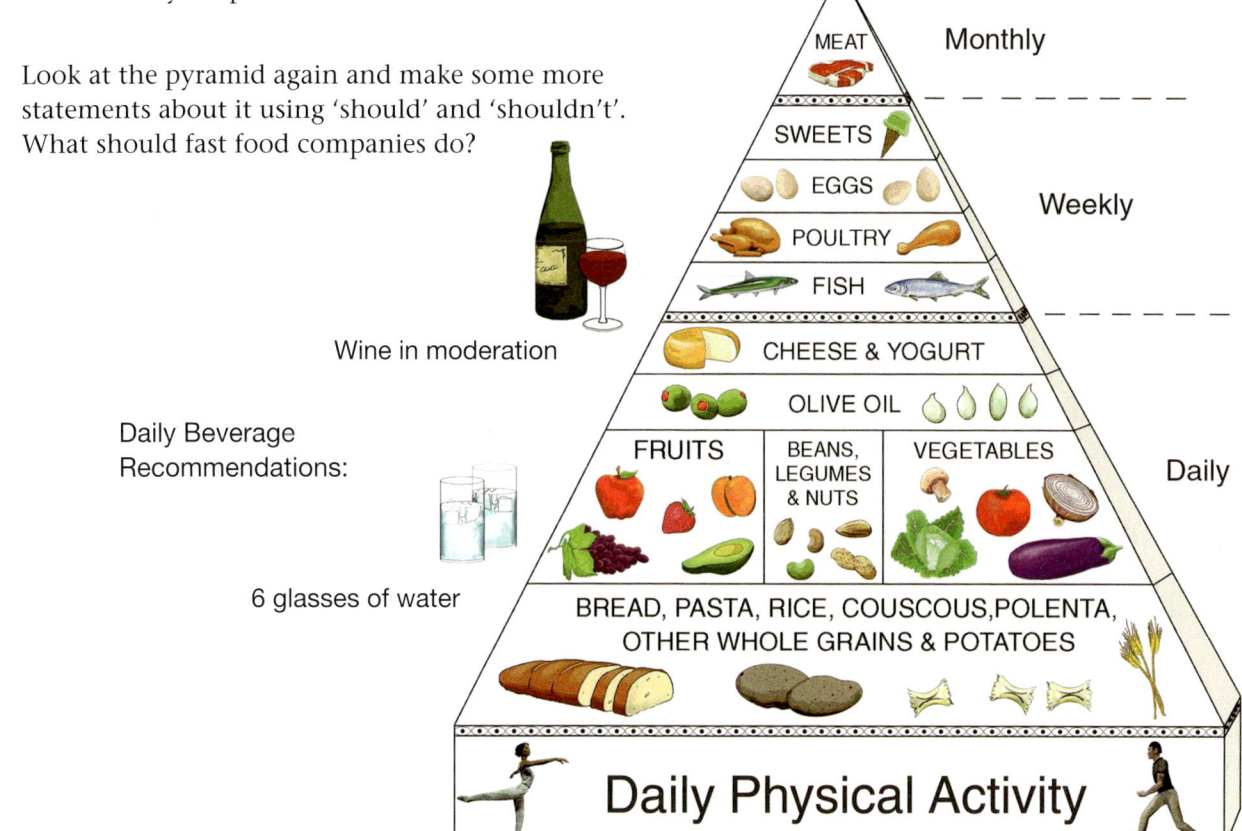

Wine in moderation

Daily Beverage Recommendations:

6 glasses of water

© 2000 Oldways Preservation & Exchange Trust   www.oldwayspt.org

---

Should / shouldn't
You use 'should' to talk about something that is a good idea.
Example: You **should** eat a lot of fruit.

You use 'shouldn't' to talk about something that is a bad idea.
Example: You **shouldn't** eat chocolate.

4 Doctors!

a Doctors often tell us what we should and shouldn't eat so that we are healthy. When we are ill, doctors tell us what we have to do and what we mustn't do.

 Listen to these telephone calls when friends ring up and ask questions. Why can't the friends meet?

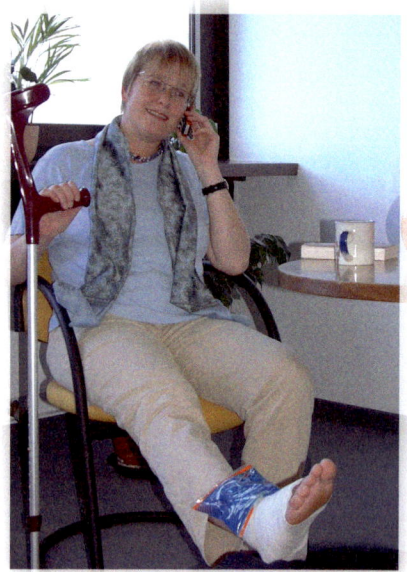

	has to	mustn't
Janet		
Brian		
Anita		

Mustn't
You use 'mustn't' when you talk about something that is wrong to do (so don't do it).
Example: Sally **mustn't** carry heavy shopping bags.

Have to / has to
You use 'have to' / 'has to' when you talk about something that is 100% necessary.
Examples: I **have to keep** my arm in a sling.
Brian **has to** keep off alcohol.

b A few weeks later Roger, Jim and Sally ring their friends and ask about their health. They are better now.
– Janet doesn't have to use crutches now.
– Brian doesn't have to take tablets for hay fever so he doesn't have to keep off alcohol.
– Anita doesn't have to keep her arm in a sling.

Don't have to / doesn't have to
You use 'don't have to' / 'doesn't have to' to talk about something that isn't necessary.
Example: Anita **doesn't have to** keep her arm in a sling.

 Look in the grammar reference section on page 131 for more help and in the back-up on page 86 for more work with 'should', 'shouldn't', 'mustn't', 'have to' and 'don't have to'.

5 Come to Utopia!

a Utopia is very good country to live in. Choose a group of people (e.g. children) and make some sentences from this chart.

In Utopia …

cyclists	should	eat healthy food
children	shouldn't	help parents with the washing up
car drivers	have to	wear crash hats
dog owners	mustn't	ride on the pavement
parents	don't have to	keep their dog on a lead
		be careful of pedestrians
		slow down near schools
		give their children a lot of pocket money
		pay for hospital treatment

b Now work in groups of three and think of a new country, a wonderful country where everything is ideal. Write ten sentences about your country using the verbs from the table in **5a**. Tell the other groups about your country.

Which is the best country? Which country would you like to live in?

6 Sunday lunch

a Sunday in England is not a day to think about what you should and shouldn't eat but it's often a day when the whole family goes for a pub lunch.

Make a list of all the words for food that you know.

b Then look at the menu on the next page and find the names of the following:

2 sorts of cheese	*2 sorts of fish*	*4 sorts of vegetables*

something hot/for a curry	*something yellow*	*something that smells*

c Now look at the menu more carefully and decide what the following people would order from it.

1. Bob isn't very hungry. He doesn't like fish or garlic.
2. Janie wants a traditional Sunday lunch. She doesn't eat red meat.
3. Andrew is hungry and he's vegetarian.
4. Wendy likes fish but she only has £10 in her purse.
5. Lee says that a meal without soup is like a day without sunshine and he also wants a traditional Sunday lunch. He doesn't like plums.

What do you have to remember in a British pub? You buy your drink and then you sit down. If a small group of friends go out for a drink together each person buys 'a round', in other words a drink for himself or herself and one for everyone in the group. Are there any traditions like this in your country?

PUBS OF LONDON

Serving from 12 noon until 9.30 pm.
Please place your orders at our food order bar.

S t a r t e r s

Fresh Tomato Soup £2.95
Made with the finest sun-ripened Spanish tomatoes.
Comes with a wedge of crusty fresh bloomer bread.

Crab and Salmon Fish Cakes £5.25
Beautifully prepared and flavoured with hints
of wild chilli and coriander, served with lemon
mayonnaise and a dressed mixed salad.

Breaded Mushrooms £3.25
Deep-fried to perfection served with a creamy
garlic dip.

S u n d a y   R o a s t s

Freshly Carved Sirloin of Beef £7.25
Served with Yorkshire pudding, roast potatoes,
glazed Charlotte potatoes, freshly steamed
vegetables and a rich gravy.

**Roast Norfolk Turkey with Victoria
Plum Stuffing** £6.55
Accompanied by roast potatoes, glazed Charlotte
potatoes, freshly steamed vegetables and a bacon-
wrapped sausage served with a rich gravy.

M a i n   C o u r s e s

Cajun Chicken on Bow Tie Pasta £7.25
A tender breast of chicken, lightly grilled and
seasoned with Cajun spices and served on pasta
mixed with red and green peppers. Accompanied
by tomato and garlic bread.

Baked Sea Bass £10.95
A whole baked sea bass finished with a lemon
and parsley butter.
Served with Charlotte potatoes and freshly
steamed vegetables.

Roast Nut, Mushroom and Spinach Loaf £6.95
This nut loaf is stuffed with creamy Brie and
accompanied by a mushroom mascarpone sauce.
Served with roast potatoes, glazed Charlotte
potatoes and freshly steamed vegetables.

Classic Chicken Caesar Salad £7.25
Lightly grilled chicken, parmesan slices, ciabatta
croutons and lettuce with our Caesar dressing.

d If you were in this pub for lunch, what would you choose from the menu and why?

7 The Sunday lunch wasn't a great success

a Some people had a pub lunch and there were a few problems.
Listen to the short dialogues and fill in the missing words in the problems.

problem	apology
1. waiting for _____	I'm really sorry. I'll send it back.
2. chicken served without _____	I really do apologise. Would you like ...?
3. _____ isn't done in the middle	I'm sorry about that. I'll get you some now.
4. _____ is cold	Sorry about that. ... I'll check for you.

b Now listen again and match the apologies to the problems. Some problems are more serious than others.

c How serious are the following situations? How would you apologise?

1. You spill wine on a friend's coat.
2. You spill wine on someone's coat. You don't know the person.
3. You break a wine glass when you are at a wedding. It's very expensive.
4. You break a water glass at a friend's house.
5. You arrive late at a friend's house.
6. You arrive very late for an appointment at the dentist's.

Note
a water glass – *the glass is empty*
a glass of water – *the glass is full*

8 The pub lunch

a Businessmen in London often go out to the pub for lunch. Pubs are often crowded at lunchtime. Imagine you are in a pub. How would you reply if someone asked you these questions?
Look in the key to see if your ideas were possible.

Can I take this chair?	Sure. Help yourself.	I'm sorry, it's taken.
Can I look at your menu?	Sure. Here you are.	Well, I'd rather you didn't.
Can I borrow your ashtray?	Sure. Go ahead.	Sorry, I haven't finished yet.
Can I have the salt and pepper?		Sorry, we need it.
Is it OK if I smoke?		
Is it OK if I open a window?		
Can I take your plate?		

b Stand in a circle. Your teacher will start and ask one of the questions from **8a** and throw you a ball. Give an answer. Then say another sentence and throw the ball to someone else.

9 Cherry or sherry?

a Listen and repeat the pairs of words you hear.

	A /ʃ/		B /tʃ/	
1.	she's	☐	cheese	☐
2.	sherry	☐	cherry	☐
3.	sheep	☐	cheap	☐
4.	ships	☐	chips	☐
5.	shop	☐	chop	☐
6.	shoe	☐	chew	☐

b Now listen again and tick the word that you hear from either column A or B.

Learning Tip – Pronunciation
You could have a page in your word bank where you collect a lot of words that have the sound [ʃ] and ones where you have words with the sound [tʃ] .

Back-up

1 If

Make questions using these prompts and then answer them for yourself.

Example: What / do / win a million Euro?
What would you do if you won a million Euro? – I'd go on a world tour.

1. Where / spend holiday / money be not a problem?
2. What / say to him/her / meet your favourite film star/pop singer?
3. What / do / forget partner's birthday?
4. How / feel / company offer you or your partner a new job in Australia?
5. What / do / hear strange noises in the night?
6. Who / phone / tree fall on your roof in a storm?
7. What / do / police arrest you on a demonstration?
8. What / do / get bad marks in an English test?
9. What new pet / buy / your cat/dog run away?
10. What / say / police stop you for speeding?

2 Necessary or not necessary? A good idea or a bad idea?

a Put mustn't / have to / has to / should / shouldn't / don't have to / doesn't have to in the blanks in these sentences.

1. You _____ drink and drive in Ireland.
2. The young children _____ wear a uniform but the older ones do.
3. The thing I like best about holidays is that I _____ get up early.
4. I know I _____ eat a lot of chocolate, but I love it. I'm a chocoholic.
5. You _____ eat chicken every day on a Mediterranean diet.
6. He _____ take tablets for hay fever every spring.
7. For healthy teeth you _____ clean your teeth twice a day.
8. I know you are sitting in the back but you still _____ wear a seat belt.
9. Passengers _____ smoke in the underground because it is dangerous.
10. Pedestrians _____ drop litter in Singapore or they may go to prison.
11. First you _____ buy a valid ticket.
12. I _____ be at the airport very early. The flight takes off at 12 noon.
13. Pamela _____ to drive into London every day. She has a flat near the office during the week.
14. You _____ phone her after 9.30 because she goes to bed then.
15. Bob _____ use crutches at the moment because he has a broken leg.
16. You _____ drink two litres of water a day.
17. Don't forget your passport. You _____ show it when you arrive in England.
18. You _____ be rich to be happy.
19. In some countries you _____ wear a crash helmet when you drive a motorbike.
20. She _____ worry about what she eats, she's very fit and healthy.

b   Now complete the sentences so that they are true for you.

I should _____ but I don't!

I shouldn't _____ but I do!

I love _____ because I don't have to _____.

I have to _____ regularly because _____.

3   Vocabulary

In these words the vowels a, e, i, o, u are missing.
Fill in the missing words and then write a sentence with each word.

1. s _ r _ _ _ s

2. _ v _ d _ n c _

3. c _ m p l _ _ n t

4. f _ l _ v _ r

5. c _ _ g h

6. _ p p _ _ n t m _ n t

7. d _ n g _ r

8. v _ _ c _

9. _ p _ l _ g _ s _

10. _ l _ m _ s t

11. _ r g _ n t l y

12. _ n s t _ _ d

13. b _ r r _ w

14. _ d v _ r t _ s _ n g

4   Permission or an apology?

What would you say in these situations?

1. You stand on someone's foot in the bus.
2. You are sitting near the window and it is very hot.
3. You are away on business and you want to check your e-mails in a friend's office.
4. You are driving your car with one passenger and you put your brakes on suddenly.

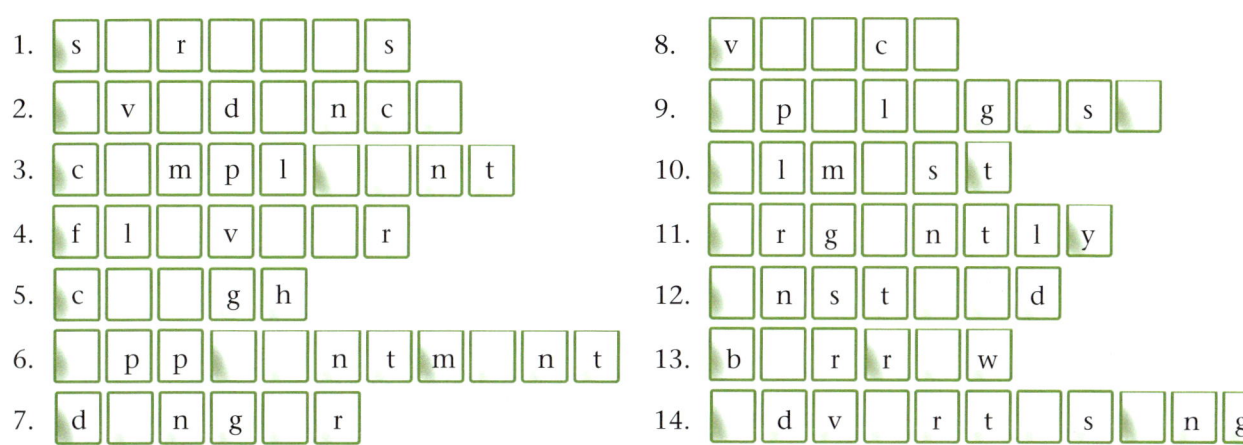

At the end of this unit I ... :

✓✓   ✓   ✗

● can express how I'm feeling.

● can talk about health problems.

● can use 'should/shouldn't' to talk about good/bad ideas.

● can understand and explain simple rules.

● can listen to problems and apologise.

✓✓ = I can do this easily.
✓ = I can do this.
✗ = I need to work on this.

Words and expressions from this unit for my personal **word bank** are:

_____

_____

Celebrations

4.6. Charlotte

18.8. Paul

29.2. Lisa

1 A special date

a Look at these photos and read the sentences before you match the names to the sentences below.

He's celebrating his eightieth birthday. _____

She's celebrating her first birthday. _____

She's celebrating her sixth (!) birthday. _____

b In the sentences below fill in the birthday dates.

The baby is celebrating her first birthday on ...
Lisa is celebrating her twenty-fourth birthday on ...
Paul is celebrating his eightieth birthday on ...

> **Note**
> People who have their birthday on
> 29th February were born in a leap year.

> **Note**
>
> | | | | | | | | |
> |---|---|---|---|---|---|---|---|
> | 1st | first | 5th | fifth | 11th | eleventh | 13th | thirteenth |
> | 2nd | second | 8th | eighth | 12th | twelfth | 30th | thirtieth |
> | 3rd | third | 9th | ninth | 20th | twentieth | 14th | fourteenth |
> | 4th | fourth | 10th | tenth | | | 40th | fortieth |

 Look in the back-up section on page 94 for work with the pronunciation of numbers, e.g. 14 and 40.

c When is your birthday? What day is your birthday on this year? What did you do on your last birthday?

d Now write down three dates that are special to you. Show them to your partner. He or she has to ask questions to find out why they are special to you.

Examples: Did you pass your exam on that day?
Was it the first day in your new flat?
Was it your wedding day?
Did you meet your partner on that day?

2 Birthdays and weddings

38

a Do you always celebrate your birthday or your wedding anniversary? If so, how? Do you give a party or do you go out for a meal in a restaurant?
Listen to the CD and fill in Sandra's answers to a questionnaire about parties.

Have you ever organised a party	on a beach?	Yes, I have.
	at the top of a mountain?	Yes, _____.
	for more than 100 people?	No, _____.
	by a lake?	_____
	by a river?	_____

b What has she done?
Sandra has organised a party on a beach and she has organised one
_____ but she has never organised a party for more than 100 people.

What about you?
I have organised a party _____ but I have never

organised one _____ .

c Make six sensible questions from this table and write them on a piece of paper.
Then stand up, go round the class and ask three people the questions and put down the answers.

Have you ever	attended a wedding	on a beach?
	celebrated a birthday	at the top of a mountain?
	got drunk	in a beer garden?
	celebrated a wedding anniversary	on a ship?
	given a speech	in Hawaii?
		in a foreign country?
		by a lake?
		at a wedding/at a party?
		in a cathedral?
		by a river?
		of friends from a different culture?

Now tell the group three things that you found out.

Examples: Helga has never celebrated a birthday in a foreign country.
Robert has given a speech at a wedding.

39

d "Have you ever celebrated a birthday in a foreign country?" – "Yes, I have."
In this answer we don't know 'when' she celebrated a birthday.
To find out listen and fill in the missing information in this short dialogue.

- ● _____ you _____ given a speech at a wedding?
- ■ Yes, I have.
- ● When _____ that?
- ■ At my brother's wedding in 2002.

e Over to you. – Work in groups of four. One person sits in the 'hot seat'. He or she has to give information and the other three have to ask questions. It doesn't HAVE to be about celebrations.

Examples: I have organised a party on a beach.
When was that?
Two years ago. It was my partner's thirtieth birthday.

I have eaten octopus.
When was that?
Last year on holiday in Greece.

Talk about three things and then change the person in the 'hot seat'.

Remember how to sound interested from unit 6 on page 62.

The present perfect
You use the present perfect to talk about experiences, but you don't say when it happened. You use it in sentences with no definite time signals.

Positive form
Present of the verb 'to have' + past participle.
Example: I **have celebrated** a birthday on a beach.

The past participle is the same as the past simple for regular verbs. For irregular verbs look on page 133.

Negative form
Present of the auxiliary verb 'to have' + never + past participle.
Example: I **have never attended** a wedding at the top of a mountain.

Question form
Present of the verb 'to have' + person + ever + past participle.
Examples: **Have** you **ever been** a bridesmaid at a wedding? – No, never.
Have you **ever given** a speech at a wedding? – Yes, I have.

To ask or say 'when' something happened, you use the **past simple**.
Example: When **was** that? – **Last year**. It **was** my brother's birthday.

Here you use the past simple because you are talking about a definite time in the past.

 Look in the back-up section on page 94 for more work with the present perfect and on pages 128/129 in the grammar reference section.

3 # Wedding customs

Work with a partner. Partner A reads the text about weddings in India on the next page and partner B reads the text about weddings in Mexico on page 115.

Partner A

Your partner will ask you questions about your text, so make a note of the answers.
– What happens before the wedding ceremony?
– What does the bride do and wear on her wedding day? Are there any reasons?
– What does the groom wear and do on his wedding day? Are there any reasons?
– What do the relatives and guests do on the wedding day? Are there any reasons?

world-wedding-traditions.net

An Indian wedding

Sweets, eggs and money are all very important in an Indian wedding so that the couple has a sweet life, many children and enough money. When the couple has made their wedding vows the groom's father or a brother showers flower petals on the couple; then he holds a coconut over the bride and groom's heads and circles it around three times to protect them from evil spirits.
Traditional Indian brides wear pink and red saris on their wedding day and as much jewellery as possible. On the evening before her wedding female members of her family bathe the bride in a traditional way and then also stain her hands and feet with henna in beautiful patterns.
The groom gives his wife a special wedding gift, a necklace, on their wedding day. When she wears the necklace everyone she meets knows that she's married.
To find out more about weddings in different countries visit the web-site:

www.world-wedding-traditions.net

4 Away on honeymoon

a Sarah is getting married again next Saturday and it is the school holidays. She and her new husband are going to Mexico on their honeymoon. Her ex-husband, Tim, can't look after the children, as he is going into hospital. She asked her mum, Joan, and she agreed at once to look after them.

Joan has organised a lot of things for her grandchildren to do while their mum is away and she's written everything down in her diary. Joan and her husband usually play golf with friends on Tuesdays, Wednesdays and Saturdays so Joan rings them.

40 Listen and complete her diary.

Saturday 13th	Sarah's wedding
Sunday 14th	
Monday 15th	
Tuesday 16th	
Wednesday 17th	
Thursday 18th	Cheshire ice cream farm
Friday 19th	
Saturday 20th	Llangollen Wharf horse-drawn boat centre
Sunday 21st	
Monday 22nd	
Tuesday 23rd	take the kids back to Stockport

What's happening each day? And what are the children doing with their grandparents?
– On Saturday Sarah is getting married. On Monday Joan is …

b What are you doing next week? Make notes in your diary.

c Work together with a partner to find out what he/she is doing next week.

Example: What are you doing next Monday? – I'm going to the dentist's.

> **Present progressive for future meanings**
> You use the **present progressive** to talk about definite arrangements in the future.
> Form: the verb **to be** plus **-ing** form of the verb.
> *Examples:* I**'m going** to the dentist's on Tuesday.
>   She**'s getting** married next Saturday.
>
> For the negative add 'not'.
> *Example:* They **aren't** (are not) **flying** to Rome on their honeymoon.
>
> For questions change round the verb and the person.
> *Examples:* **Is** she **getting** married on Saturday?
>   **Are** they **flying** to Rome?

Look on page 129 in the grammar section for more explanations of the present continuous for future meaning and on page 95 in the back-up section for some more work with this grammar point.

5 The invitation

a You are Mr/Mrs Gladstone. You get home after 2 weeks' holiday and hear the following message on your answering machine. You make a note of it on the notepad by the phone.

Message from: _____

Message: _____

> Mr and Mrs Bradbury request the pleasure of the company
> of Mr and Mrs P. Gladstone to a cocktail party on Friday 15 July
> at 6 p.m. on the occasion of Mr Bradbury's retirement after
> 40 years with the company.
> R.S.V.P.

Accept
We would be delighted / very happy / to attend the cocktail party.

Refuse
Unfortunately, we can't accept the kind invitation to the cocktail party because …

Decide if you want to accept or refuse the invitation.

b Now you want to speak to Mr Bradbury's assistant, but she isn't in her office.
Leave a message on her answering machine.
– Give your name and spell it.
– Apologise that you haven't replied. Give a reason why you haven't replied.
– Accept or refuse the invitation. If you refuse, give a reason; say what you are doing on that Friday. (It must be something important!)
– Send good wishes to Mr Bradbury.

c While you were away, you have also received this invitation.

> You are invited to a party at Jeff's place.
> When: Saturday 16th July from 8.00 p.m.
> Why: I've passed my driving test!
> Bring a bottle!

Your partner is Jeff or his wife Pamela. Phone him/her to accept or refuse the invitation.

Accept	Refuse
We'd love to come. Thanks.	I'm really sorry, but we can't come because we're …

Plan what you are going to say before you make the call! Look at the phone call in this unit on page 139 (track 40) for some help with the beginning of a call.

6 At the party

a You accept Jeff's invitation to his party. Match a sentence from column A with one from column B to make short dialogues you would hear at the party.

A
Sorry, I'm late.
Can I take your coat?
Would you like another drink?
What a pretty blouse. The colour
   suits you.
Congratulations.
Thanks for a lovely evening.
The food is wonderful.

B
Thanks. I'm glad you like it.
Not at all. Thank you for coming. Drive carefully.
Thank you. Nice of you to say so.
Thanks.
No, problem. Go through and help yourself to
   a drink.
Oh, yes. Thank you.
Yes, please, but just something soft. I'm driving.

b Listen to see if you were right.

Should you take a present when you are invited to a party? If yes, what? Is there anything that you should not take as a present when you go to a party in your country? When you receive a present should you open it immediately or some time later? Should you say thank you and how much you like the present?

Back-up

1 Have you ever ... ?

Make questions from these prompts and then answer the questions for yourself.

Example: visit / Majorca?   Have you ever visited Majorca?   – Yes, I have. Last year.
                                                                    – No, never.

1. watch / grand prix on TV
2. get lost / in / foreign country
3. have / car accident
4. attend / cocktail party
5. stay / five star hotel
6. sleep / by a lake / by a river
7. drive / car / foreign country
8. break / arm or leg

2 What happened?

a What happened on the dates you are going to hear on the CD? Do you know the answers? Write them down.

1. _____
2. _____
3. _____
4. _____
5. _____

b What date did you say?

Listen and decide which date you hear. Tick the correct box.

1. 13th ☐   30th ☐
2. 15th ☐   50th ☐
3. 13th ☐   30th ☐
4. 17th ☐   70th ☐

5. 14th ☐   40th ☐
6. 15th ☐   50th ☐
7. 17th ☐   70th ☐
8. 14th ☐   40th ☐

3 The family diary

a Match a word from column A with one from column B.

A		B
have		meeting / wedding / christening / cocktail party
give		swimming / to the dentist's / to the hairdresser's
go to / attend a		a violin lesson
go		tennis
play		Geneva
fly to / back from		a presentation

b Everyone in the Thomson family is very busy next week. Look at their diaries.

	Peter	Carol	The children
Monday	presentation to Marketing Manager 10 a.m.	sales meeting 10.30	Bob tennis 6 p.m.
Tuesday	Dentist's 4 p.m.		Jane swimming 2 p.m.
Wednesday	LH Berlin to Geneva	sales meeting 11.00	Jane violin lesson 3.30
Thursday	LH Geneva to Berlin		
Friday	cocktail party 6 p.m.	cocktail party 6 p.m.	Sally babysitting
Saturday	Maria & Michael's wedding	Maria & Michael's wedding	Maria & Michael's wedding
Sunday	Paul's christening	Paul's christening	Paul's christening

Write some sentences about what the members of the family – Carol / Peter / Bob / Jane – are doing.

c What are you doing next week? Next Saturday? When are you going on holiday? On your next business trip?

4 Birthday

Look back in this unit and in the book. How many words can you find beginning with the letters of the word 'birthday'?

b before, _____
i ill _____
r reason, _____
t traditional, _____
h help yourself, _____

d decide, _____
a advantage, _____
y yesterday, _____

At the end of this unit I ... :

- can talk and ask about special occasions and dates.
- can congratulate people.
- can talk about arrangements in the future.
- can accept or refuse an invitation.

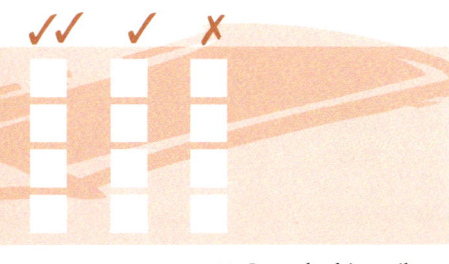

✓✓ = I can do this easily.
✓ = I can do this.
✗ = I need to work on this.

Words and expressions from this unit for my personal **word bank** are:

_____

_____

UNIT 10 What does the future hold?

1 What couldn't you live without in your home?

a Our great-grandparents lived in houses or flats with no fridges or washing machines but we probably couldn't live without them now.

Look at this list. Which three things couldn't you live without in your home? Add two ideas of your own if necessary.

– a freezer	– a radio	– an alarm clock
– a microwave	– a DVD player	– …
– a TV	– a PC	– …

b Now talk to a partner and tell him/her why these things are so important to you.

2 Furniture

a Look at the picture on the right and say if the sentences on page 97 are true or false.

	True	*False*
1. The TV is opposite the sofa on the carpet.	☐	☐
2. The standard lamp is in the corner next to the armchair.	☐	☐
3. The fireplace is between the windows.	☐	☐
4. The flowers are to the left of the TV against the wall next to the writing desk.	☐	☐
5. The coffee table is on the carpet behind the sofa.	☐	☐
6. The picture is on the wall above the fireplace to the right of the bookshelves.	☐	☐
7. The sofa is in front of the window and opposite the TV.	☐	☐
8. The DVD player is under the stereo system on the shelves.	☐	☐

b Do you have your TV in the sitting room? If so, where is it? If not, where is it?

3 The house of the future

a The house in **2a** is a traditional home. The Softroom British team of architects predict that the way we will live will change dramatically over the next century.

What do you think they will predict?

1. We won't have simple square or rectangular rooms.
2. Furniture in a home will be very different in the future.
3. We won't hear traffic noise in a home of the future.
4. Businessmen won't stay in hotels but will take their mobile home with them on business trips.
5. We will have a lot more technology in our homes.
6. The rooms in an ideal home will be flexible, will change to suit our mood.
7. Rooms will be very full of big pieces of technological equipment.

b Now read an article written by Oliver Salway who founded the company Softroom (www.softroom.com) and see if you were right.

Ideas about what makes an ideal home have changed, but we at Softroom still believe that you should be able to relax and forget the stress of the day in the comfort of your own home.

Everyone has their own idea about what comfort is. In the West it means, to most people, a good sofa, a good bed, carpets on the floor, a hot shower when you want it. I don't think that this will change dramatically so that we see Japanese-style homes in Europe. What will change, however, is the influence technology has on the way that we live.

It already has a very big influence in our homes that we don't think about. It turns on our central heating so that the home is warm when we want it to be. It turns on the cooker so that our meal is ready when we get home from a long day at work and it closes the garage door for us when we have put the car away. I think the technology that controls the automatic house will become cheaper, simpler and much more efficient so that everyone will be able to afford the technology that dims the lights and chooses the music and the colour of the living room walls to suit your mood, moves the walls and the position of the furniture so that a room can be suitable for a romantic evening for two or a family birthday celebration.

When there is a problem a technician will solve it with the click of a mouse from a computer anywhere in the world. The average family will hardly notice the technology. Rooms will not be filled with complicated machines, on the contrary they will have a calm and peaceful atmosphere.

We will use modern building materials so that noise from traffic and the neighbour's stereo will not be a problem and won't spoil this peaceful atmosphere. We mustn't make the rooms of the house of the future too relaxing, however. Human beings want to feel protected and secure in their home, but humans also need some sort of stimulation. Each room should, therefore, have something unusual in it, something that you see immediately when you come

in – a window with an unusual shape for example. Rooms shouldn't always be square or rectangular. We can design rooms with curves now, thanks to computer technology.

A home to relax in will always be important but we as architects have to remember that life-styles are changing and we have to design homes that will suit these new lifestyles. Already at the beginning of the twenty-first century patterns of employment are changing. Top executives and experts will travel all over the world for their job more and more often and when they do, we at Softroom predict that they will take their home with them by plane or helicopter. We have invented our penknife apartment for this sort of person, a 7-metre mobile home with a bedroom, a bar, bathroom and a lot of storage space with floor-length curtains instead of walls. This is just the beginning. Anything is possible.

Did you predict right?

C Now read more carefully and answer these questions.

1. Which will be the biggest change in the house of the future?
2. Oliver Salway describes a lot of technology that could be in the house of the future.
    Why don't more people have it now?
3. How will technicians make repairs in the future?
4. Why does Oliver Salway think it isn't a good idea to have total peace in a room?
5. How will business travel change in the future?

> **The future with 'will'**
> When you are predicting the future – the future that is not 100% sure – you use 'will' + the infinitive of verbs.
> *Examples:* Businessmen **will take** their home with them.
>   Technology **will become** cheaper.
>
> **Negative form**
> Add 'not' after 'will'.
> *Example:*   Rooms **will not (won't)** be filled with complicated technology.
>
> **Question form**
> Change round the 'will' and the infinitive
> *Example:*   **Will** the rooms **be** square in the future?

d Salway says we all have our own idea of comfort. What's your idea of comfort in a home? What technology that is mentioned in the text would you like to have in your home in the future?

What do you know about homes in other countries?

4 Over to you

Work in small groups and complete the following sentences. Make two predictions of your own.

We think that the price of petrol will _____ .

We think the price of flats in our cities will _____ .

We think the average temperature next summer will be _____ .

We think air in cities will get _____ in the future.

We think the number of cars on our roads will _____ .

We think that we will eat more _____ in the future.

_____

_____

Tell the class about your group's predictions.

5 I want to move

Your friend lives in the city and she's thinking about moving to the country.
She's an optimist so her predictions are positive.

Examples: If I move to the country, the price of flats will be cheaper.
   If I move to the country, the air will be better.

What other advantages of life in the country can you think of? Tell your friend about them.

> **Yes** I think it's a great idea. If you move to the country, you will …

There are also disadvantages. Tell your friend about them.

> **Yes** Yes, rents will be cheaper. But: if you leave the city, you will/won't …

'if' sentences type 1
When you talk about a possible condition that may happen in the future, you can use the following combination of tenses:

'if' part	main part
present simple	will + infinitive

Examples: If you **move** to the country, you **will pay** more in train fares to get to work.
   If you **stay** in the city, you **won't need** a car.

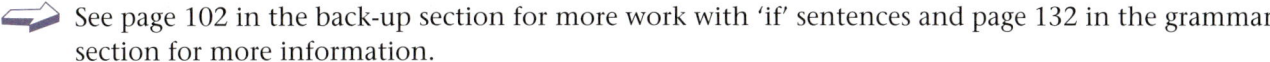

See page 102 in the back-up section for more work with 'if' sentences and page 132 in the grammar section for more information.

6 A house or a home?

a What do you miss when you are away from home on a business trip or visiting friends in a different area? Why do you enjoy coming home? Why do your children enjoy coming home? Did you enjoy going back to your parents' home after moving away?

b Here are some words from a song. Can you match the words that have the same sounds?

breaks ▮ around ▮ free ▮ moon ▮ frowns ▮ land ▮ mistakes ▮
clowns ▮ me ▮ girls ▮ town ▮ hand ▮ buffoon ▮ curls

breaks – mistakes

 Listen to check the words that sound the same.

 **c** Now listen to the song and as you do put the lines in the correct order.

_____ I've travelled the land
_____ Had my share of the breaks
_____ And an eye ever open for some fun.
_____ I've made some mistakes
_____ Seen the boys on the make
_____ With a guitar in my hand
_____ And on the bum.

_____ I've been to the places in the town
_____ Screamed at the moon
_____ Where the faces hang round
_____ I've looned with them
_____ But I soon discovered.
_____ Just to stare at each other.
_____ Behaved like a buffoon

_____ Running for home
_____ Run as fast as I can
_____ Run for home
_____ Oh running man

_____ Run for home ...

_____ Just to be free
_____ I've seen all the frowns
_____ And the downs that they take
_____ I've seen all the girls
_____ But they don't mean a lot to me.
_____ In their pretty frocks and curls
_____ On the faces of the clowns.

_____ I've travelled the land
_____ Heard the noise
_____ Seen the faces in the places misunderstand.
_____ Yes I've travelled the world
_____ Seen the pretty boys and girls
_____ That destroys and commands.
_____ Made mistakes out of hand

_____ Run for home ...

Run for home

Why is the man in the song running for home? What do you think will happen when he gets home?

d Have you got some favourite pieces of music that remind you about special things you have done in your life? Can you tell us why?

7 So now what?

Now you have almost finished the course. What are you going to do now? Have you got any plans about learning more English in the future? Are you going to do any of these things?

> I'm going to learn ten new words a week.

> I'm going to listen to the CD again on the way to work.

> I'm going to take another English course.

> I'm going to read some simple English books.

> I'm going to visit some web-sites to find an English chat room.

> I'm going to join a 'Stammtisch' where I can listen to and speak English.

> We are going to meet in a beer garden once a month and talk English.

> We are going to e-mail each other in English.

Your teacher is going to show you some ideas about learning vocabulary and some useful web-sites.

> **The future with 'going to'**
> You use going to when you talk about a plan in the future (with no final arrangements).
> You use the verb 'to be' + going to + infinitive.
> *Examples:* **I'm going to learn** vocabulary.
> **He's going to visit** a web-site.

8 It's time to say goodbye

 47

Match the replies below to the ways of saying goodbye. Then listen to check.

1. Goodbye. Thank you for inviting me.
2. Bye, Bill. Give our love to Angela.
3. I hope you soon settle into your new home. Keep in touch.
4. Bye. Have a good flight. Give us a ring when you arrive in Sydney.
5. Good night. Sleep well.
6. Cheers mate. I'm off home now.

a. Thanks – yes, I will. Bye.
b. Thanks, you too.
c. Thank you for coming. Drive carefully. Goodbye.
d. I will. Bye.
e. Yeah. Cheers. See you tomorrow.
f. Thanks. We will.

Learning Tip – Speaking

There are a number of accepted short phrases in spoken English, e.g., 'See you tomorrow.' Collect them as you go along and try to use them when you speak to others. It helps to make you sound more 'at home' in English.

Back-up

1 We can't decide

You are going on holiday in August but you can't decide: Italy or Sweden? So you make a list.

	advantages	disadvantages
Italy	hotter, more exciting	noisier
Stockholm	quieter	colder, more boring?
train	cheaper	longer journey
plane	faster	more expensive
hotel	comfortable, more relaxing	more expensive
campsite	cheaper	more work, noisier

Write some sentences.

Examples: If we go to Italy in August, the weather will be hotter than in Sweden.
If we go by plane, it will be more expensive but the journey will be shorter.

Look in the key for some suggested answers.

2 A prediction or a plan?

Decide which verb form goes into these sentences.

1. The weather on the coast _____ (be) hot and sunny.
2. I don't think the price of petrol _____ (rise) above 3 Euro a litre.
3. Next year after university Jim _____ (travel) around the world for a year.
4. The Dickinson family _____ (visit) Prague next spring because Mr Dickinson may get a new job there.
5. I think Steve _____ (pass) his exams because he has worked very hard.
6. I'm _____ (buy) a new car soon, because I don't think my old one _____ (pass) its inspection.
7. We haven't got a dining room table for our new flat yet but we _____ (buy) a new one this weekend at IKEA.
8. Bob _____ (take) his Mum on a cruise next July because it's her sixtieth birthday.
9. I _____ (take) the train into the city because it _____ (be) difficult to park because of the football match.
10. Do you think your team _____ (win)?
11. I _____ (spend) the money I won on a new kitchen.
12. The party starts at about 8 o'clock ad I don't think it _____ (finish) before 2 in the morning.
13. When we go to London Russell _____ (visit) the British Museum and I _____ (do) some shopping in Harrods.
14. Take a raincoat because it _____ (be) wet when you are in Thailand in August.
15. You _____ (improve) your English if you do some work on it every week.

In this book you have learned three ways of talking about the future.
Look back and find the third way.

Back-up

Wordsearch

Can you find 16 words in this wordsearch puzzle?

N	E	C	E	S	S	A	R	Y	A
E	X	X	S	A	L	A	R	M	U
E	E	T	I	S	O	P	P	O	D
W	C	H	O	O	S	E	X	L	I
T	E	A	N	X	L	L	A	W	E
E	C	A	R	P	E	T	X	M	N
B	R	E	M	E	M	B	E	R	C
X	F	U	R	N	I	T	U	R	E
C	L	O	C	K	M	E	A	L	X
P	R	E	F	E	R	G	R	O	W

4 | Likes and dislikes

Look at these words from all units of this book.
Do you like or dislike them? There is no right answer.
How do you FEEL about the words?

Examples: I like the word 'grandmother' because I love my grandmother very much.
I don't like the word 'chopsticks' because I can't eat with them.

> grandmother ▮ chopsticks ▮ platform ▮ newspaper ▮ advice ▮ ordinary ▮
> surgery ▮ entertainment ▮ neighbourhood ▮ cancel ▮ departure ▮ windy ▮
> elevator ▮ appointment ▮ dog owner ▮ valid ▮ cathedral ▮ tall ▮ freezer

Look at the word list on pages 151–167. What other words from the book do you like or dislike and why?

5 | Goodbye

Sort out the words in these sentences to make three small dialogues.

1.
● home I'm going now. bye.
▲ bye. good have weekend a.
● you thanks too.

2.
■ wedding lovely a was it. thank you inviting us for.
● you glad could come. goodbye.
■ goodbye.

3.
▲ good a summer have.
● same you to. next term you see.
▲ bye.
● bye.

✓ At the end of this unit I ... :

● can name the place of objects in a room.
● can read a text about predictions in the future.
● can talk about advantages and disadvantages.
● can talk about future plans.
● can use different ways to say 'goodbye'.

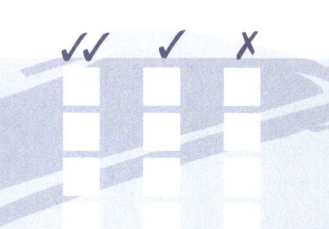

✓✓ = I can do this easily.
✓ = I can do this.
✗ = I need to work on this.

Words and expressions from this unit for my personal **word bank** are:

Reading

Simon has received an invitation from an old pen friend and wants to visit your country for two weeks. He looked up a website to find out a little bit more about his holiday destination and found this entry in a chat room for travellers. He thinks it is a little strange – can you read it and mark anything you think is wrong?

Example:

You ~~have to~~ *should* bring a present …

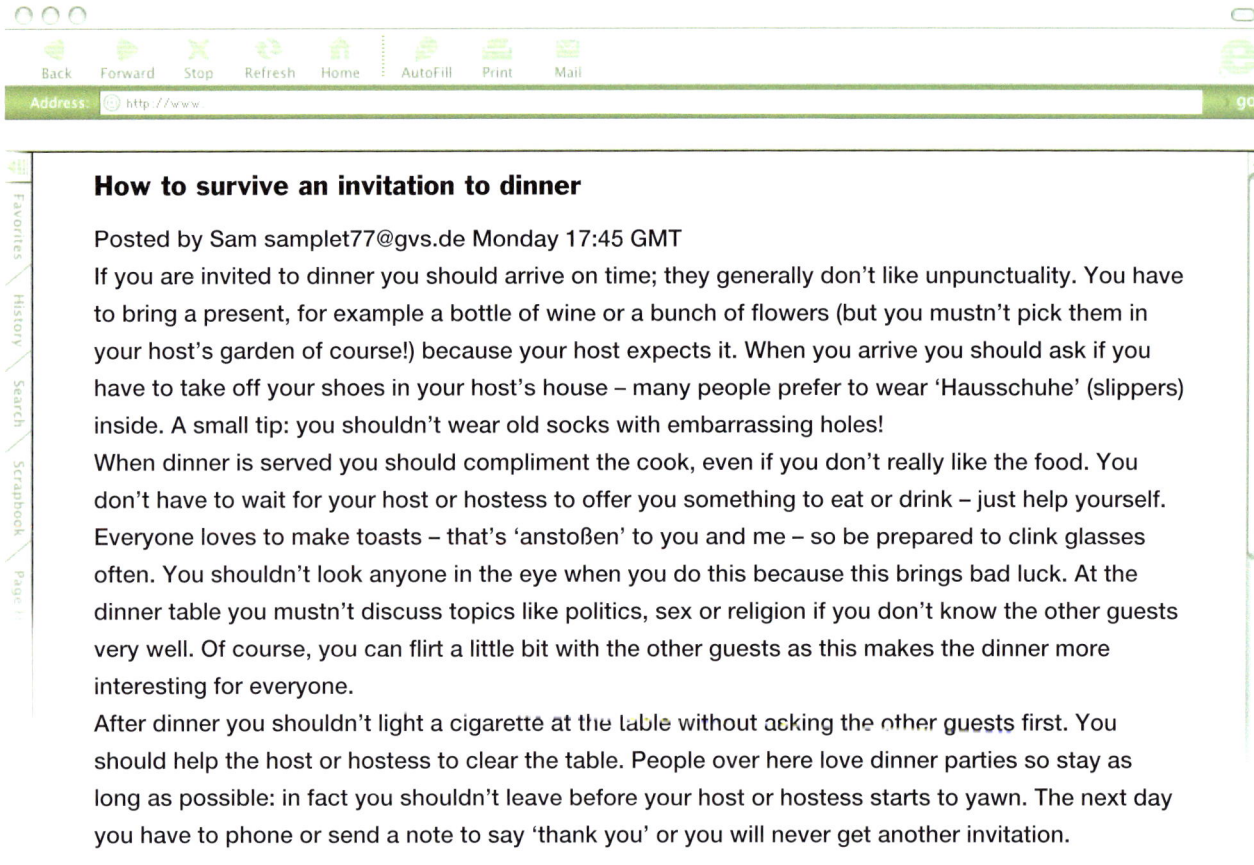

How to survive an invitation to dinner

Posted by Sam samplet77@gvs.de Monday 17:45 GMT

If you are invited to dinner you should arrive on time; they generally don't like unpunctuality. You have to bring a present, for example a bottle of wine or a bunch of flowers (but you mustn't pick them in your host's garden of course!) because your host expects it. When you arrive you should ask if you have to take off your shoes in your host's house – many people prefer to wear 'Hausschuhe' (slippers) inside. A small tip: you shouldn't wear old socks with embarrassing holes!

When dinner is served you should compliment the cook, even if you don't really like the food. You don't have to wait for your host or hostess to offer you something to eat or drink – just help yourself. Everyone loves to make toasts – that's 'anstoßen' to you and me – so be prepared to clink glasses often. You shouldn't look anyone in the eye when you do this because this brings bad luck. At the dinner table you mustn't discuss topics like politics, sex or religion if you don't know the other guests very well. Of course, you can flirt a little bit with the other guests as this makes the dinner more interesting for everyone.

After dinner you shouldn't light a cigarette at the table without asking the other guests first. You should help the host or hostess to clear the table. People over here love dinner parties so stay as long as possible: in fact you shouldn't leave before your host or hostess starts to yawn. The next day you have to phone or send a note to say 'thank you' or you will never get another invitation.

In groups of three, compare your corrections. Do you agree on all points?

Writing

Work with a partner and write a short text for visitors to your country about eating out at a restaurant. Think about these points:

| reserving a table | arriving at the restaurant | ordering from the menu |
| table manners | communicating with the waiter | paying | leaving a tip |

Use phrases like:
You should … You shouldn't … You mustn't … You have to … You don't have to …

Language practice

Choose the correct alternative.

1. I think I *should / have to* do something to feel fitter. – Have you tried yoga? My doctor says it helps you also to lose weight so you *don't have to / mustn't* go on a diet.
2. Have you ever been to Hungary? – Yes, I have. I *travelled / 've travelled* round there a few years ago.
3. How long will it take to repair? – I *will finish / finish* it by Thursday if the parts *arrive / will arrive* tomorrow.
4. Would you like to go out later? – I don't know, I'm tired. – Oh, well, never mind. But if you *will change / change* your mind, call me.
5. What are your plans? – I think I'*m going to take / 'm taking* another English course.

Listening

Thomas is going away for the weekend so he has asked his friend Katie to look after his flat and his cat. Before you listen to the message he leaves on her answering machine, match the parts of the sentences below.

1. If you're hungry,
2. If you're thirsty,
3. If the cat starts meowing in front of the door,
4. If you forget her,
5. I'll call again later on so

a. she'll scratch the backdoor till you let her in.
b. she'll want to go out.
c. you'll find food in the fridge.
d. if you have any questions you can ask me then.
e. you'll have to drink water or milk.

 Listen to check you were right.

Speaking

How well do you know your partner?

Student A: look at the statements below. Student B: look at the statements on page 111. Read the statements and try to imagine which statements are true for your partner, crossing out the part that you think isn't correct. Don't say anything to him/her and don't ask him any questions!

Your partner …	Am I right?
1. … has/hasn't attended a wedding abroad.	☐
2. … has/hasn't broken a mirror.	☐
3. … has/hasn't visited Buckingham Palace.	☐
4. … has/hasn't found a message in a bottle.	☐
5. … has/hasn't organised a party for more than 30 people.	☐
6. … has/hasn't lost his/her keys.	☐
7. … has/hasn't cried at a film.	☐
8. … has/hasn't celebrated his/her birthday in the open air.	☐
9. … has/hasn't read a newspaper or magazine in English.	☐
10. … has/hasn't driven on the left side of the road.	☐

Now compare answers with your partner.

Example: Have you ever attended a wedding abroad? – Yes, I have. / No, I haven't.

If you guessed correctly, put a tick in the box. When you both have checked your answers, see who has the most correct answers!

Unit 2

7 Games in different countries

a Work in two groups. Group B reads the text on this page about the game 'Kudoda' and Group A reads the text about 'Sepak Takraw' on page 23.

First look at these questions:

Is it an energetic game?
Is it a dangerous game?
Is it an expensive game?
Is it a team game or can you play alone?

How many people can play?
Do you need a lot of equipment to play this game?
Do you play this game inside or outside?
Can you have a winner? Who wins?

Group B

Kudoda

This game comes from Zimbabwe in Africa. You can play alone but it's more fun if you play with friends because then you can have a winner. It isn't an energetic or dangerous game and it isn't expensive because you don't need a lot of equipment to play it. You only need a metal bowl and some small stones or marbles. In a game of 'Kudoda' players sit in a circle round the bowl. It is better if you play outside because in the house you might break something. The first player takes a small stone from the bowl and throws it up in the air. He or she then tries to pick up as many stones as he can before the stone lands in the bowl again. The winner is the person who has got the most stones at the end of the game.

Ask the people in your group or your teacher if you don't understand all the words.

b Your teacher will give you a number. Find the person with your number from group A and answer his/her questions about 'Kudoda'.

c If you have access to the Internet you can look at some more games from around the world:
http://www.ga.k12.pa.us/academics/MS/6th/MCGAMES

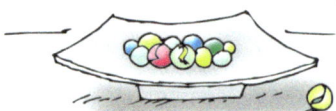

Unit 3

2 c Numbers

Partner A

Dictate these phone numbers to your partner.

1. Mr Ishiguro: 0081 3529955568
2. Ms Wallner: 0043 14567252
3. Mr & Mrs May: 0044 1296776290
4. Mr Sigasa: 0027 124216302

Example: Mr Ishiguro's number is …
I think he's from …

Then listen to you partner's numbers and fill them in on page 29.

Note
How do you say the number 0 for a telephone phone?

Revision Unit 1

Speaking

Who is it?

Student B
Look at this family tree. Some of the names are missing – where do these names belong?

| Sebastian | ▮ | Tim | ▮ | Liam | ▮ | Robbie |

Ask your partner. Use the words you learned in Unit 1. For example:
A: Who is Evelyn?
B: She's Steven's wife. She's Tom and Emma's mother, and Sebastian's grandmother!
A: Ok, thanks. Who is …?

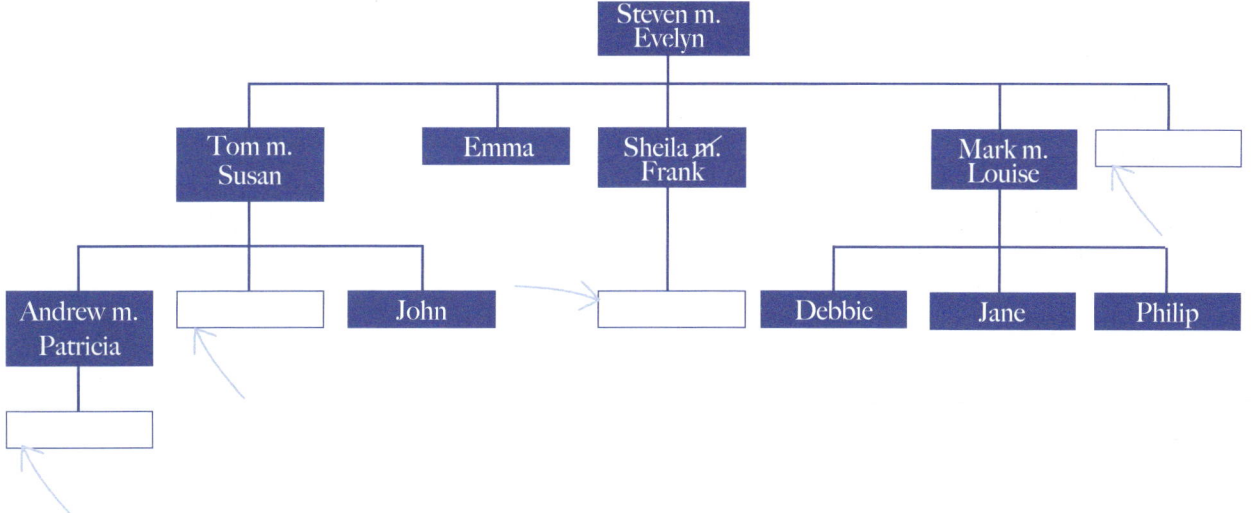

Unit 5

 4 ## An exciting event

Group B

You are standing in the streets of London so you can watch the wedding of a famous person. Send a text message from your mobile phone to tell your friends in Canada what is happening.

Before you start use dictionaries to find out some vocabulary you might need or ask your teacher.

Write the text and then give it to another group in the class.

7 b Food and your job

Read this text to answer the questions.
Does Tim eat things that are good for him? – Yes, he does because he eats _____.
No, he doesn't because he doesn't eat _____.

No queues in Dr. Young's surgery

Dr. Young doesn't have a black bag and patients don't come to his surgery,
but he has thousands of patients from all over the world. How does he do it?
He gives advice via the Internet in his weekly newsletter.

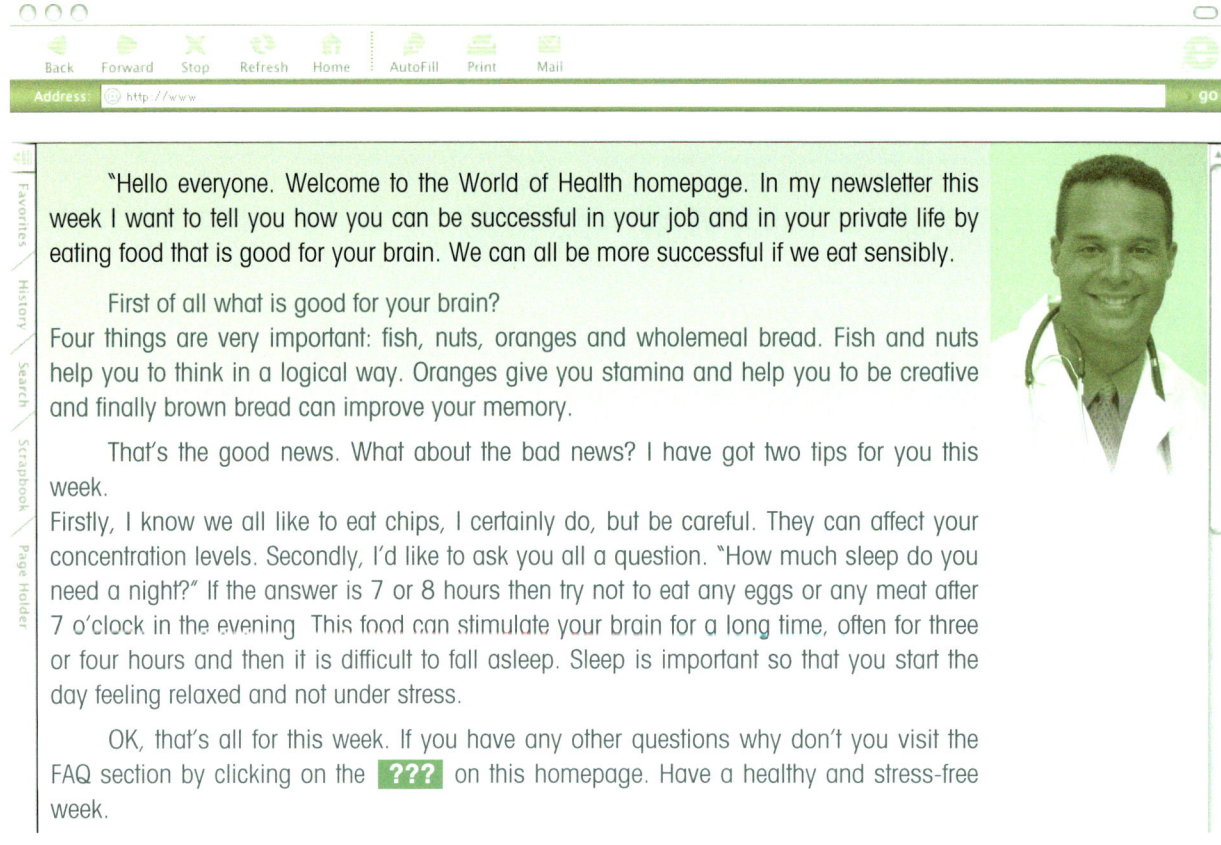

"Hello everyone. Welcome to the World of Health homepage. In my newsletter this week I want to tell you how you can be successful in your job and in your private life by eating food that is good for your brain. We can all be more successful if we eat sensibly.

First of all what is good for your brain?
Four things are very important: fish, nuts, oranges and wholemeal bread. Fish and nuts help you to think in a logical way. Oranges give you stamina and help you to be creative and finally brown bread can improve your memory.

That's the good news. What about the bad news? I have got two tips for you this week.
Firstly, I know we all like to eat chips, I certainly do, but be careful. They can affect your concentration levels. Secondly, I'd like to ask you all a question. "How much sleep do you need a night?" If the answer is 7 or 8 hours then try not to eat any eggs or any meat after 7 o'clock in the evening This food can stimulate your brain for a long time, often for three or four hours and then it is difficult to fall asleep. Sleep is important so that you start the day feeling relaxed and not under stress.

OK, that's all for this week. If you have any other questions why don't you visit the FAQ section by clicking on the **???** on this homepage. Have a healthy and stress-free week.

 4 An exciting event

Group D

You are watching a demonstration in a city you know. Send a text message from your mobile phone to tell your friends in the UK what is happening.
Before you start use dictionaries to find out some vocabulary you might need or ask your teacher.

Write the text and then give it to another group in the class.

Unit 8

 c This is serious

Group D

Read the posting in the chat room and make sure you all understand the main point in it.

Then your teacher will give you a number. Find people who have got the same number as you and work with them in a new group. Tell them about your chat room posting.

Example: I read about Jeff. He thinks fast food is cheap and tasty.

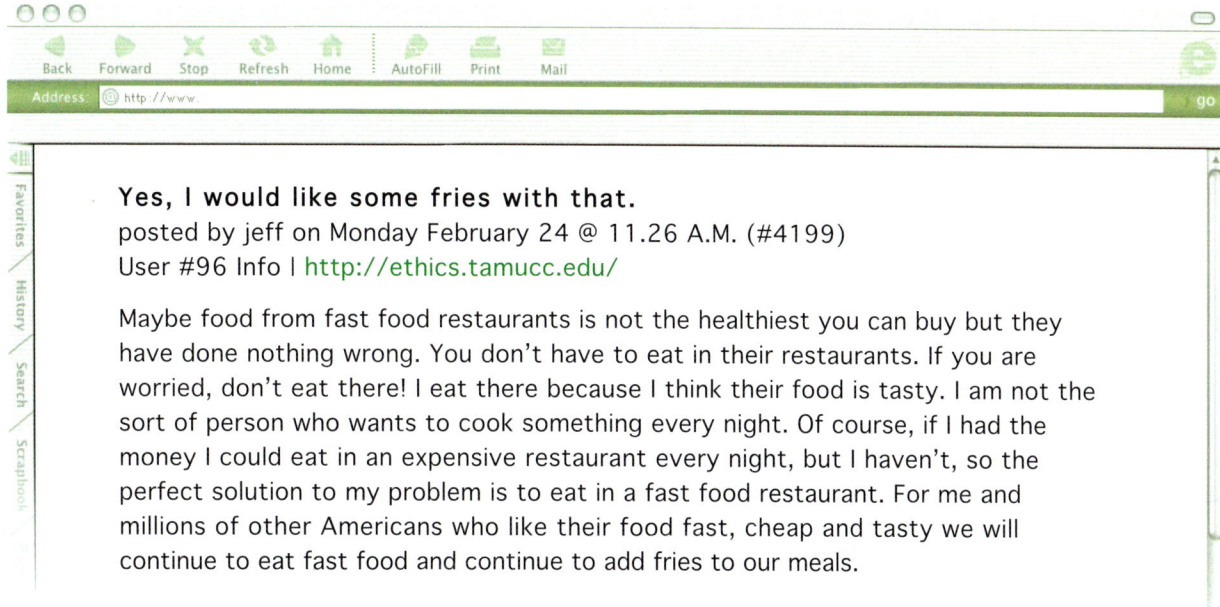

Yes, I would like some fries with that.
posted by jeff on Monday February 24 @ 11.26 A.M. (#4199)
User #96 Info | http://ethics.tamucc.edu/

Maybe food from fast food restaurants is not the healthiest you can buy but they have done nothing wrong. You don't have to eat in their restaurants. If you are worried, don't eat there! I eat there because I think their food is tasty. I am not the sort of person who wants to cook something every night. Of course, if I had the money I could eat in an expensive restaurant every night, but I haven't, so the perfect solution to my problem is to eat in a fast food restaurant. For me and millions of other Americans who like their food fast, cheap and tasty we will continue to eat fast food and continue to add fries to our meals.

What do *you* think about fast food?

Unit 3

 c Numbers

Partner B

Dictate these phone numbers to your partner.

1. Mr Kashino: 0081 744227698
2. Ms Häberli: 0041 264675257
3. Mr President: 001 7032629196
4. Mr Hewitt: 0061 262451 5277

Note
How do you say the number 0 for a telephone phone?

Example: Ms Häberli's number is …
I think she's from …

Then listen to you partner's numbers and fill them in on page 29.

7 **c Food and your job**

Partner B
This is Brian's kitchen.

Give your partner the information he or she asks for:

Example: Your partner asks: You answer:

Are there any nuts in his kitchen?   No, there aren't.
Is there any tea in his kitchen?   No, there isn't.

Ask your partner about Paula's kitchen.

Example: Is there any coffee?

Mark your answers here:

	Yes	No
coffee	☐	☐
herbal tea	☐	☐
nuts	☐	☐
oranges	☐	☐
chocolate	☐	☐
eggs	☐	☐
meat	☐	☐
gin	☐	☐
water	☐	☐
beer	☐	☐

So does Paula eat things that are good for her brain? –
I think so … / I don't think so because …

Unit 6

b Where to stay

Group C

Read this short text to find out about one of the leading hotels of the world.
Then fill in the table on page 58.

The Rambagh Palace Hotel, Jaipur, India
This hotel was once a palace and all the 73 rooms and all the 17 suites still have an atmosphere of royalty.
The hotel is situated in 47 acres of gardens and near the main shopping area and historical monuments.
There are two excellent restaurants. The Suvarna Mahal which serves continental Chinese, Indian or Rajasthani cuisine. The Nell Mahal offers light meals 24 hours a day. The Polo bar is a must for our visitors. There you can gently sip your gin and tonic and admire the Maharajah's polo trophies. We have facilities for a wide variety of sports. You can play billiards, badminton, tennis, squash, table tennis and there is a putting green. There is also a jogging track and a large indoor swimming pool and a fitness centre with sauna, steam bath and jacuzzi. If you are an enthusiastic golfer then we can arrange a round for you.

We have a shopping arcade where you can choose an exceptional gift for your family.
Room rates range from US $225 to US $400 a night which includes continental breakfast.

Revision Unit 3

Speaking

How well do you know your partner?

Student B

Read the statements and try to imagine which statements are true for your partner, crossing out the part that you think isn't correct. Don't say anything to him/her and don't ask him any questions!

Your partner…	*Am I right?*
1. … has/hasn't lost his/her wallet.	☐
2. … has/hasn't complained in a restaurant.	☐
3. … has/hasn't spilled wine in a friend's house.	☐
4. … has/hasn't seen the Eiffel Tour in Paris.	☐
5. … has/hasn't locked him/herself out of the house.	☐
6. … has/hasn't been to a rock concert.	☐
7. … has/hasn't had breakfast at a fast food restaurant.	☐
8. … has/hasn't moved house more than once in the last 10 years.	☐
9. … has/hasn't given a speech to more than 50 people.	☐
10. … has/hasn't sung in public.	☐

Now ask your partner and compare answers.

Example: Have you ever lost your wallet? – Yes, I have. / No, I haven't.

If you guessed correctly, put a tick in the box. When you both have checked your answers, see who has the most correct answers!

Unit 6

b Where to stay

Group A

Read this short text to find out about one of the leading hotels of the world.
Then fill in the table on page 58.

The Madison, Washington D.C.
Come to where all presidents of the USA stay. From many of the 311 rooms and the 42 suites you have a view of the Washington Monument and the Jefferson Memorial. This hotel which is now beautifully restored is only 5 miles from Ronald Reagan Washington National Airport.

The Federalist restaurant serves breakfast, lunch and dinner. You can forget stress as you relax in the Postscript Bar and Lounge. In the beautiful restaurant Palette your food is carefully prepared and served in an atmosphere of quiet elegance. Contemporary art collections are displayed regularly in this restaurant.

Explore all the exciting sights of this cosmopolitan city and then come back to your home to relax and slowly unwind in our health and fitness club.

Room rates range from $150 to $197.

Unit 7

British or American?

Partner A
First guess what these words are in American English. Then check with a partner.

British English	American English
petrol	
lift	
bill	
torch	
tap	
handbag	
taxi	
underground	
film	
motorway	
mobile phone	
rubber	

Unit 5

 An exciting event

Group A

You are at a Champions League football match and it is half-time. Your team is playing against Manchester United. ManU is losing. Send a text message from your mobile phone to tell your friends in Manchester what is happening.
Before you start use dictionaries to find out some vocabulary you might need or ask your teacher.

Write the text and then give it to another group in the class.

Revision Unit 2

Speaking

New Year's Resolutions

Student A

Student A looks at this part of William's list of New Year's Resolutions. Did he do all the things he wanted to do? Ask your partner questions to fill in the missing information and answer his/her questions.

Example: Student A: Did he learn to drive?
Student B: Yes, he did. He learned to drive in the summer.

Learn to drive before September.	Yes! Driving test in July!
Stop smoking.	No ... Next year ...
Lose 10 kg.	----------
Start going to the fitness centre.	----------
Do an evening course – French? Karate?	Did an evening course in Tai Chi.
Remember my mum's birthday in February.	No.
Remember my dad's birthday in April.	----------
Bring all my old newspapers to the recycling centre every week.	Yes.
Learn to cook Thai food.	No – Indian food.
Give money to charity.	----------

Unit 8

2   **c**   **This is serious**

Group B

Read the posting in the chat room and make sure you all understand the main point in it.

Then your teacher will give you a number. Find people who have got the same number as you and work with them in a new group. Tell them about your chat room posting.

Example: I read about Minnie. She thinks fast food companies should inform customers what's in the food.

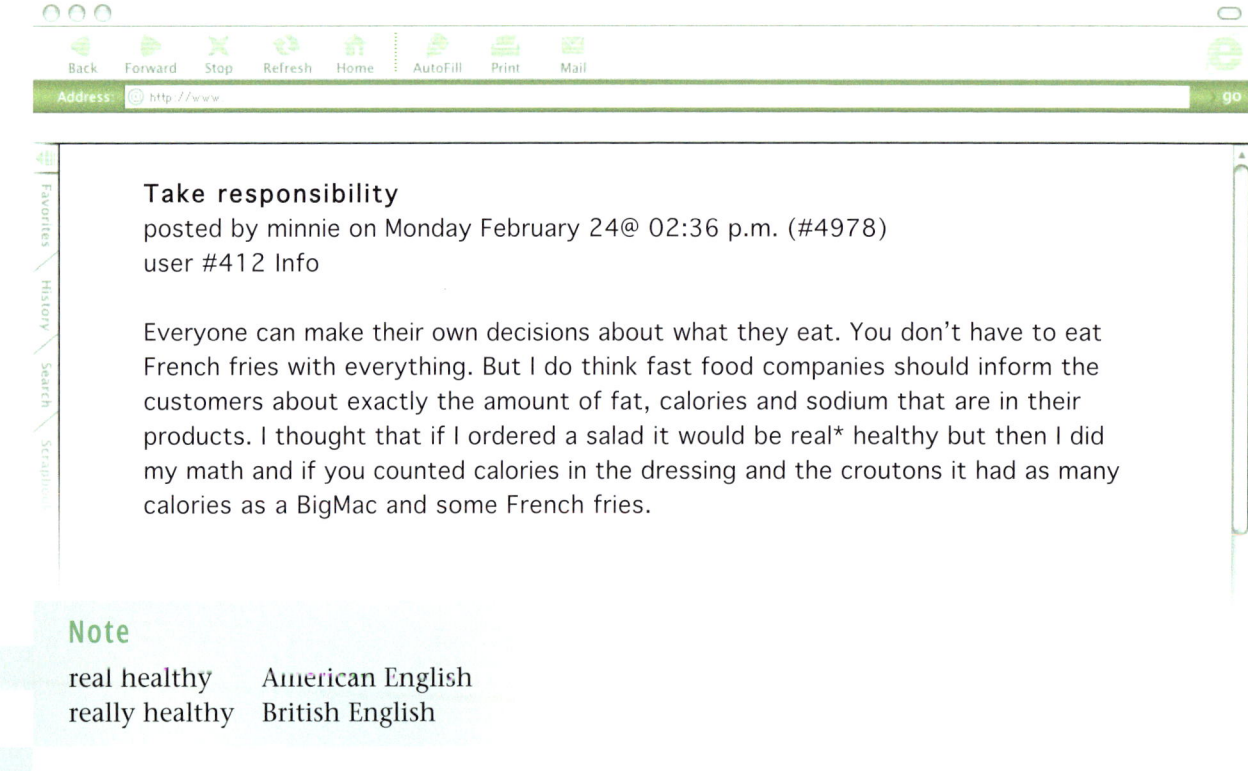

Back   Forward   Stop   Refresh   Home   AutoFill   Print   Mail

Address: http://www.

go

Favorites   History   Search

Take responsibility
posted by minnie on Monday February 24@ 02:36 p.m. (#4978)
user #412 Info

Everyone can make their own decisions about what they eat. You don't have to eat French fries with everything. But I do think fast food companies should inform the customers about exactly the amount of fat, calories and sodium that are in their products. I thought that if I ordered a salad it would be real* healthy but then I did my math and if you counted calories in the dressing and the croutons it had as many calories as a BigMac and some French fries.

Note

real healthy	American English
really healthy	British English

What do *you* think about fast food?

Unit 5

4   **An exciting event**

Group C

You are celebrating New Year in a city you know. Send a text message from your mobile phone to tell your friends in Australia what is happening.

Before you start use dictionaries to find out some vocabulary you might need or ask your teacher.

Write the text and then give it to another group in the class.

3 Wedding customs

Partner B

Your partner will ask you questions about your text, so make a note of the answers.
– What happens before the wedding ceremony?
– What does the bride do and wear on her wedding day? Are there any reasons?
– What does the groom wear and do on his wedding day? Are there any reasons?
– What do the relatives and guests do on the wedding day? Are there any reasons?

world-wedding.traditions.net

Mexican weddings

In Mexico Godparents or 'Padrinos' organise the wedding and in fact look after the couple throughout their married life. During the wedding ceremony a white ribbon called a 'lasso' is tied loosely round the necks of the couple and this shows that they will spend their lives together and not as two single people. The Godparents give the couple a rosary and a Bible and the groom gives his wife thirteen gold coins. The priest blesses these coins and when the groom gives them to the bride he promises to look after her.

As the couple leave the church friends and members of the family throw red beads at them for good luck and at the party afterwards all the guests hold hands and stand in a heart shape around the newly married couple as they dance together as man and wife for the first time. Also at the party a paper maché container called a 'pinata' and shaped like a heart or an animal hangs from the ceiling. The children try to break it and when they do sweets fall out and all the guests share them.

To find out more about weddings in different countries visit the web-site: www.world-wedding-traditions.net

5 British or American?

Partner B
First guess what these words are in British English. Then check with a partner.

American English	British English
gas	_____
elevator	_____
check	_____
flashlight	_____
faucet	_____
purse	_____
cab	_____
subway	_____
movie	_____
highway	_____
cell phone	_____
eraser	_____

Unit 8

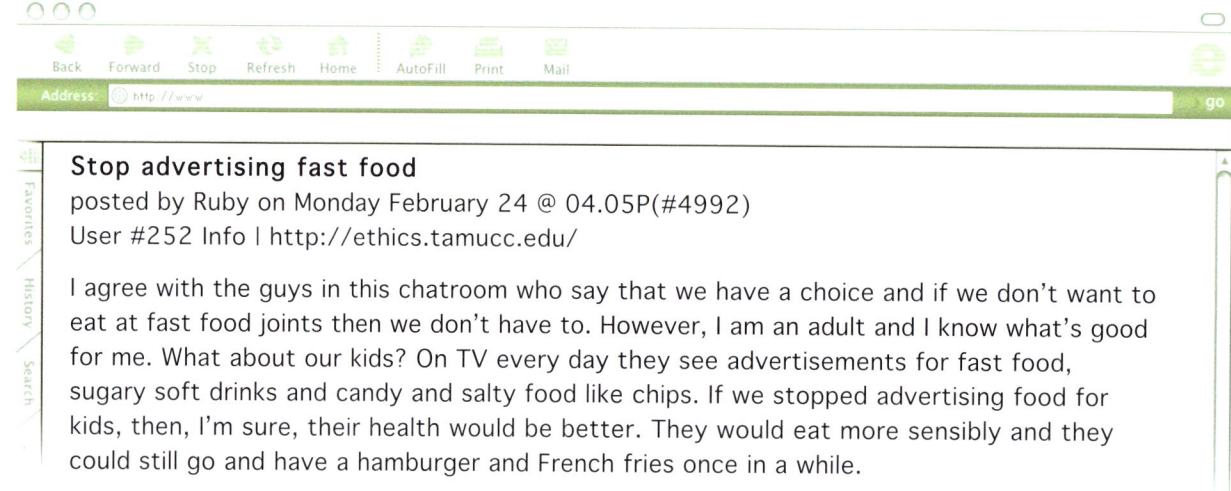
2   **c**   **This is serious**

Group C

Read the posting in the chat room and make sure you all understand the main point in it.

Then your teacher will give you a number. Find people who have got the same number as you and work with them in a new group. Tell them about your chat room posting.

Example: I read about Ruby. She thinks it would be a good idea to stop advertising.

Back	Forward	Stop	Refresh	Home	AutoFill	Print	Mail

Address: http://www   **go**

Stop advertising fast food
posted by Ruby on Monday February 24 @ 04.05P(#4992)
User #252 Info | http://ethics.tamucc.edu/

I agree with the guys in this chatroom who say that we have a choice and if we don't want to eat at fast food joints then we don't have to. However, I am an adult and I know what's good for me. What about our kids? On TV every day they see advertisements for fast food, sugary soft drinks and candy and salty food like chips. If we stopped advertising food for kids, then, I'm sure, their health would be better. They would eat more sensibly and they could still go and have a hamburger and French fries once in a while.

Favorites   History   Search

What do *you* think about fast food?

Unit 6

1   **b**   **Where to stay**

Group B

Read this short text to find out about one of the leading hotels of the world. Then fill in the table on page 58.

Banyan Tree in the Maldives
You can find this wonderful hotel on a small coral island in the Indian ocean. Time moves slowly in the Maldives so be prepared for a relaxing and unforgettable holiday. The hotel has got 48 rooms and is 12 miles from Malé International Airport.

We have two restaurants which offer Maldivian and international cuisine where you can enjoy a romantic dinner under the stars.

Of course, the main recreation in this tropical paradise is in the sea. You can enjoy diving, snorkelling, deep sea fishing. If you are less energetic, you can go sightseeing in Malé or shopping in the Banyan Tree Gallery where you can buy exotic gifts or elegant accessories. You can also relax on the deck of your room overlooking the sea and read or play board games. There is of course a health club for those who need a workout.
Room rates per night range from US $395 for bed and breakfast to US $660 full board.

Functions

Introducing yourself
- Hello. My name's Albert. Nice to meet you.
- Nice to meet you, too. My name's Franziska.

Spelling
- Can you spell your surname, please?
- T-I-N-C-K-E-R

Asking for and giving information
- Excuse me, does this bus go to Oxford Circus?
- Yes, it does.

- Excuse me, does the train for Manchester leave from here?
- No, it doesn't. You want platform three.

Making and responding to offers
- Would you like a cup of coffee?
- That would be very nice, thanks.

- Would you like to go to a football match on Saturday?
- I'm sorry, I can't this weekend.

Asking for and giving phone numbers
- What's your telephone number?
- 0207 263 4802

Asking for and giving the time
- Have you got the time?
- Yes, it's quarter past seven.

- What time do you make it?
- Half past eleven.

Making, accepting and rejecting suggestions
- Why don't you have a massage?
- Yes, that's a great idea.

- How about going to a concert?
- Thanks, but I'm not very keen on that idea because I don't like music.

Asking for and expressing opinions and responding politely
- I think it's dangerous to transfer money via the Internet.
- I'm afraid, I don't think so. It's really secure now. I do it all the time.

- It's quick and easy to buy books via the Internet.
- Yes, I think so, too.

- Do you think office routines are different now?
- Yes, I think so.

Expressing sympathy and enthusiasm
- We can't come to the party, I'm afraid, because Bob is in hospital.
- Oh, dear. I'm sorry about that.

- Our hotel room in San Francisco had a view of the Golden Gate Bridge.
- Oh, that sounds wonderful.

Requesting politely and responding to requests
- Could you book me a rental car for next Monday?
- Sure. Big or small?

- Could you copy these papers for me?
- I'm sorry, but this copier isn't working. Ask Jane. I'm sure she can help.

Complaining and apologising
- This fish is cold.
- I'm really sorry. I'll send it back.

- I ordered my meal thirty minutes ago and I'm still waiting.
- Sorry about that. I'll check for you.

Asking for permission: Granting and refusing permission
- Can I borrow your ashtray?
- Sure. Help yourself.

- Can I take this chair?
- I'm sorry, it's taken.

- Is it OK if I smoke?
- Well, I'd rather you didn't.

Invitations and responding to them

Formal (often in a written form)
Invitation
Mr and Mrs X request the pleasure of the company of Mr and Mrs Z to a cocktail party on …

Accept
We would be delighted / very happy to attend the party.

Refuse
Unfortunately, we can't accept the kind invitation to the cocktail party because …

Informal
Invitation
You are invited to a party at Clare's place.

Accept
We'd love to come. Thanks.

Refuse
I'm really sorry, but we can't come because we're going on holiday that weekend.

Complimenting and replying to compliments
- What a pretty blouse. The colour suits you.
- Thank you. Nice of you to say so.

- It was a great party.
- Thank you. Glad you enjoyed it.

Congratulating
- Congratulations.
- Thank you.

- Happy Birthday. Many happy returns of the day.
- Thank you.

Saying goodbye
- Goodbye. Keep in touch.
- Yes, I will. Goodbye.

- Cheers mate. I'm off home now.
- Yeah. Cheers. See you on Monday.

- Good night. Sleep well.
- Thanks. You too.

Pronouns

Personal pronouns – subject

I	I'm from Hungary.
You	You're Spanish.
He	He's a commuter.
She	She's a member of a fitness club.
It	It's cold.
We	We've got a garden.
You	You're under 40.
They	They've got a big house.

Personal pronouns – object

me	He loves **me**.
you	She gave **you** the money.
him	I see **him** every morning.
her	They like **her** very much.
it	The car hit **it**.
us	Mary showed **us** the new car.
you	We phoned **you**.
them	I see **them** every day.

my	**my** first name
your	**your** e-mail address
his	**his** surname
her	**her** bicycle
its	**its** tail
our	**our** teacher
their	**their** names

Nouns

Regular plural forms

For most nouns, you add an **-s**.

    student – student**s**
    book – book**s**

For nouns which end in **-s, -sh, -ss, -ch, -x,** you add **-es**.

    bus – bus**es**
    dish – dish**es**
    address - address**es**
    box – box**es**

For some nouns which end in **-o**, you add **-es**.

    potato – potato**es**
    tomato – tomato**es**

For most nouns which end in a consonant and **-y**, you change the **-y** to **-ies**.

    country – countr**ies**
    dictionary – dictionar**ies**

For nouns which end with a vowel and **-y**, you add **-s**.

    day – day**s**
    boy – boy**s**

Irregular plural forms

    child – children
    man – men
    woman – women
    foot – feet
    wife – wi**ves**
    knife – kni**ves**

G4   Possessive forms

You use the possessive **'s** and not **of** when you talk about people and what 'belongs' to them.
> Violet is Richard**'s** wife.
> Jim**'s** dog is very old.

You add **'** to regular plural nouns.
> Their daughters**'** names are Angela and Melanie.

But you use **'s** for the plural nouns 'men', 'women' and 'children'.
> I like children**'s** books.

For things you use **of** and not **'s**
> The door **of** the house is red.

G5   Countable and uncountable nouns

Countable nouns are things you can count. They can be both singular or plural.
> a nut, some nuts
> a chip, some chips

Uncountable nouns are things you cannot count. They do not normally have a plural.
> sleep, gin

Some and any

G6   Some and any

You use **some** in positive sentences with countable and uncountable nouns when you do not say the exact amount.
> There's **some** coffee in Brian's kitchen.
> There are **some** bottles of beer in the fridge.

You normally use **any** in questions and in negative sentences with countable and uncountable nouns.
> There aren't **any** nuts in Brian's kitchen.
> There isn't **any** chocolate in the kitchen.
> Is there **any** fish in Paula's kitchen?
> Are there **any** eggs in the fridge?

Much and many

G7   Much and many

You use **many** in questions with plural countable nouns.
> How **many** cups of coffee do you drink a day?

You use **much** in questions with uncountable nouns.
> How **much** water do you drink a day?

Articles

A/an and **the** are called articles. **The** is the definite article and **a/an** are indefinite articles.
You use **a/an** when you talk about things in general or when you don't know or it isn't important which one. You use **the** when you know which thing you are talking about.

> We need **a** doctor. *(it's not important which doctor)*
> **The** doctor is here. *(the one you need)*

You use **an** before a, e, i, o, u and sometimes before h (when you don't hear it) and **a** before other letters of the alphabet.

> Golf is **an** expensive hobby.
> He's **an** honest man.

You use **a** or **an** when you talk about a person's job.

> She's **an** engineer and he's **a** teacher.

Adjectives

Comparatives
For most one-syllable words, the comparative form of adjectives is **-er + than**.

> This hotel is **cheaper than** that one.

Some adjectives double the final consonant before adding **-er**.

> The weather is **hotter** this summer **than** it was last year.
> Berlin is a **bigger** city **than** Budapest.

For two-syllable words ending in y, change the **-y** to **-i** before adding **-er**.

> The streets in Hong Kong are **noisier than** in London.
> The homework this week was **easier than** the homework last week.

For other two-syllable and longer words, you use **more + adjective + than**.

> A good bed is **more important** for me **than** a good breakfast in a hotel.

Superlatives
For one-syllable words and two-syllable words ending in -y, the superlative form is **-est**.

> Today was the **hottest** day in August.
> When I was thirty it was the **happiest** time of my life.

For other two-syllable and longer words, you use **most + adjective**.

> The jade market was the **most interesting** part of Hong Kong.
> The Peninsular is the **most expensive** hotel in Hong Kong.

Irregular comparatives and superlatives
good – better – best
bad – worse – worst
far – further – furthest

Adjectives and adverbs

You can use **adjectives** to describe nouns and after the verb 'to be'. They answer the question 'What is it/he like?'

He is a **patient** man.   'patient' is an adjective
The music is very **loud**.   'loud' is an adjective

You use **adverbs** with other verbs.

He is waiting **patiently**.   'patiently' is an adverb
She is singing **loudly**.   'loudly' is an adverb

Adverbs of manner answer the question '**How?**'.
How do the drag queens dress? – **Outrageously**.
How is she singing? – **Loudly**.

You normally add **-ly** to change an adjective into an adverb.
careful – careful**ly**
beautiful – beautiful**ly**
wonderful – wonderful**ly**

Adjectives ending in **-ic** add **-ally** to form the adverb.
enthusiastic – enthusiastic**ally**
tragic – tragic**ally**

Adjectives ending in **-y** usually change the **-y** to an **-i.**
angry – angr**ily**
happy – happ**ily**

With adverbs of frequency you can say **how often** something happens.

100%   **0%**

always   usually   often   sometimes   seldom   never

In a sentence these words come **before a full verb:**
We **always** go on holiday to Italy.
I **never** drink coffee.

… and **after** the verb **to be** and **auxiliary verbs** (have, can, must).
He is **sometimes** late for work.
I have **never** eaten octopus.
I can **never** remember his surname.

Prepositions

G12   Prepositions of time

You use **prepositions of time** to say **when** something happens.

You use 'at' for clock times.
at one o'clock
at 4 p.m.
at nine fifteen

You use 'in' for longer periods of time:
parts of the day, months, seasons, years.
in August
in 2003
in summer
in the afternoon

You use 'on' for days and dates.
on Saturday
on 29th February
on Christmas Day
on my birthday

Note
at night
at the weekend (UK)
on the weekend (US)

G13   Prepositions of place

You use **prepositions of place** to describe **where** something or someone is.

It's | **in** the corner.
between the lamp and the coffee table.
on the left.
to the left of the desk.
next to the bookcase.
in front of the window.
on the wall **above** the table
behind the sofa.

Where were you yesterday? – **At** home.
At the office.
At the doctor's.
At the cinema.
At a party.
In bed.

Verbs

G14 The verb 'to be'

The verb **to be** is irregular.

Present simple

> They**'re** married.
> She **isn't** from Spain.
> **Is** he a commuter?

Positive form	Short form	Negative form	Question form
I **am**	I'm	I **am not** (I'm not)	**Am** I …?
You **are**	You're	You **are not** (aren't)	**Are** you …?
He **is**	He's	He **is not** (isn't)	**Is** he …?
She **is**	She's	She **is not** (isn't)	**Is** she …?
It **is**	It's	It **is not** (isn't)	**Is** it …?
We **are**	We're	We **are not** (aren't)	**Are** we …?
They **are**	They're	They **are not** (aren't)	**Are** they …?

Past simple

> They **were** late.
> I **was** late.
> The plane (it) **wasn't** late.
> We **weren't** late.

I			
He	**was**		
She			
It		not (n't)	late.
You			
We	**were**		
They			

For the question change round the subject (e.g., I, he, they) and the verb.
Were you late?
Was he late?

G15 The verbs 'have' and 'have got'

British usage: The verb 'have got'

Present simple
Positive form
The form is the same for all persons except 'he' / 'she' / 'it'.

I**'ve got** a bicycle (**have got**).
You**'ve got** a beautiful garden (**have got**).
We**'ve got** a large family (**have got**).
They**'ve got** a new e-mail address (**have got**).

She**'s got** a sports car (**has got**).
He**'s got** a dog and a cat (**has got**).
It**'s got** three rooms, a kitchen and a bathroom. (**has got**)

Question form
Have I / you / we / they **got** ...?
Has he / she / it **got** ... ?

Negative form
I / you / we / they **haven't got** ...
He / she / it **hasn't got** ...

In the **past simple** 'got' is not often used with 'have'.
> When I was a child I **had** a dog.

American usage: The verb 'have'
In American English you don't use 'have got' but 'have'.
> I **have** a car.
> They **have** a new e-mail address.

The negative and question forms of **have** are the same as for regular verbs. See the next section G16.

The verb 'have' is irregular in the past simple. See page 133 for the past and the past participle of this verb.

Other verbs

G16   Present simple

You use the **present simple** to talk about things which are facts.
> I **come** from Austria.
> She **lives** in Bern.

When you talk about regular habits, you also use the present simple.
> He always **goes** shopping on Sunday.
> He seldom **reads** a newspaper.
> They **go** on holiday twice a year.

The verb form is the same for all persons except 'he' / 'she' / 'it'. Remember the 3rd person **s** .
> he listen**s**
> she like**s**
> it run**s**

Remember these irregular verb forms for 3rd person singular:
> watch – watch**es**
> go – go**es**
> do – do**es**

Negative form
When you use the negative form, you need a signal word (do not / does not).
> I **don't have** an e-mail address.
> She **doesn't take** the bus to work.

Question form with 'do' and 'does'
> **Do** you like reading?
> **Do** you have a dog?
> **Does** he/she play the piano?

Present progressive

You use the **present progressive** for descriptions of actions and people in pictures.
> She**'s wearing** a pink hat.

You also use the present progressive to talk about things which are happening at the moment of speaking.
> I**'m sending** this message from an internet café.
> The band **is playing** in the square.

Positive form

I**'m renovating** my flat.
You**'re working** hard.
He**'s watching** TV.
She**'s reading** a good book.
We**'re learning** English.
They**'re singing and cheering.**

Negative form
Add 'not' after the form of 'be'.

I**'m not renovating** ...
You **aren't working**...
He **isn't watching** ...
She **isn't reading** ...
We **aren't learning** ...
They **aren't singing**...

Question form
Change round the subject (e.g., I, you, they) and the form of 'be'.
Are you working ...?
Is he watching ...?
Is she reading ...?
Are they singing ...?

Past simple

You use the **past simple** to talk about something that happened in the past. You also say when it happened – 'yesterday', 'in 2003', 'last week', ' two years ago'.
> I **lived** in Bremen in 2001.
> We **flew** to Hong Kong two years ago.

Regular verbs in past simple
You use the same form for all persons.

The past simple for regular verbs ends in **-ed**.
> relax – relax**ed**
> watch – watch**ed**

If the verb ends with an **-e**, you add only **-d** to the verb.
> move – move**d**

Most verbs that end with a **-y** change the **-y** to **-ied**.
> marry – marr**ied**

For verbs which end with a vowel and **-y** you add **-ed** to the verb.
> stay – stay**ed**

You double the final consonant of some one-syllable verbs.
> stop – stop**ped**

Think carefully about the pronunciation of the **-ed** in regular verbs in **past simple**.

For verbs that end in /ð/, /b/, /v/, /z/, /ʒ/, /dʒ/, /g/, /m/, /n/, /ŋ/, /l/ it is pronounced /**d**/.
failed /feɪld/
moved /muv:d/

For verbs that end in /θ/, /p/, /f/, /s/, /tʃ/, /ʃ/, /k/ it is pronounced /**t**/.
washed /wɒʃt/
watched /wɒtʃt/
worked /wɜːkt/

After /t/ and /d/ it is pronounced /**ɪd**/.
wanted /wɒntɪd/
started /stɑːtɪd/
mended /mendɪd/

Irregular verbs in past simple
Irregular verbs have a special form in the past simple. Again it's the same form for all persons.
   buy – **bought**
   give – **gave**
   have – **had**
For a list of irregular verbs turn to page 133.

Negative form
In a negative sentence you need a signal word 'did not' (short: 'didn't').
   They **didn't enjoy** the food.
   We **didn't have** a wonderful holiday.

Question form and answers
Did they **enjoy** the food? – Yes, they **did**. / No, they **didn't**.
Did you **have** breakfast late last Sunday? – Yes, I **did**. / No, I **didn't**
When **did** you last **sell** an old car? – (I **sold** one) three years ago.
When **did** his car fail its inspection? – (It **failed** the inspection) last year.

Present perfect

G19	Present perfect

When you talk about the past but there are **no definite time signals** you use the **present perfect**. You use the adverbs 'ever' and 'never'.

Have you **ever celebrated** a birthday on a beach? – No, I **haven't**.   *(you only want a yes/no answer, it is not important when)*

Have you **ever got** drunk at a party? – Oh, yes, **I have**.   *(we don't know when)*
I **have** (**never**) **visited** Hong Kong.

He **has given** a speech at a wedding.   *(we don't know when)*

Future tenses

Form
The **present perfect** contains two parts:

– have/has +	**past participle** in positive statements and questions	
– haven't/hasn't +	**past participle** in negative statements	

I			
You	**have/haven't**	**eaten**	caviar.
We		**celebrated**	a birthday at the top of a mountain.
They			

He			
She	**has/hasn't (has never)**	**given**	a speech at a wedding.
It		**organised**	a party for fifty people.

The past participle is the same as the past simple for regular verbs. For the past participle of irregular verbs see page 133.

Future tenses

G20   Simple present as future tense

You use the simple present when you talk about something in the future based on an official timetable.
What time **does** the bus **leave**?
The next train **leaves** at 10.30.

G21   'going to' as future tense

You use 'I'm going to …' when you talk about your plans.
I**'m going to** take another English course.
I**'m not going to** forget all my English.

You form this tense with the verb **to be + going to + the infinitive**.
She **is** (she's) **going to** meet her friends and speak English once a week.
They **are** (they're) **going to** visit their grandmother.

For the negative add **not** after the verb **to be**.
He **is not (isn't) going to** work on Saturday.
We **are not (aren't) going to** buy a new car.

G22   The present progressive (continuous) as future tense

You use the present progressive (continuous) to talk about future arrangements. It is all organised.
He**'s flying** to Rome on Saturday. *(I've got the tickets.)*
They **are spending** their honeymoon in Barbados. *(They've booked the hotel and the flight.)*
I**'m going** to the dentist's tomorrow. *(The appointment is at 10 o'clock.)*

For the form of this tense see G17 on page 127.

G23   'will' as future tense

You use the will-future to talk about things in the future you cannot change.
> I **will** be 40 in December.

You also use it when you say what you think will happen in the future.
> The price of petrol **will** rise.
> I think Germany **will** win the next football championships.

Positive and negative form
The form of the verb is the same for all persons.

I You She He It We You They	**will / 'll** **will not / won't**	win the next game.

Modal verbs

G24   'can'

can expresses the idea of ability.

Positive form
The form is the same for all persons.
> I **can** type.
> He **can** use chopsticks.

Negative form
> I **can't** understand all text messages. (cannot)
> He **can't** use chopsticks. (cannot)

Questions and short answers
> **Can** you understand all text messages? – Yes, I **can**. / No, I **can't**.
> **Can** he use chopsticks? – Yes, he **can**. / No, he **can't**.

G25   must not (mustn't)

Must not (mustn't) is used to express what is forbidden, what is wrong to do. (So don't do it!)
> She **mustn't** walk without crutches.
> He **mustn't** drink alcohol when he takes his tablets for hay fever.
> You **mustn't** ride your bike on the pavement.

Imperatives

G26   'have to'

Have to / has to expresses the idea of necessity – what the rules or people tell you. It is 100% necessary to do.

> I **have to** go the hospital for a check-up every year. *(The doctor tells me.)*
> He **has to** take tablets for hay fever. *(The doctor tells him.)*
> You **have to** keep your dog on a lead in this park. *(The rules tell me.)*

Form

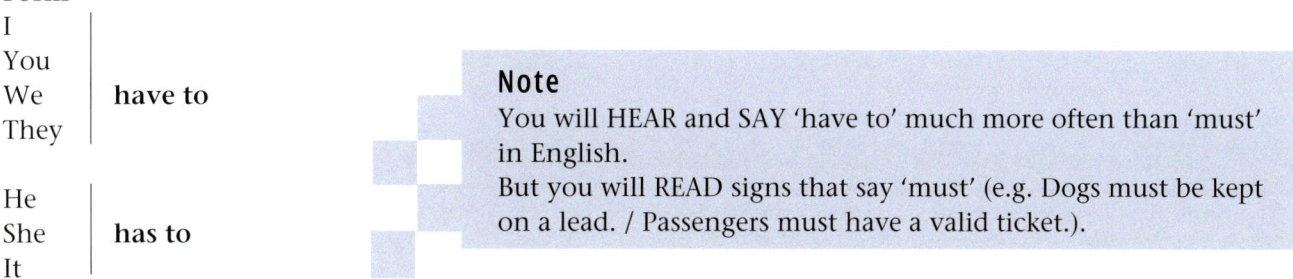

I You We They	**have to**
He She It	**has to**

Note
You will HEAR and SAY 'have to' much more often than 'must' in English.
But you will READ signs that say 'must' (e.g. Dogs must be kept on a lead. / Passengers must have a valid ticket.).

G27   don't have to / doesn't have to

This expresses what is not necessary to do.

> She **doesn't have to** keep her arm in a sling now.
> I **don't have to** get up early on a Sunday.
> You **don't have to** eat the spinach if you don't like it.

Imperatives

G28   Imperatives

The imperative is used to give instructions and advice.

> **Wear** gloves.
> **Take** a flashlight when you dumpster dive at night.
> **Wash** your hands when you finish.

It has the same form as the infinitive without 'to'.

Negative form
For the negative imperative you need the signal word 'don't'.

> **Don't** climb over a fence to reach a dumpster.
> **Don't** take more than you need.

'If' sentences

You use the word 'if' to talk about something which must happen before something else happens. This is a condition. There are different sorts of 'if' or conditional sentences to talk about possible situations, some that we think *may* happen and others we think *may not* happen.

G29   'If' sentences type 1

'If' sentences are made up of two parts: the if-clause and the main clause.
To talk about possible situations that we think *may* happen in the future and the results, you can use two combinations of tenses:

if-clause	main clause
present simple	will-future
present simple	imperative

If I **move** to the city, I **will go** to the cinema more often. (*I am thinking of moving to the city so this may happen.*)

If you **want** to save money, **buy** your clothes in the sale. (*Everyone wants to save money so this may happen.*)

G30   'If' sentences type 2

To talk about possible situations (and possible results) that we think *may not* happen, you use the following combination of tenses:

if-clause	main clause
past simple	would + infinitive (conditional)

What **would** you **do if** your car **broke** down on the motorway? (*I know you have a very good car, so this may not happen.*)

If someone **stole** my wallet, I **would go** to the police. (*This is possible, but I live in a very safe area, so this may not happen.*)

> **Note**
> The verb 'to be' has a special form in this sort of if-clause.
> – **If** I **were** you, I **would** (I'd) **go** to the doctor's.
> (In spoken English you will also hear: If I was you, I'd go to the doctor's.)

List of irregular verbs

infinitive	past simple	past participle
be	was / were	been
begin	began	begun
break	broke	broken
bring	brought	brought
build	built	built
buy	bought	bought
choose	chose	chosen
come	came	come
do	did	done
drink	drank	drunk
drive	drove	driven
eat	ate	eaten
find	found	found
fly	flew	flown
forget	forgot	forgotten
get	got	got
give	gave	given
go	went	gone
have (got)	had	had
hear	heard	heard
know	knew	known
learn	learned, learnt	learned, learnt
leave	left	left
lose	lost	lost
make	made	made
meet	met	met
pay	paid	paid
put	put	put
read	read	read
say	said	said
see	saw	seen
sell	sold	sold
send	sent	sent
shine	shone	shone
sleep	slept	slept
speak	spoke	spoken
spend	spent	spent
steal	stole	stolen
take	took	taken
teach	taught	taught
tell	told	told
think	thought	thought
throw	threw	thrown
understand	understood	understood
wake up	woke up	woken up
win	won	won
write	wrote	written

Unit 1 About you and me

1b Names

1.
Think of a person.
OK.
He or she?
He.
Can you spell his surname?
Right. It's G-I-B-S-O-N.
I know. It's Mel Gibson.
Yeah. That's right.

2.
Think of a person.
OK.
He or she?
He.
Can you spell his first name?
Sure. It's P-A-U-L.
I know. Paul McCartney.
No. Try again.
Paul Newman.
No.
Help! Can you spell his surname?
H-O-G-A-N.
Got it. Paul Hogan.
Yeah. That's right.

3.
Think of a person.
OK.
He or she?
She.
Can you spell her first name?
Sure. It's N-I-C-O-L-E.
I know. It's Nicole Kidman.
That's right.

2 Nice to meet you

Robert: Hello, my name's Robert.
    Nice to meet you.
Ludmilla: Nice to meet you, too. My
    name's Ludmilla.
Robert: And what's your surname?
Ludmilla: Taguieva.
Robert: Can you spell that, please,
    Ludmilla?
Ludmilla: Sure. It's T-A-G-U-I-E-V-A.
Robert: Thanks.
Ludmilla: You're welcome.

5 My family

Sandy: Have you got any pictures of
    your family, Jennifer?
Jennifer: I keep all my family photos in
    this album. Let's have a look. Look,
    this is Alan. It's an old picture. He
    was 29 then and now he's over 50!
    He's my husband.
Sandy: Who's this?
Jennifer: This is Angela. She's my
    daughter. And this is Melanie.
    She's my second daughter.
Sandy: Have you got a son, too?

Jennifer: Yes, I have. One. Here's a
    picture of him. His name's Philip.
Sandy: And who's this?
Jennifer: Joe. He's my Dad and this is
    my mum Joan.
Sandy: My mum's name's Joan, too.
Jennifer: Really!
Sandy: Yeah. It was a popular name in
    the late 1920's!
Jennifer: Yeah.
Sandy: Have you got any brothers and
    sisters?
Jennifer: I haven't got any sisters, but
    I've got a brother. His name's
    Peter. Peter's married and his wife's
    name's Sarah.
Sandy: This is an old photo.
Jennifer: Yes, that's a picture of my
    grandparents on their wedding day
    in 1923. Their names were Violet
    and Richard. They were mum's
    parents.

Unit 2 In my free time

3 In winter or in summer?

1.
This is Jan and he's from Australia.
Tell us about your hobbies Jan. What
about the summer?

Your summer or my summer?! The
long summer holidays are in
December in Australia. In December
and January I go surfing along the
coast in Queensland and go diving on
the barrier reef. Diving is wonderful
but it's an expensive hobby. In the
winter I go skiing. Of course, there
isn't a lot of skiing in Australia as
there is in Europe but we have snow
in the Blue Mountains north of
Sydney. When I go skiing I take a lot
of photographs. I do a lot of
photography in the winter.

2.
What are your hobbies Bob?

Well, I live in Canada so in the winter
I play ice hockey on the lake near my
house because it's very cold and the
lake is often frozen. It's a very
energetic and dangerous sport. I broke
my nose last winter. And in summer.
Well, I also go hunting in the forest
with my friend Paul and I play
basketball. I play in a team but I'm not
very good.

3.
Hi, I'm Doug and I'm from San Diego
in California.

Tell us about your hobbies Doug.
My main hobby is soccer. In Europe
you call it football. OK, that's in the

winter and in the summer I play
baseball, a typically American sport.
It's an energetic sport but it's not
really dangerous and I go swimming,
but not outside. There's a big indoor
swimming pool near my house.

4.
Shashi's from India. Tell us about your
hobbies Shashi.

Well, I play cricket. A lot of people
think that cricket is very boring but I
love it. It's a complicated sport but it
isn't boring at all. We don't have
winter and summer in India. We have
the wet and the dry season. From June
to September it can be very wet and
then I don't play cricket, I like reading
books then.

4 Sounds /z/ and /s/

pens	[z]
bus	[s]
zoo	[z]
place	[s]
said	[s]
lose	[z]
juice	[s]

6 Why not?

Do you like chatting on the Internet?
No, I don't.
Why not?
Well, I can type but I can't type fast
and I don't understand all text
messages.

Can YOU text?
Yes, I can. It's easy!

9 Everyday English

Excuse me, does this train stop in
Birmingham?
No, it doesn't. You want the one from
platform 9.
Cheers mate.
You're welcome.

Excuse me, does this bus go to
Heathrow?
Yes, it does. It goes to all four London
airports. Heathrow, Gatwick, Stansted
and Luton.
Thanks a lot.
Not at all.

Excuse me, does the coach to Bath
leave from here?
No, it doesn't. You need stop number
4. Over there where there's a queue.
Thanks.
Not at all.

Unit 3   On the Road

2b   Numbers

What's your telephone number?
It's 0044 1729830468.

What's your extension number?
3920.

What's your credit card number?
3750 30123822006.

What's your PIN number?
It's a secret!

What's your mobile number?
0177 456 4540.

4b   Excuse me, have you got the time?

1.
Excuse me, have you got the time?
Sure. It's quarter to four.
Thanks.

2.
Excuse me, have you got the time?
Yeah. It's eleven thirty.
Thanks very much.
You're welcome.

3.
Got the time mate?
Ten to nine.
Cheers.

4.
What time do you make it?
Twenty-five past.
I think my watch is slow. I make it
twenty past.
Never mind. We're not late. I said
we'd meet Jim and Ann in the bar at
half past so we can have a drink before
the concert starts at 8.

Revision Unit 1

Receptionist: The Black Swan Hotel,
    good morning. How can I help
    you?
Holli: Hello, I'd like to book a hotel
    room, please. For two nights.
Receptionist: Certainly, madam. A
    double room or single room?
Holli: A single room, please. With a
    bath.
Receptionist: That's no problem, all
    our rooms have baths. From when
    to when?
Holli: From the 10th June to the 12th
    June ...
Receptionist: The 10th – that's a
    Saturday, isn't it?
Holli: That's right.

Receptionist: Ok ... a single room for
    two nights ... the twelfth ...Can I
    have your name, please?
Holli: Yes, it's Holli Blanchfield.
Receptionist: H – O – double L – Y?
Holli: No, I.
Receptionist: Sorry?
Holli : I ... eh ... I for, for Iceland!
Receptionist: Ok! H – O – double L – I
    – and your surname?
Holli: Blanchfield – B – L – A ...
Receptionist: B – L – A –
Holli: N – C – H ... F – I – E – L –D.
Receptionist: Blanchfield?
Holli: Yes, that's right.
Receptionist: Can I have your
    telephone number, please?
Holli: Sure, it's 00 44 161 802 ... and
    my extension number is 9143.
Receptionist: Can you repeat that,
    please?
Holli: It's 00 44 161 802 9143. That's
    my work number. Do you want my
    fax number?
Receptionist: Yes, please. I can send
    you a copy of the reservation by
    fax.
Holli: Great. My fax number is the
    same as the telephone number –
Receptionist: The same as the
    telephone number?
Holli: Eh, no, not exactly, the last four
    numbers are different. The
    extension number is different. It's
    9145 at the end.
Receptionist: Oh, I see. Thank you. So,
    Ms Blanchfield, I'll send you your
    reservation immediately.
Holli: Super. Thanks a lot!
Receptionist: You're welcome. Bye!

Unit 4   No time

2a   Routines in Maria's life

Interviewer: Welcome to our
    programme "Ordinary People". In
    it we ask people, like you, the
    listeners, to talk about their
    working day in the twenty-first
    century. We want to answer the
    question: are routines different
    today? Maria is in our studio today
    and she is a wife and mother and
    also personal assistant to the
    manager of a small textile
    company. So Maria, how do you
    do it?
Maria: Good question! I suppose I
    organise my day carefully and I am
    lucky because my husband is an
    architect and he often works at
    home and my Mum lives near us
    so they both help me with the
    children.

I: So when do you start and finish
    work?
M: Well, I start at 8.30 and officially I
    finish at 5.30.
I: Why do you say officially?
M: Well, I work overtime two or three
    times a week and if we have a big
    conference I work in the evening.
I: So what does a typical day look
    like?
M: At 8.30 I answer my e-mails and
    again at about 4.30. I still write
    some letters but most office
    communication is now by e-mail
    and once a week I book all flights
    and hotels for my boss online. I do
    that sort of thing in the morning. I
    also phone our partners in India or
    Hong Kong before lunch because
    the time there is eight hours ahead
    of us in the UK. I sometimes phone
    partners in Brazil and Mexico and
    that is, of course, in the afternoon.
    If I have a conference to organise I
    surf the net for information about
    venues and catering facilities. I
    read trade journals too after lunch
    and mark anything interesting for
    my boss. I don't have a lot of time
    to read during the week when I'm
    not in the office. I never read a
    newspaper. That's about it at the
    office I think.
I: A full day! When do you go
    shopping?
M: I go shopping for food once a
    week. Of course shops are open on
    Sundays in the UK so that's when I
    usually go shopping and with most
    supermarkets you can order
    groceries online, so I sometimes
    buy groceries that way.
I: And relaxation? Do you have time
    for that?
M: Not a lot! But I always try to listen
    to a music CD in the car on the
    way home and, oh, the children go
    swimming with Bob every Friday
    night and that's when I go to my
    yoga classes.
I: Your family is obviously important
    to you. How often do you go on
    holiday as a family?
M: We try to go away twice a year. We
    go skiing after Christmas, usually
    for a week, and then we always
    have a summer holiday with the
    children. We can't go on holiday
    when the children are in school so
    our main holiday is usually in July
    or August. It depends.
I: It sounds as though you deserve
    good holidays, Maria. Thank you.
M: Thank you.

Tapescripts

3b Come out of the darkness

Get up, alarm clock, lip gloss, what a shock.
Get dressed, front door, more stress, what for?
Trapped in your world
You know you're trapped in your world
Lunch hour, fast food, telephone, more abuse.
V.U. headache, cigarettes, coffee break.
Trapped in your world
You know you're trapped in your world.
(Come out of the darkness)
Come out of the darkness, over the tower blocks
Into the light.
Go into the rush hour, out of the factory
Leave it behind
Turn on your TV. Back to suburbia, every night.
Come out of the darkness, over the offices, into the light.
(Come out of the darkness)
Leave work, happy hour, too drunk by far
Bus full, Waterloo, fall asleep on the tube.
Trapped in your world
You know you're trapped in your world.
(Come out of the darkness)

Vodka, lemonade, ashtrays what a shame
Poor cow, sits alone, pubs close, go home.
Trapped in your world
You know you're trapped in your world.
(Come out of the darkness)

(by Republica)

5a Pronunciation

1. men – man
2. ten – tan
3. bend – band
4. send – sand
5. pet – Pat
6. lend – land

5b

men, ten, band, send, Pat, land

5c

1. I play in a rock band.
2. The man over there is my brother.
3. Be careful there is a dangerous bend in the road near here.
4. Linda hasn't got a pet.

5. You can get a tan in our sun studio.
6. Can you lend me some money?

8 Making a booking

1.
● Lotus restaurant. Can I help you?
■ I'd like to book a table for six for Friday 13th February at 1 p.m., please.
● Sorry, for how many people?
■ 6.
● Er – let me see. Yes, that's fine. Can I have your name, please?
■ The table is for Mr Sutcliffe. That's S-U-T-C-L-I-F-F-E.
● Fine. That's a table for six on Friday 13th February at 1p.m.
■ Thanks very much.
● Not at all. Goodbye.
■ Goodbye.

2.
● Hilton Hotel Heathrow Airport. Can I help you?
■ I'd like to book a small conference room for the morning of the 4th July.
● For how many people?
■ About fifteen.
● Sorry, was that fifty or fifteen?
■ Fifteen.
  I'm sorry, madam, but the small conference rooms are not available then. One small one is free in the afternoon or there's one that seats fifty that's free in the morning.
● No, I really need a small one for the morning but thanks anyway.
■ Not at all. Goodbye.
● Goodbye.

Unit 5 Communication

2 Family photos

Rachel: Who are all these people? They all look very dressed up.
Clare: Well, yes, of course they are. The photos were taken on Pamela and Andy's wedding day. Well, let's see. The woman who's wearing this turquoise dress and this fabulous hat is my Mum, you don't know her, do you?
Rachel: No, I don't. And who's the man next to Andy?
Clare: Oh, you mean the man who's wearing the dark suit and dark red tie? That's Simon.
Rachel: Ah, right, is he still living in that bachelor flat in London?
Clare: Oh no. He's married now and he and his wife Kate are renting a flat in Windsor. They want to buy a

house but everything is so expensive.
Rachel: Yeah, I know. And who are the people in this next picture? Who's the man with the dark grey suit and the blue tie?
Clare: That's Roger!
Rachel: Gosh that's Roger? I don't recognise him. How old is he now?
Clare: 24. He's in Rio at the moment. He and a friend are travelling round the world in his gap year after university and before he starts work.
Rachel: And the woman sitting next to him? Is that his girlfriend Natalie?
Clare: Yeah, that's right. That dress looks good on her, doesn't it? Pink suits her.
Rachel: Yeah, it does. And is she travelling with him?
Clare: Not at the moment. She's training to be a nurse and she can't interrupt her course. They may meet in Mexico after her exams.
Rachel: Remember me to them if you are in contact by e-mail.
Clare: Yeah, I will.

5a Are they cheering or jeering?

1. cherry – Jerry
2. cheap – jeep
3. choke – joke
4. chill – Gill
5. chest – jest
6. chin – gin
7. choose – Jews
8. cheer – jeer

5b

cherry, cheap, joke, Gill, chest, gin, choose, jeer

5c

Gill is in bed with a chill.
Jerry is eating a cherry.
The jeep is cheap.
The Turin fans are cheering and the Manchester United fans are jeering.

6c Shopping

Dialogue 1
Sales assistant: Can you find the colour you want, madam?
Customer: Do you have these pullovers in red?
Sales assistant: Yes, we do. Here you are. Would you like to try them on?
Customer: Yes, please.
Sales assistant: The fitting rooms are over there.
(pause)
Customer: They are a bit small. Have you got a bigger size?

Sales assistant: No, I'm sorry, we haven't.

Customer: Oh, well, I'll leave it then.

Dialogue 2

Sales assistant: Are you looking for a shirt to go with those trousers, sir?

Customer: Yes, I am.

Sales assistant: Any particular colour?

Customer: Have you got anything in green?

Sales assistant: How about this one?

Customer: Yes, it's nice. Can I try it on?

Sales assistant: Certainly. The fitting rooms are over there.

(pause)

Customer: Yes, it fits very well. How much is it?

Sales assistant: £23.

Customer: Fine, I'll take it.

7c   I'm sorry, we haven't

Do you know his phone number? I'm sorry, I don't.

Are you free on Sunday? I'm sorry, I'm not.

Is the rental car insured for my wife? I'm sorry, it isn't.

Can I smoke in here? I'm sorry, you can't.

Excuse me, is there an Internet café near here? I'm sorry, there isn't.

Excuse me, does this bus stop at the main station? I'm sorry, it doesn't.

Can you give me a lift to the airport? I'm sorry, I can't.

Have you got a double room free for tonight? I'm sorry, we haven't.

8   Telephone expressions

1.
- This is Michael Grundy. Can I speak to Mr. Sutton, please?
- I'm sorry, he's having lunch at the moment. Can I take a message?
- It's OK. It's not urgent. I'll ring back later.
- Fine.

2.
- This is Charles Morton. Can I speak to Mr Archer, please?
- I'm sorry, he's attending a conference in Rome at the moment. Can I take a message?
- It's rather urgent. Can I have his mobile number?
- Of course. It's 01717 480567.
- Thank you for your help.
- Not at all. Goodbye.

Unit 6   On holiday

3   Honeymoon in Hong Kong

Pat: 6267887

Anna: Hi, Pat. This is Anna.

Pat: Anna! You're back. Did you have a good time?

Anna: Oh Pat, it was wonderful.

Pat: So what was the hotel like? Was it worth all that money?

Anna: Every penny – well, every dollar. Our room was on the fifteenth floor and the view over the harbour was really spectacular, the food was good, all the people in the hotel were always friendly and helpful.

Pat: Well, you sound happy. When did you arrive back?

Anna: Yesterday.

Pat: How's the jet lag?

Anna: Bad! It was a long uncomfortable flight. We didn't sleep very well so we were very tired when we arrived back.

Pat: Oh, that's a shame. A bed at The Peninsular is more comfortable than a seat on a Boeing 747, I suppose!

Anna: You can say that again. By the way, did you get the postcard?

Pat: No.

Anna: That's strange, I posted it ten days ago. Never mind. Look, can we meet up sometime next week so that I can tell you all about it?

Pat: Sure. How about Monday?

Anna: Fine, see you then.

Pat: Great. Bye.

Anna: Bye.

Unit 7   Too much waste?

1b   Recycle it

Interviewer: Welcome to our environmental series "Don't Throw It Away". This week I am talking to Heather Steele who is a dumpster diver. Someone who searches other people's garbage to see what they can find and recycle. So – how did you first become a dumpster diver Heather?

Heather: I read about this hobby on a web-site. I didn't have an exciting hobby and I thought it sounded fun and interesting.

Interviewer: So what did you do then?

Heather: Well, before I began I went to the library to check that it was legal. I didn't want to have any problems with law enforcement officers. My husband's dad is a cop!

Interviewer: So what then?

Heather: Well, I was very nervous about my first dumpster dive but it was no problem. I didn't plan to do it. I was in a supermarket car park. I was by my car and a man came out with a cart full of bottles of orange juice and threw them away. I saw the juice was still OK so I took ten bottles out of the dumpster and put them into the trunk of my car.

Interviewer: So when was that?

Heather: That was three years ago and I am now a real enthusiast and know where to go to get the best results.

Interviewer: So where do you go dumpster diving?

Heather: My three favourite dumpsters are at the back of an apartment block, next to a furniture store and by a toy store.

Interviewer: Why there?

Heather: Well, people from the apartment block move quite often and you know what it's like when you move. You throw things away. At this block people throw away clothes mostly. I sent about 4,000 items of clothing to a hostel for homeless people last year and all from one dumpster!

Interviewer: Wow! Do you always give things away that you find in the dumpsters?

Heather: Not always. Two weeks ago I found a TV in the furniture store dumpster and my husband repaired it and we gave it to our daughter.

Interviewer: What is the best thing you found so far?

Heather: That's easy. Twenty soft toy animals. They were at the bottom of the toy store dumpster and were dirty and had ears or eyes missing, but we washed and repaired them and spent a wonderful day at a children's home where we gave each kid a toy for Christmas.

Interviewer: So a worthwhile hobby, but isn't it a dirty one?

Heather: Not at all. A lot of sports are much dirtier than dumpster diving. It's like a treasure hunt. I think it is a wonderful way to recycle and have fun. Why don't you try it!

Interviewer: Maybe I will.

3b   That's not right

1. She didn't begin it <u>four years ago</u>, she began <u>three years ago</u>.
2. She didn't give it to a <u>children's home</u>, she gave it to their <u>daughter</u>.
3. She didn't send <u>5,000</u> items, she sent <u>4,000</u>.

4. She didn't read about it in a <u>newspaper</u>, she read about it on a <u>web-site</u>.
5. They didn't take them to a <u>school</u>, they took them to a <u>children's home</u>.

6 Can you lend it to me?

1.
● Look, Ian, I left my mobile in my hotel room. Could you phone a taxi for me at about four thirty?
■ Sure.
● Thanks.

2.
● Hi, Jane. An emergency. I left my purse in the hotel room. Could you possibly lend me £15 to pay the taxi?
■ Of course. Let me see … OK. Here you are.
● Thanks a lot. You saved my life.

3.
● Hello, John. Look, I left my laser pointer in my hotel room. Could you lend me one, just for this morning?
■ Sorry, I need it this morning. Why don't you ask Peter?
● OK. Thanks.

4.
● Morning Julia.
■ Hi.
● Look, I left my stapler in the hotel room this morning. Could you staple these papers for me?
■ I'm sorry, but my stapler doesn't work. Ask Judith. She can do it for you.
● Thanks.

7b Rules

Bill: Welcome to the phone-in program about dumpster diving. Our first caller is Karen. So what's your question, Karen?
Karen: Hi, Bill. I'm new to this hobby. I went to the police and asked about it. It is legal in our area but are there any other things I should think about?
Bill: Hi, Karen. Well, it's good to know that it's legal in your area but don't climb over a fence to reach a dumpster and remember it's a hobby for people who care about waste and the environment, so don't take more than you need, leave the area cleaner than you found it and don't make a lot of noise.
Karen: OK. You mentioned leave the area tidy. Do you get dirty dumpster diving?
Bill: Well, not if you are careful. Wear gloves, wash your hands when you finish and, er, don't forget a first aid kit.
Karen: Thanks a lot.
Bill: No problem. Have fun.

Back up Unit 7

4 Sentence stress

1. I didn't buy the computer from Dixons, I bought it from Currys.
2. I didn't throw the TV away, I threw the radio away.
3. I didn't buy the new mobile phone for my son, I bought it for my daughter.
4. I didn't buy a computer last year, I threw one away.
5. I didn't recycle the shoes, I recycled the coat.

5b Vocabulary

salary, dirty, suddenly, behind, apartment, nervous, reduction, ago

Revision Unit 2

Richard: "Oh God … oh, my head … six messages … oh, no …"
Message 1: "Richie! It's James and, yes, Clare is here, too. We just wanted to say thanks for the party. It was so much fun. It was crazy; you were dressed so outrageously! Where did you get that pink hat? It really suited you … Only joking! Thanks again."
Richard: Pink hat?

Message 2: "Hi Richie, Angela here … Mmm … thanks for the party, it was brilliant. You danced so … enthusiastically! It was the funniest thing I've seen in years! And that pink hat! Oh my God! I hope you're ok this morning. I'll call you later, bye."
Richard: What hat?

Message 3: "Rich, it's Tom. You ok, mate? When I left last night you were on the table singing … eh … don't know what you were singing but you were singing very loudly, anyway. Sorry about the kitchen window by the way, it was an accident, I swear. Talk to you later. Bye."
Richard: Oh God, not on the table …

Message 4: "Hello Richard. This is Katie. Remember me? I'm your girlfriend; at least, I was your girlfriend till yesterday evening but I'm not sure now. You had a long and interesting conversation with that Angela Jones – I don't know what was so interesting but you were talking very, very quietly. I would like an explanation. Today. Call me. And by the way, I put that stupid pink hat in the dustbin."

Message 5: "Richard. This is Mrs Leach from next door. I am calling to complain about that party last night. I actually called yesterday evening but you were very drunk and you spoke to me very angrily. You called me 'an old bag', in fact. I'm telling your parents about this, young man!"
Richard: "An old bag? …"

Message 6: "Richard, love, it's mum. I hope you're not missing us! Remember I ordered a hat on-line for cousin Sylvia's wedding? Well, if a parcel arrived yesterday, that's it. Please be careful with it, sweetheart, put it somewhere safe because it's really quite expensive. Thanks … Mmm, that's all. We'll be home at about six this evening. Bye, dear …"
Richard: "The hat?! I'm dead!"

Unit 8 What would you do?

2b This is serious
The two teenagers from New York who took a big fast food chain to court lost their case today. The boys said they had health problems because they ate in the fast food restaurant and lawyers argued that the company didn't tell the truth about the contents of the food or warn their customers about the health risks. Food activists are saying that this case could be the beginning of a lot of legal problems for the multinational fast food companies.

4a Doctors!

1.
Janet: Haltwhistle 56921
Roger: Hi, Janet. This is Roger.
Janet: Roger! Nice to hear from you. How are you?
Roger: Fine. Look, Janet, I'm sorry to bother you but could you do me a favour and give me a lift to the station? My car won't start.

Janet: I'm sorry but I've got a problem with my ankle and I mustn't walk on it. I have to use crutches.
Roger: Oh dear. I'm sorry to hear that. Is it painful?
Janet: It's better than it was last week.
Roger: Good. Get well soon.
Janet: Thanks. Sorry I couldn't help.
Roger: Never mind.

2.
Brian: 6224586
Jim: Brian?
Brian: Speaking.
Jim: Hi, Brian. I didn't recognise your voice. This is Jim. Would you like to come to the pub for a beer with Sam and me?
Brian: Well, I'd love to, mate, but I'm taking strong tablets for hay fever at the moment so I have to keep off the alcohol.
Jim; I don't believe it. You off the alcohol!
Brian: 'Fraid so. I mustn't drive either. So life's no fun at the moment.
Jim: Not for too long, though, eh?
Brian: No, see ya around.
Jim: Yeah, see ya.

3.
Anita: Watford Library. Can I help you?
Sally: Anita?
Anita: Yeah?
Sally: Hi, Anita. This is Sally. Look would you like to come shopping after work?
Anita: Normally I'd love to, but I've got problems with my arm and I have to keep it in a sling.
Sally: Oh dear. And I suppose you certainly mustn't carry heavy shopping bags!
Anita: You guessed it.
Sally: Does your arm hurt?
Anita: Not much. It's just annoying.
Sally: Oh, well, another time. Get well soon. Bye.
Anita: Bye for now.

7a The Sunday lunch wasn't a great success

1.
Customer: Excuse me.
Barman: Yeah.
Customer: I ordered a Caesar salad half an hour ago and I'm still waiting for it.
Barman: Sorry about that. We're short-staffed today. I'll check for you.

2.
Customer: Excuse me.
Waiter: Yes. Is everything all right?

Customer: Well, I ordered the Cajun chicken and it says on the menu it is served with tomato and garlic flat bread but I haven't got any.
Waiter: I'm sorry about that. I'll get you some now.
Customer: Thanks.

3.
Customer: I'm afraid I have a complaint to make.
Barman: What seems to be the trouble?
Customer: This fish isn't done in the middle.
Barman: Oh dear. I really do apologise. Would you like a new portion?
Customer: No, thanks. I'll have the Cajun chicken instead.
Barman: Fine. I'm afraid it will take about fifteen minutes.
Customer: That's OK.

4.
Customer: Excuse me.
Barman: Yes?
Customer: This soup is almost cold.
Barman: I'm really sorry. I'll send it back. I'll bring you some fresh soup in a minute.

9a Cherry or sherry?
1. she's   cheese
2. sherry   cherry
3. sheep   cheap
4. ships   chips
5. shop   chop
6. shoe   chew

9b
1. Cheese, please.
2. Would you like a sherry?
3. This is cheap.
4. The ships are very big.
5. This is an expensive shop.
6. New shoes?

Unit 9   Celebrations

2a   Birthday and weddings
● Sandra, have you ever organised a party on a beach?
■ Yes, I have.
● And have you ever organised a party at the top of a mountain?
■ Yes, I have.
● And have you ever organised one for more than 100 people?
■ For 50 people, yes, but for 100 – no, never.
● OK, so one 'no' so far. What about the next question? Have you ever organised a party by a lake?

■ Yes, I have.
● You obviously like parties. Have you ever organised one by a river?
■ Yes, I have.

2d
Have you ever given a speech at a wedding?
Yes, I have.
When was that?
At my brother's wedding in 2002.

4   Away on honeymoon
Dorothy: Norwich 48026
Joan: Hello, Dot. This is Joan.
Dorothy: Oh, hello Joan. How are you?
Joan: Fine, thanks. And you? Is your cold better?
Dorothy: Yes, I'm fine now, thanks. Are you coming next Tuesday?
Joan: 'Fraid not. That's why I'm ringing. You know Sarah's getting married again on Saturday?
Dorothy: Yes. Is everything alright?
Joan: Yes, everything's fine with Sarah and Alec, but it's Tim. He's going into hospital and he can't look after the children, so we're collecting them on the Monday and then on Tuesday we're taking them to The Anfield experience.
Dorothy: Oh, you mean the tour round the Liverpool football ground. So no golf on Tuesday this week then. And Wednesday?
Joan: Well, we're not doing anything special, but we won't have time to see you I'm afraid.
Dorothy: So when are Sarah and Alec coming back?
Joan: On Monday the 22nd at 7 in the evening. So no golf on Saturday 20th either, I'm afraid.
Dorothy: Ah, well. Never mind. By the way have you ever taken the kids to the Blue Planet Aquarium or to the Llangollen horse-drawn canal boat centre? I've never been, but my grandson Sam has. It was with his school last summer and he had a wonderful time.
Joan: Oh, I'm glad because I've never been, but we're going to Llangollen on Saturday and to the aquarium on Monday.
Dorothy: I'm sure the kids will enjoy it.
Joan: I hope so. So I'll see you on the 13th for the big day.
Dorothy: Yes. Fingers crossed that it doesn't rain and that 13 is a lucky number! Bye.
Joan: Bye.

5a The invitation

Hello. You have reached Henley 9846721. Peter and Alison Gladstone can't take your call at the moment, but if you leave your name and number we'll ring you back as soon as possible.

Hello. This is Janie Clayton speaking. I'm Mr Bradbury's assistant. As you know Mr Bradbury is retiring at the end of next month after 40 years with the company. I hope you have received the invitation to the cocktail party on Friday 15th July at 6 p.m. Could you ring me back as soon as possible to let me know if you can attend? My number is 020 457 9821. Thank you.

6b At the party

Hi. Sorry, I'm late. The traffic was very bad.
No problem. Go through and help yourself to a drink.
Thanks.

Can I take your coat?
Oh, yes. Thank you.

Would you like another drink?
Yes, please, but just something soft. I'm driving.
Orange juice OK?
Fine.

What a pretty blouse. The colour suits you.
Thank you. Nice of you to say so.

Congratulations.
Thanks.

Thanks for a lovely evening.
Not at all. Thank you for coming. Drive carefully.
I will. Bye.
Bye.

The food is wonderful.
Thanks. I'm glad you like it.

Back up Unit 9

2a What happened?

1. What happened on 1st January 2000?
2. What happened in New York on September 11th 2001?
3. What happened in Paris on 31st August 1997?
4. What happened to Neil Armstrong on 20th July 1969?
5. What happened in Tibet on 1st June 1953?

2b

1. The next meeting is on the thirteenth of July.
2. It's his fifteenth birthday on Saturday.
3. I'm sorry, Mrs Robinson is away until the thirtieth of May.
4. His new daughter was born on the seventeenth of August.
5. His office is on the fourteenth floor.
6. It is their fiftieth wedding anniversary next month.
7. He finished seventieth in the Marathon.
8. Where did you celebrate your fortieth birthday?

Unit 10 What does the future hold?

6b A house or a home?

breaks – mistakes
around – town
free   – me
moon   – buffoon
frowns – clowns
land   – hand
girls   – curls

6c Run for home

I've travelled the land
With a guitar in my hand
And an eye ever open for some fun.
I've made some mistakes
Had my share of the breaks
Seen the boys on the make
And on the bum.

Run for home
Run as fast as I can
Oh, running man
Running for home

I've seen all the frowns
On the faces of the clowns
And the downs that they take
Just to be free.
I've seen all the girls
In their pretty frocks and curls
But they don't mean a lot to me.

Run for home …
I've been to the places in the town
Where the faces hang round
Just to stare at each other.
I've looned with them
Screamed at the moon
Behaved like a buffoon
But I soon discovered.

Run for home …
I've travelled the land

Made mistakes out of hand
Seen the faces in the places
misunderstand.
Yes I've travelled the world
Seen the pretty boys and girls
Heard the noise
That destroys and commands.

(by Lindisfarne)

8 It's time to say goodbye

1.
Goodbye. Thank you for inviting me.
Thank you for coming. Drive carefully. Goodbye.

2.
Bye, Bill. Give our love to Angela.
I will. Bye.

3.
I hope you soon settle into your new home. Keep in touch.
Thanks. We will.

4.
Bye. Have a good flight.
Thanks.
Give us a ring when you arrive in Sydney.
Yes, I will. Bye.

5.
Good night. Sleep well.
Thanks, you too.

6.
Cheers mate. I'm off home now.
Yeah. Cheers. See you tomorrow.

Revision Unit 3

Hi Katie – thanks for offering to look after my flat this weekend. I left a list of instructions on the kitchen table for you. If you're hungry, you'll find food in the fridge and if you're thirsty, you'll have to drink water or milk because I forgot to buy anything else, I'm really sorry. There's a bottle of white wine in the fridge too, so help yourself. What else? Oh yes, if the cat starts meowing in front of the door, she'll want to go out. She usually comes back after about half an hour. If you forget her, she'll scratch the backdoor till you let her in, so please don't forget! I think that's everything. I'll call again later on so if you have any questions you can ask me then. Thanks a million, I owe you one!

Key

Unit 1

1b
1. Mel Gibson
2. Paul McCartney, Paul Newman, Paul Hogan
3. Nicole Kidman

2a
Robert	Ludmilla
meet	Nice
surname	Sure
spell	welcome

3
Austria
Russia
Hungary
Switzerland
Italy
Czech Republic
Croatia
Spain
Persia (Iran)
Japan
Romania

4a
I've got: a partner, a son, a bicycle, three children, a dog, a cat, a car, an e-mail address, a daughter.
I am (I'm): married, single, divorced, a member of a fitness club, over 20, interested in football, under 40, from Germany, a commuter, retired.

5
From the top of the tree left to right:
Violet and Richard
Joe and Joan
Alan and Jennifer / Peter and Sarah
Angela and Melanie and Philip

6
The Chinese family
1. false (husband)
2. true
3. false (mother and father)
4. false (Lee See Chai's grandmother)
5. true

The Malaysian family
1. false (first name)
2. true
3. true
4. false (two brothers and one sister)
5. false (she's got a cat)

7
1. Write down the names that you hear.
2. Fill in the missing information.
3. Work with a partner.
4. Ask your teacher.
5. Tell your partner.
6. Look in the Back-up section.
7. Sort them out.

8. Show the names to your partner.
9. Tell the group three things about your partner.
10. Choose the words that are true for you.
11. Stand in a circle.
12. Your teacher will begin.

Back up Unit 1

1a
1. sisters
2. students
3. countries
4. families
5. daughters
6. children
7. addresses
8. dictionaries

1b
1. students
2. addresses
3. children; daughters
4. sisters
5. dictionaries
6. countries
7. families

4a
1. brother-in-law
2. sister-in-law
3. mother
4. grandmother
5. nephew
6. grandfather
7. uncle
8. aunt
9. niece
10. cousin
11. grandson
12. granddaughter

4b
Her; She; They; Their; They; his; Their

5
1. Peter is …
2. Who is …
3. He is …
4. Jason's (possessive 's) wife is …
5. Her daughter is …
6. His wife's (possessive 's) name is …
7. His surname is …
8. My sister is …
9. Fatimah is …

Unit 2

1a
(suggestions)
Number 3 is an energetic hobby.
Number 1 is an expensive hobby.

Number 4 is a dangerous hobby.
Number 2 is a relaxing hobby.
Number 2 is a creative hobby.
Number 3 is an exciting hobby.

2a
like:	could be for any of the words (must be for: watching TV, chatting on the Internet, reading, singing)
go:	windsurfing, jogging, skating, skiing, birding, hiking
go to:	the cinema, art galleries
play:	tennis, golf, ice hockey, the piano
do:	silk painting, pottery, aerobics, Tai Chi, crossword puzzles

3
Jan
In the summer he goes surfing and diving.
In the winter he goes skiing and does photography.
true, true, false (in the winter)

Bob
In the winter he plays ice hockey.
In the summer he goes hunting and plays basketball.
true, true, false (in the summer), false (a basketball team)

Doug
In the winter he plays soccer.
In the summer he plays baseball and goes swimming.
false (soccer and baseball), true

Shashi
In the dry season he plays cricket.
In the wet season he likes reading.
false (in the dry), true

4a
see tapescripts

6a
1.
Well, I can [kən] type but I can't [kɑ:nt] type fast and I don't understand all text messages.

2.
Can [kən] YOU text?
Yes, I can [kæn]. It's easy!

6b
Text messages:
Tonight.
Happy birthday.
Happy holidays.
Thank you.
You are great.
See you.
Money, money, money, money
Are you OK?

7

Kudoda	Sepak Takraw
1. No, it isn't.	Yes, it is.
2. No, it isn't.	Yes, it is.
3. No, it isn't.	No, it isn't.
4. A team game but you can play alone, too.	A team game.
5. Any number.	Three.
6. No, you don't: stones/marbles and a bowl.	No, you don't. A net and a ball.
7. Outside.	Outside or inside.
8. Yes, you can. The person who picks up the most stones.	Yes, you can. The team that wins 2 sets.

8a

1.
Do you play golf?
Yes, I do. My handicap is not very good, though. It's 18.
That's no problem. Would you like to play on Saturday?
That would be very nice.
Good. See you on Saturday.
Fine. I look forward to it.

2.
Are you interested in ice hockey?
Yes, I am. The local team in Canada is very good.
Would you like to go to a game on Saturday? I can get tickets from a friend.
I'm sorry, I can't this weekend.
And next week?
Yes, that would be fine.
Fine. See you on Saturday then.

3.
Is this your first visit to Munich?
Yes, it is.
Would you like to go on a tour of Ludwig's castles?
Oh, yes. I'd like that very much.
Good. I can book the tour for Saturday. See you then.
See you then. I look forward to it.

4.
Good morning. Can I help you?
Good morning. I've got an appointment with Mr. Harris.
I'm sorry, Mr Harris is still in a meeting.
That's OK. I'm early.
Do sit down. Would you like a coffee?
Sorry, I don't drink coffee, but tea would be nice.
With milk and sugar?
Black with no sugar.

9
1c; 2a; 3b

Back up Unit 2

1

1.	a	8.	a
2.	an	9.	an
3.	a	10.	an
4.	a	11.	an
5.	an	12.	a
6.	an	13.	an
7.	an	14.	a

2a
Cameron comes from New Zealand and lives in Christchurch. He works as a lorry driver. In his free time he plays rugby.
Aznan comes from Malaysia and lives in Penang. He works as a doctor. In his free time he plays badminton.
Janet comes from Wales and lives in Cardiff. She works as an artist. In her free time she goes bird watching.
Gary comes from Northern Ireland and lives in Belfast. He works as an airline pilot. In his free time he goes fishing.

2b

live	comes
they	like
works	go
gets	doesn't like
doesn't travel	go
works	swim
gets	swim
starts	love
collects	says
finish	are
makes	enjoy
have	

3

Do you get to work by train?
drive to work?
drive a BMW?
drink tea for breakfast?
live near Berlin?
play football in a team?
watch TV in the evening?
like chocolate?
play tennis in the summer and in the winter?

Can you eat with chopsticks?
swim?
ride a bicycle?
drive a tractor?
play chess?
speak Italian?

Can you ...? Yes, I can./No, I can't.
Do you ...? Yes, I do./No, I don't.

4
ice hockey; pottery; piano; cinema; photography; operate; winner; equipment; exciting; dangerous

Unit 3

1
1. photo 4
2. photo 1
3. photo 3
4. photo 2

2a
telephone
extension
mobile
identity card
passport
PIN
credit card

2b
telephone
extension
credit card
PIN
mobile

2c
Partner A
The people are from: Japan, Austria, England, South Africa

Partner B
The people are from: Japan, Switzerland, USA, Australia

3a
When; Where; Who; How; Who; Why; Where; Why;

3b

When?	at Christmas, at six o'clock, in the winter, in the summer, on my birthday
Where?	in London, in Italy, in the city
What?	coffee, toast, squash
Why?	because it helps me to sleep, because it's good exercise, because it's cheap
How?	on foot, by plane, by car, by bus
Who?	my brother, two colleagues, my boss

4a
1. photo 4   3. photo 1
2. photo 3   4. photo 2

4b
1. quarter to four (3.45)
2. eleven thirty (11.30)
3. ten to nine (8.50)
4. twenty-five past (7.25), twenty past (7.20), half past (7.30), eight (8.00)

5b
1. in; 2. at, at; 3. at, on; 4. in, in;
5. at; 6. on, on; 7. on, in

6

Tom and Lisa: Renault Espace
Jana and Alex: Vauxhall Omega
Sarah: Peugeot 307
Ranjit and Romy: Ford Focus

Back up Unit 3

1

1. Who
2. Where
3. Where
4. Who
5. Where
6. Who

2

1. When do you get up during the week?
2. What do you eat for breakfast?
3. How do you get to work?
4. When does your boss start work?
5. What do you do when you are on holiday?
6. What do your colleagues do on holiday?

3

1. It's a quarter past four.
2. It's a quarter to six.
3. It's ten past seven.
4. It's twenty past eleven.
5. It's twenty-five past twelve.
6. It's thirty-five past two. / It's twenty-five to three.
7. It's twenty to nine.
8. It's ten to five.
9. It's five to ten.
10. It's five past one.

4

1. in, in; 2. at; 3. at, on; 4. on; 5. in

5

Across	Down
3. queue	1. suitcase
5. company	2. newspaper
8. colleague	4. rent
9. extension	6. cheap
	7. flight
	8. celebrate

Revision Unit 1

Reading

a

What do you do in your free time?
How do you play it?
What are the rules?
How does a team win?
How often do you practise?
Is it dangerous?

b

1c; 2b; 3c

Listening

Surname: Blanchfield
Name: Holli
Fax no.: 0044 161 802-9145
Single room: 1
No. of nights: 2

Speaking

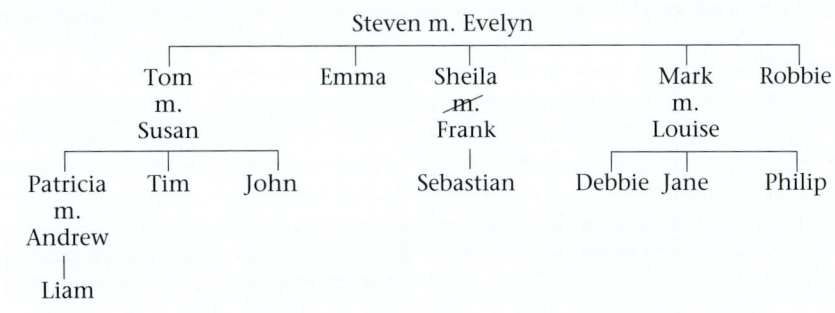

Unit 4

1

once a day, twice a week, three times a month, four times a year

2a

1. 2-3 times a week
2. twice a day
3. once a week
4. once a day
5. once a week
6. once a week
7. once a week
8. twice a year

2c

1c; 2d; 3e; 4f; 5a; 6b

2d

1. seldom
2. always
3. often
4. usually
5. always; sometimes (x2)
6. never

3a

alarm clock
get dressed
front door
coffee break
leave work
rush hour
go home
fast food
turn on your TV
fall asleep

3b

clock, dressed, door, food, break, hour, on, TV, work, fall, home

5b

men, ten, band, send, Pat, land

5c

1. band; 2. man; 3. bend;
4. pet; 5. tan; 6. lend

6a

countable nouns – How many …?
uncountable nouns – How much …?

You can count 'glasses' of wine. You can't count wine.
You can count 'bottles' of gin. You can't count gin.
You can count 'litres' of water. You can't count water.

6b

How much gin/water/herbal tea do you drink a day?
How many cups of coffee do you drink a day?
How much gin do you buy a week?
How many bottles of wine do you buy a week?

7b

Tim doesn't eat brown bread, fish or nuts. – This is not very good for his brain. But he eats oranges.

Tim sometimes eats chips and he sometimes eats his dinner late at night (at 8.30 or 9p.m.). – He should be careful because this can affect his concentration level and his sleep.

8

see tapescripts

Back up Unit 4

1
1. I never look at my e-mails after seven o'clock in the evening.
2. She is usually relaxed because she always does yoga on Friday evening.
3. She sometimes plays the piano in the evening.
4. He often goes on business trips to Dubai.
5. I never go jogging in the morning.
6. I seldom work overtime.
7. We usually play tennis on Saturday morning.
8. He always hires his car from Sixt.
9. I have a stressful job so I am often tired.
10. We sometimes go to art galleries.

2
1. How many days can you buy a London travel card for? – 1, 2, 3, 4, or 7.
2. How much does a three-day travel card for zones 1-6 cost? – €28 for adults and €12.50 for children.
3. How many zones are there in the London underground system? – 6
4. How much does a Historic Scotland Explorer Pass cost for a child for 7 days? – €24.
5. How many Euro does a Great British Heritage Pass cost for 4 days? – 30.
6. How much money can you save if you buy a London Pass when you visit London? – £200.
7. How many interesting places can you visit with a London Pass? – 50.

3
1. How much wine do you drink a day?
2. I'm sorry, we don't have any information about the London Eye here.
3. There isn't any wine in the house.
4. How many eggs do you eat a week?
5. We don't have any fish or meat in the house because we're vegetarians.
6. Is there any coffee in the cupboard? Sorry, I don't drink coffee, only tea.
7. How much water do you drink a day? About 2 litres.
8. How many glasses of beer do you drink at the weekend?
9. You should eat some brown bread every day.
10. How many hours do you spend in front of the computer screen? – Too many! Seven or eight.

11. Do you eat nuts? Yes, I eat some in my muesli every morning.
12. Where are the oranges? There aren't any in the fruit bowl.

4

1.	2.	3.
pen	red	hat
pan	dress	hit
son	send	chat
rose	sand	chart
nose	sad	cart
lap	read	cat
personal	darkness	tear
		reach
		cheat
		architect

Unit 5

1a
1. true
2. true
3. false
4. false / possible
5. true / possible
6. possible

2b

She's wearing a turquoise hat.	Mum
He's living in Windsor with his new wife.	Simon
He's travelling round the world.	Roger
She's studying to be a nurse.	Natalie

3b
The e-mail is from Rio at carnival time.

3c
Thousands of people are singing and cheering <u>enthusiastically</u> and dancing <u>wildly</u>.
The drag queens dress <u>outrageously.</u>
No-one is shouting or complaining <u>loudly</u>.

3d

cheering	wildly, noisily, loudly, enthusiastically
singing	loudly, noisily, beautifully, enthusiastically
laughing	loudly
dancing	wildly
jeering	wildly, loudly, noisily, angrily
waiting	patiently, nervously
crying	noisily
shouting	loudly, wildly, angrily
playing	dangerously, carefully
screaming	loudly, noisily

5b
cherry, cheap, joke, Gill, chest, gin, choose, jeer

5c
In bed with a chill.
He's eating a cherry.
No, it's cheap.
The Turin fans are cheering.

6c
see tapescripts

7b
A
I'm sorry, we haven't.
I'm sorry, there isn't.
I'm sorry, it doesn't.
I'm sorry, it isn't.

B
I'm sorry, I don't.
I'm sorry, I can't.
I'm sorry, I'm not.
I'm sorry, you can't.

7c
see tapescripts

8
see tapescripts

9a
1. sports
2. gossip columns
3. home news
4. entertainment pages
5. human interest
6. business and the economy
7. science and technology
8. world news

9b
Human interest section.

9c
1. He's trying to help people with junk mail.
2. People write about junk mail stories and ask for help.
3. Companies who are trying to sell trekking holidays.
4. In Tring.
5. In Reading.
6. He runs a web-site and writes letters and e-mails to give information about junk mail.
7. She can register with the Mailing Preference Service.
8. www.readgroup.co.uk
9. No web-site can help them with their legal problems.
10. No, he throws them into the dustbin.

9d
four-week
who is 95
children's
32-year-old
expensive

Back up Unit 5

1
1. The dog is eleven years old.
2. At the moment they are living in a flat in Oxford.
3. He's wearing a dark grey suit.
4. She's wearing a black skirt.
5. Her son is travelling round the world in his gap year.
6. The football fans are cheering enthusiastically.
7. The people in the crowd are cheering noisily.
8. Jim and Hanna are renovating their holiday flat.
9. Companies send a lot of junk mail.
10. She is preparing a big wedding party for her daughter.
11. It is hot and humid in Rio and a lot of tourists are having problems with the heat.
12. The phone is an important fashion accessory.
13. The dog tried to pull junk mail from the letterbox.
14. I read the science and technology section of the newspaper because I am interested in developments in the world of computers.
15. There is a big crowd watching the football match.

2
1. a dress; 2. a suit; 3. a pair of jeans; 4. a pullover; 5. a blouse; 6. a shirt; 7. a skirt; 8. a swimming costume; 9. a pair of swimming trunks; 10. a bikini; 11. a pair of gloves; 12. a tie; 13. a pair of tights; 14. a pair of socks

3
1. dangerous
2. quietly
3. slowly
4. outrageous
5. loudly
6. careful
7. wild
8. superb; hard
9. patiently
10. nervous; dangerously

4
starts, lasts, compete, work, is employing, sell, prepare, wear, come, begins,
am speaking, come, are sending, is sending,
starts, is arriving, open, are waiting, attend, watch

Unit 6

1a
On holiday you can stay in a: hotel, Bed & Breakfast, guest house, tent, caravan or mobile home, holiday flat, rented flat, youth hostel or on a campsite.

1b
see file section

3a
The room was on the 15th floor.
The view was spectacular.
The people were friendly and helpful.
The flight was long and uncomfortable.

3b
hotel: very comfortable, expensive, good, dirty, clean
beach: dirty, clean, sandy
people: noisy, helpful, friendly
food: spicy, boring, hot, international
rooms: very comfortable, cold, quiet, noisy, beautiful
weather: hot, humid, cold
view: beautiful, spectacular

4a
By limousine.
They relaxed by the pool.
They walked round the markets.
They watched the laser show at 8 o'clock in the evening.

4b
did
ed
I didn't believe it …/I didn't buy any …

6
1. false; 2. true; 3. false; 4. possible; 5. possible; 6. false; 7. possible; 8. false; 9. possible; 10. false;

Back up Unit 6

1
1. and
2. but
3. and
4. and
5. but
6. and
7. but
8. so
9. because
10. but
11. so
12. and, so
13. but, because
14. but, so
15. because

2
1. He started his holiday in Rio.
2. We didn't book the hotel in advance.
3. She visited the famous museum.
4. He paid more than $100 a night for this hotel.
5. I walked along the harbour promenade.
6. We didn't watch a big laser show in the evening.
7. They didn't want to buy any jade in the market.
8. We didn't stay in a five-star hotel.
9. We enjoyed the holiday.
10. We booked the holiday on-line.
11. She didn't arrive at the hotel after midnight.
12. They didn't play tennis every morning.
13. I reserved a seat on the train.
14. The children didn't try the local food.
15. The parents relaxed by the swimming pool.

3a
(suggestions)
Berlin is more expensive than Paris but London is the most expensive.
Munich is bigger than Zurich but Berlin is the biggest.

A Renault Clio is more expensive than a Fiat Punto.
A Toyota Yaris is more comfortable than a Renault Clio.

Golf is more expensive than tennis but scuba-diving is the most expensive.
Hang-gliding is more dangerous than scuba-diving.

3b
1. highest
2. most expensive
3. most cosmopolitan
4. nearest
5. quickest

4
1. famous
2. harbour
3. recommend
4. spicy
5. popular
6. noisy
7. sympathetic
8. view
9. journey
10. stay

missing word: facilities

Unit 7

1b

a. 1; b. 5; c. 4; d. 7; e. 2; f. 6; g. 3;

1c

1. on a web-site
2. the library
3. bottles of orange juice / the trunk of her car
4. three years ago
5. 4,000
6. TV / daughter
7. 20 soft toy animals
8. a children's home

1d

began	went	spent
found	read	took
gave	sent	put

2a

(possible answers)

He or she ate some donuts. He/she ate pretzels, macaroni & cheese, chocolate, soup. He/she drank a bottle of Californian wine. He/she flew to New Orleans.

3a, b

1. She didn't begin this hobby <u>four years ago</u>. She began it <u>three years ago</u>.
2. She didn't give the TV to a <u>children's home</u>. She gave it to her <u>daughter</u>.
3. She didn't send <u>5,000 items</u> of clothing to a hostel for homeless people, she sent <u>4,000</u>.
4. She didn't read about this hobby <u>in a newspaper</u>, she read about it <u>on a web-site</u>.
5. Heather and her partner didn't take the toys to a <u>school</u>, they took them to a <u>children's home</u>.

5

AE	BE
garbage	rubbish
trunk	boot
store	shop
apartment block	block of flats

(File section)

BE	AE
petrol	gas
lift	elevator
bill	check
torch	flashlight
tap	faucet
handbag	purse
taxi	cab
underground	subway
film	movie
motorway	highway
mobile phone	cell phone
rubber	eraser

6a

1. mobile phone; 2. purse;
3. laser pointer; 4. stapler

6b

1. Could you phone me a taxi at about four thirty?	Sure.
2. Could you lend me £15 to pay the taxi?	Of course. Let me see. Here you are.
3. Could you lend me one, just for this morning?	Sorry, I need it.
4. Could you staple these papers for me?	I'm sorry, but my stapler doesn't work.

7

Don't take more than you need.
Check if this is legal in your area.
Don't make a lot of noise.
Wear gloves.
Wash your hands when you finish.
Leave the area cleaner than you found it.
Don't climb over a fence to reach a dumpster.
Don't forget a first aid kit.

8b

1c; 2b; 3e; 4d; 5a; 6f

8c

1. false (rust)
2. false (people from the charity)
3. false (he got a tax reduction)
4. true
5. true
6. false (the driver screamed and shouted at the patrolman)

Back up Unit 7

1

(suggestions)

If you want to reduce waste, join a toy library.
If you want to save trees, don't send paper cards for birthdays, send e-mail ones.
If you want to reduce waste and grow vegetables in your garden, put kitchen waste on a compost heap.
If you want to reduce waste, buy second-hand electrical goods.
If you want to give help to people who need it, send old clothes to the Red Cross.
If you want to support a good cause, donate your old mobile phone to charity.
If you want to save oil, don't buy fruit packed in plastic.
If you want to make some money, don't throw away your old computer, sell it through eBay.
If you want to reduce waste, give cinema tickets as birthday presents.

2

1. sent
2. didn't buy, bought
3. bought, sold
4. didn't join, took
5. didn't buy, bought
6. recycled
7. broke, didn't throw, took (sold), didn't buy, bought
8. didn't have, read

3

1. Could you reserve a table for two in restaurant x, please?
2. Could you book me a hotel room for two nights, please?
3. Could you speak up, please? (speak a bit louder, please)
4. I'm sorry, he's in a meeting. Could you ring back later?
5. Could you find me an overhead projector?
6. Could I have some more water, please?
7. Could you give me a lift to the airport?
8. Could you send her/him some flowers?
9. Could you copy these documents for me, please?
10. Could I have an early morning call, please?
11. Could I have some more ice, please?
12. Could you take my suitcases to my room, please?

4

(stressed words)

1. Dixons / Currys
2. TV / radio
3. son / daughter
4. buy / threw away
5. shoes / coat

5

Oo	dirty, nervous
oOo	apartment, reduction
Ooo	salary, suddenly
oO	behind, ago

Revision Unit 2

Reading

a

1. howdy; 2. a bookworm; 3. a label

b

1. true; 2. false; 3. false; 4. true; 5. true

Listening

a

1. James and Clare; 2. Angela; 3. Tom,
4. Katie; 5. Mrs Leach; 6. Richard's
mum

b

1. He dressed outrageously.
2. He danced enthusiastically.
3. He sang very loudly.
4. He chatted very quietly.
5. He spoke very angrily.

Reading/Job talk

a. heard; applied; got
b. attended; did
c. went; did; wanted; changed; went
d. started; saw; applied; was; got
e. left; moved; found; worked
f. started; studied
g. did; liked
j. discovered; worked; spent; stayed
k. worked

1i; 2c; 3k; 4f; 5g; 6e; 7b; 8a; 9j; 10d;
11h

Unit 8

1a

picture 1: tired, picture 2: sad;
picture 3: happy, picture 4: bored,
picture 5: angry, picture 6: cold

1d

What would you do if ...?
– your car broke down on the
  motorway?
– you lost your voice?
– you locked yourself out of the
  house?
– you saw someone trying to steal a
  car?
– someone stole your handbag/wallet
  when you were on holiday?
– your family pet ran away?
– you needed a lot of money
  urgently?
– you broke your glasses / lost your
  contact lenses?

2a

The missing word in the headlines is:
fast food.

2b

see tapescripts

3a

1. True; 2. False; 3. True; 4. False;
5. False; 6. True; 7. True; 8. True

3b

You shouldn't eat eggs/fish every day.
You should eat some cheese every day.

You should eat a lot of potatoes.
You should eat nuts ever day.
You shouldn't eat meat every week.
You shouldn't eat chicken every day.
You should go for a walk ever day.
You shouldn't drink a lot of wine.

4

Janet mustn't walk on her ankle and
has to use crutches.
Brian has to keep off alcohol and
mustn't drive.
Anita has to keep her arm in a sling
and mustn't carry heavy shopping
bags.

6b

2 sorts of cheese: Brie, parmesan
2 sorts of fish: salmon, sea bass
4 sorts of vegetables: tomato, potato,
    mushroom, peppers
something hot / for a curry: chilli,
    coriander, spices
something yellow: lemon mayonnaise
something that smells: garlic

6c

Bob: tomato soup
Janie: roast Norfolk turkey
Andrew: roast nut, mushroom and
spinach loaf
Wendy: crab and salmon fish cake
Lee: tomato soup, sirloin of beef

7a, b

	problem	apology
1.	waiting for food (salad)	Sorry about that. … I'll check for you.
2.	chicken served without bread	I'm sorry about that. I'll get you some now.
3.	fish isn't done in the middle	I really do apologise. Would you like …?
4.	soup is cold	I'm really sorry. I'll send it back.

8

?	😊	😟
Can I take this chair?	Sure. Go ahead. / Help yourself.	I'm sorry, it's taken.
Can I look at your menu?	Sure. Here you are. / Help yourself.	Sorry, we need it.
Can I borrow your ashtray?	Sure. Help yourself. / Here you are.	Sorry, we need it.
Can I have the salt and pepper?	Sure. Help yourself. / Here you are.	Sorry, we need it.
Is it OK if I smoke?	Sure. Go ahead.	Well, I'd rather you didn't.
Is it OK if I open a window?	Sure. Go ahead.	Well, I'd rather you didn't.
Can I take your plate?	Sure. Go ahead.	Sorry, I haven't finished yet.

9b

1. cheese   4. ships
2. sherry   5. shop
3. cheap   6. shoes

Back up Unit 8

1

1. Where would you spend your
   holiday if money were not a
   problem?
2. What would you say to him or her
   if you met your favourite film
   star/pop singer?
3. What would you do if you forgot
   your partner's birthday?
4. How would you feel if the
   company offered you or your
   partner a new job in Australia?
5. What would you do if you heard
   strange noises in the night?
6. Who would you phone if a tree fell
   on your roof in a storm?
7. What would you do if the police
   arrested you at a demonstration?
8. What would you do if you got bad
   marks in an English test?
9. What new pet would you buy if
   your cat/dog ran away?
10. What would you say if the police
    stopped you for speeding?

2a

1. mustn't   11. have to
2. don't have to   12. don't have to
3. don't have to   13. doesn't have to
4. shouldn't   14. mustn't
5. shouldn't   15. has to
6. has to   16. should
7. should   17. have to
8. have to   18. don't have to
9. mustn't   19. don't have to
10. mustn't   20. doesn't have to

2b

(suggestions)

I should go for a walk every day but I don't!

I shouldn't eat chocolate but I do!

I love Friday evenings because I don't have to go to work the next day.

I have to take my car to the garage regularly because it's ten years old.

3

1. serious
2. evidence
3. complaint
4. flavour
5. cough
6. appointment
7. danger
8. voice
9. apologise
10. almost
11. urgently
12. instead
13. borrow
14. advertising

4

1. Sorry.
2. Is it OK if I open the window?
3. Is it OK if I check my e-mails?
4. I'm (very) sorry about that.

Unit 9

2a

see tapescripts

2c

Have you ever celebrated a birthday/a wedding anniversary
    on a beach?
    at the top of a mountain?
    in a beer garden?
    on a ship?
    in Hawaii?
    by a lake/by a river?

Have you ever attended a wedding in
    a cathedral?
    on a ship?
    in Hawaii?
    of friends from a different culture?

Have you ever given a speech
    at a party/ at a wedding?

Have you ever got drunk
    in a beer garden?
    at a party/at a wedding?

2d

see tapescripts

3

	India	Mexico
Before the wedding	bathes hands and feet decorated with henna	Godparents organise everything
Bride	wears pink/red a lot of jewellery	ribbons round the neck
Groom	gives bride a necklace	ribbons round the neck a couple and not two separate individuals give thirteen coins to bride look after her
Relatives and friends	flower petals/coconut protection from evil spirits	Godparents give a rosary and a bible friends throw red beads for good luc children try to get sweets

4

On Saturday Sarah is getting married.

On Monday Joan's collecting the children.

They are going to the Liverpool football club on Tuesday.

On Thursday they're going to the Cheshire ice cream farm.

On Saturday Joan is taking the children to Llangollen.

On Monday they are going to the Blue Planet Aquarium and Sarah and Alec are coming back from their honeymoon.

On Tuesday Joan is taking the children back home.

5a

Notepad

Message from: Mr Bradbury's assistant
Message: Mr Bradbury retiring
              Cocktail party 15th
                July 6.p.m.
              Can you attend?
              Phone: 0204579821

5b

(suggested messages)

Accept

Hello, this is Mr/Mrs Gladstone. That's G-L-A-D-S-T-O-N-E.

I'm very sorry we haven't replied to the invitation.

We were on holiday and came back yesterday.

We would be delighted to accept the kind invitation. We look forward to attending the party on Friday 15th.

Refuse

Hello …

Unfortunately, we can't attend the party as we are going to my father's 80th birthday party on that day.

Please send our good wishes to Mr Bradbury.

6

Sorry, I'm late. – No problem. Go through and help yourself to a drink.

Can I take your coat? – Oh, yes. Thank you.

Would you like another drink? – Yes, please, but just something soft. I'm driving.

What a pretty blouse. The colour suits you. – Thank you. Nice of you to say so.

Congratulations! – Thanks.

Thanks for a lovely evening. – Not at all. Thank you for coming. Drive carefully.

The food is wonderful. – Thanks. I'm glad you like it.

Back up Unit 9

1

Have you ever
    watched a Grand Prix on TV?
    got lost in a foreign country?
    had a car accident?
    attended a cocktail party?
    stayed in a five star hotel?
    slept by a lake or a river?
    driven a car in a foreign country?
    broken an arm or a leg?

2a

1. The new millennium began.
2. There was a terrorist attack on the World Trade Centre.
3. Lady Di died in a car crash.
4. He was the first man on the moon.
5. Sir Edmund Hilary and Sherpa Tensing climbed Mount Everest for the first time.

2b

13th; 15th; 30th; 17th; 14th; 50th; 70th; 40th

3a

- have a violin lesson
- give a presentation
- go to/attend a meeting / wedding / christening / cocktail party
- go to the dentist's / hairdresser's / swimming
- fly to/back from Geneva
- play tennis

3b

On Monday Peter's giving a presentation and Carol is attending a sales meeting at 10.30. Bob is playing tennis at 6 p.m.
On Tuesday Peter's going to the dentist's and Jane's going swimming.
On Wednesday Peter's flying to Geneva, Carol's attending a sales meeting and Jane is having a violin lesson.
On Thursday Peter's flying back from Geneva.
On Friday Peter and Carol are attending a cocktail party and Sally is looking after the children.
On Saturday they are all going to a wedding and on Sunday they are all going to a christening.

Unit 10

2a

1. true
2. false (the lamp is next to the chair)
3. true
4. false (to the right of the TV next to the fireplace)
5. false (in front of the sofa)
6. true
7. true
8. false (under the TV on the carpet)

3c

1. There will be a lot more technology because it will be cheaper and more efficient.
2. It is very expensive.
3. They won't come to your home to make repairs, they will do it by computer.
4. Because humans need stimulation.
5. Business professionals will travel more often and they won't stay in hotels, they will take their home with them.

4

(some possible answers)
We think that the price of petrol will rise to over 2 Euro a litre / stabilise at 1.25/1.50.
We think the price of flats in our cities will rise.

We think the average temperature next summer will be 30°.
We think air in cities will get cleaner/ dirtier in the future.
We think the number of cars on our roads will increase /fall.
We think that we will eat more vegetables /fast food /genetically modified food in the future.

5

(some possible answers)
If you move to the country, you'll
- spend more money on travelling to work / on petrol.
- need a car.
- have a garden.
- have a bigger flat.
- be healthier.
If you move to the town, you'll (you won't)
- spend more money on entertainment.
- go to the theatre more often.
- need a car.
- use public transport more often.
- spend more money on food.

6b

breaks	– mistakes
around	– town
free	– me
moon	– buffoon
frowns	– clowns
land	– hand
girls	– curls

6c

see tapescripts

8

1c; 2d; 3f; 4a; 5b; 6e

Back up Unit 10

1

If we go to Italy, the weather will be hotter and it will be more exciting for the children, but it will be noisier at night.
If we go to Stockholm, the weather will be colder and the holiday will be more boring for the children but it will be quieter at night.
If we go by train, the journey will take longer but it will be cheaper.
If we fly, it will be faster but more expensive.
If we stay in a hotel, it will be more comfortable and relaxing but it will be more expensive.
If we stay on a campsite, it will be cheaper than a hotel but there will be more work for us and it will be noisier than a hotel.

2

1. will be
2. will rise
3. is going to travel
4. is going to visit
5. will pass
6. going to buy, will pass
7. are going to buy
8. is going to take
9. am going to take, will be
10. will win
11. am going to spend
12. will finish
13. is going to visit, am going to do
14. will be
15. will improve

3

alarm, clock, necessary, audience, remember, between, opposite, meal, noise, choose, furniture, prefer, tea, carpet, wall, grow

5

1.
I'm going home now. Bye.
Bye. Have a good weekend.
Thanks. You too.

2.
It was a lovely wedding. Thank you for inviting us.
I'm glad you could come. Goodbye.
Goodbye.

3.
Have a good summer.
Same to you. See you next term. Bye.
Bye.

Revision Unit 3

Language practice

1. should; don't have to
2. travelled
3. will finish; arrive
4. change
5. I'm going to take

Listening

1c; 2e; 3b; 4a; 5d

Phonetic alphabet

These phonetic symbols mean that:

[ː]	the previous sound is long.
[']	the primary stress is on the following syllable.
[ˌ]	the secondary stress is on the following syllable.
[‿]	the two sounds are linked together.

[ʌ]	bus [bʌs], run [rʌn]
[ɑː]	last [lɑːst], park [pɑːk]
[aɪ]	my [maɪ], nice [naɪs]
[aʊ]	out [aʊt], how [haʊ]
[æ]	back [bæk], stand [stænd]

[e]	egg [eg], best [best]
[eɪ]	late [leɪt], name [neɪm], safe [seɪf], pay [peɪ]
[eə]	air [eə], where [weə]
[ə]	about [əˈbaʊt], member [ˈmembə]
[əʊ]	own [əʊn], so [səʊ]
[ɜː]	firm [fɜːm], word [wɜːd]
[ɪ]	it [ɪt], film [fɪlm]
[ɪə]	near [nɪə], here [hɪə]
[iː]	please [pliːz], see [siː]
[ɒ]	not [nɒt], long [lɒŋ]
[ɔɪ]	boy [bɔɪ], noise [nɔɪz]
[ɔː]	all [ɔːl], north [nɔːθ]

[ʊ]	book [bʊk], good [gʊd]
[ʊə]	sure [ʃʊə], tour [tʊə]
[uː]	who [huː], school [skuːl]
[ŋ]	young [jʌŋ], thing [θɪŋ]
[r]	right [raɪt], friend [frend]
[s]	sir [sɜː], Miss [mɪs]
[z]	busy [ˈbɪzɪ], please [pliːz]
[θ]	thing [θɪŋ], both [bəʊθ], nothing [nʌθɪŋ]
[ð]	that [ðæt], with [wɪð]
[ʃ]	shop [ʃɒp], fresh [freʃ]
[ʒ]	television [ˈtelɪvɪʒn]
[v]	visit [ˈvɪzɪt], love [lʌv]
[w]	well [wel], what [wɒt], quiet [kwaɪt]
[tʃ]	church [tʃɜːtʃ]
[dʒ]	Germany [ˈdʒɜːmənɪ]

Within the units the words appear in alphabetic order.

Unit 1

about [əˈbaʊt]	At the information desk you can ask ~ trains. / Tell the group ~ your partner.	nach / über
(to) ask [ɑːsk]		fragen
(to) be [biː]		sein
because [bɪˈkɒz]	I'm tired ~ it's three o'clock in the morning.	weil
brother [ˈbrʌðə]		Bruder
brother-in-law [ˈbrʌðərɪnlɔː]	My wife's brother is my ~.	Schwager
(to) choose [tʃʊːz]	~ the information that is true for you.	wählen, auswählen
circle [ˈsɜːkl]	Sit in a ~.	Kreis
(to) close [kləʊz]	Close your books.	schließen, zumachen
commuter [kəˈmjuːtə]	I live in Augsburg and work in Munich. I'm a ~.	Pendler
country [ˈkʌntri]	Austria, Switzerland and Germany are countries.	Land
cousin [ˈkʌzn]	My aunt's children are my ~s.	Cousine / Cousin
divorced [dɪˈvɔːst]	She was married but now she is ~.	geschieden
eldest son [eldɪst ˈsʌn]		ältester Sohn
false [fɔːls]	not true	nicht richtig, falsch
famous [ˈfeɪməs]		berühmt, bekannt
father [ˈfɑːðə]		Vater
father-in-law [ˈfɑːðərɪnlɔː]	My wife's father is my ~.	Schwiegervater
(to) fill in [fɪl ˈɪn]	~ the information.	ausfüllen, eintragen
forbidden [fəˈbɪdn]	Can you see the no-smoking sign? Smoking is ~.	verboten, nicht erlaubt
grandfather [ˈgrænfɑːðə]	My father's father is my ~.	Großvater
grandmother [ˈgrænmʌðə]	My father's mother is my ~.	Großmutter
grandparents [ˈgrænpeərənts]	Your mother's parents are your ~.	Großeltern
(to) have (got) [hæv ˈgɒt]		haben
(to) hear [hɪə]	Write down the names that you ~.	hören
how? [haʊ]	~ do you spell the name?	wie?
husband [ˈhʌzbnd]		Ehemann
I can do this easily. [ˈiːzɪli]		Ich kann es mühelos.
I can do this. [kæn]		Das kann ich.
I need to work on this. [niːd tə wɜːk]		Das muss ich noch üben.
group [gruːp]	There are ten people in our ~.	Gruppe
interested in [ˈɪntrəstɪd]	I'm ~ in books.	interessiert sein an
in the country [ˈkʌntri]	Not in the city: in the ~.	auf dem Land
(to) know [nəʊ]	Her name is Ann. – Yes, I ~ her.	kennen, wissen
(to) listen [ˈlɪsn]	I often ~ to the radio.	hören, zuhören, horchen
(to) look [lʊk]	~ at this picture.	anschauen
married [ˈmærɪd]	Mrs Smith is ~ to Mr Smith.	verheiratet
(to) match [mætʃ]	Match the words to the pictures.	zuordnen, verbinden
(to) meet [miːt]	Nice to ~ you.	kennen lernen, treffen

member ['membə]	I'm a ~ of a club.	Mitglied
missing ['mɪsɪŋ]	Fill in the ~ word.	fehlend
mother ['mʌðə]		Mutter
mother-in-law ['mʌðərɪnlɔː]	My wife's mother is my ~.	Schwiegermutter
Muslim ['mʌslɪm]		Moslem
nephew ['nevjuː]	My sister's son is my ~.	Neffe
niece [niːs]	My sister's daughter is my ~.	Nichte
now [naʊ]		jetzt, nun
originally [əˈrɪdʒənəli]	I live in Bonn but I'm from Turkey ~.	ursprünglich
over ['əʊvə]	He's 21, so ~ 20.	über
picture ['pɪktʃə]	You can take ~s with a camera.	Bild
popular ['pɒpjʊlə]	Many people like the name. It's ~.	beliebt
(to) practise ['præktɪs]	To be a good tennis player you must ~.	üben
(to) read [riːd]	~ the text and tick the correct statements.	lesen
really ['rɪəli]	He's over 100. Really!	wirklich
retired [rɪˈtaɪəd]	He's 65 and ~.	pensioniert
second ['sekənd]	He's son number 2. He's the ~ son.	zweite
(to) show [ʃəʊ]	~ me your passport, please.	zeigen
sister ['sɪstə]		Schwester
sister-in-law ['sɪstərɪnlɔː]	My wife's sister is my ~.	Schwägerin
so [səʊ]	I was tired ~ I went to bed.	also
son [sʌn]	My boy child is my ~.	Sohn
(to) sort out [sɔːt 'aʊt]	~ your papers.	sortieren
(to) spell [spel]	How do you ~ your name? – S-M-I-T-H	buchstabieren
(to) stand [stænd]	Don't sit, ~.	stehen, aufstehen
statement ['steɪtmənt]	Tick the correct ~s.	Aussage
sure [ʃʊə]	Can you spell your name? – Sure.	sicher, natürlich
surname ['sɜːneɪm]	George's ~ is Braun.	Familienname
(to) tell [tel]	~ me about your son.	erzählen, sagen
then [ðen]		dann, danach
(to) throw [θrəʊ]	~ the ball to me.	werfen
too [tuː]	Mel Gibson's from Australia, too.	auch, ebenfalls
true [truː]	New York is in the USA. – That's ~.	richtig, wahr, stimmt
under ['ʌndə]	She is 39, so she's ~ 40.	unter
wedding ['wedɪŋ]	You get married on your ~ day.	Hochzeit
You're welcome. ['welkəm]	Thank you. – You're welcome.	Bitte schön.
where? [weə]	Where are you from?	wo, woher
wife [waɪf]		Ehefrau
who? [huː]	~ is Barbara? – She's my daughter.	wer?
(to) write [raɪt]	~ with a pen.	schreiben

Unit 2

accountant [əˈkaʊntnt]		Buchhalter, in
(to) add [æd]	~ your name to this list.	hinzufügen
again [əˈgen]	He's here on Monday and ~ on Tuesday.	wieder, noch einmal
air [eə]	The ~ is bad because of the cars.	Luft
alone [əˈləʊn]	He's ~ in the house. His wife is out.	allein
along [əˈlɒŋ]	Walk ~ Station Road.	entlang
art gallery ['ɑːt gæləri]	"The Louvre" is a museum and an ~.	Kunstgalerie
artist ['ɑːtɪst]		Künstler, in
before [bɪˈfɔː]	Lock your car ~ you leave it in the city.	bevor
bird-watching ['bɜːd wɒtʃɪŋ]	You go ~ early when the birds sing.	Vögel beobachten
boring ['bɔːrɪŋ]	Not interesting but ~.	langweilig
bowl [bəʊl]	The fruit is in the ~.	Schale
box [bɒks]	Write your name and address in this ~.	Feld, Kästchen
(to) break sth. [breɪk]		etwas zerbrechen
bus stop/coach stop ['bʌs stɒp/'kəʊtʃ stɒp]	You wait for a bus at a ~.	Haltestelle
(to) change [tʃeɪndʒ]	In November I ~ my summer tyres.	(aus)wechseln
chess [tʃes]		Schach
chopsticks ['tʃɒpstɪks]	Chinese people eat with ~.	Stäbchen

cinema [ˈsɪnəmə]	There's a good film on at the ~.	Kino
coast [kəʊst]	Switzerland hasn't got a ~.	Küste
(to) collect [kəˈlekt]	He ~s stamps.	sammeln
(to) compare [kəmˈpeə]	~ notes.	vergleichen
correct [kəˈrekt]	12 plus 49 = 61. – Correct!	richtig
creative [kriˈeɪtɪv]	He's a writer. His job is very ~.	kreativ
crossword puzzles [ˌkrɒswɜːd ˈpʌzlz]	She's interested in words and so she likes doing ~ in the newspaper.	Kreuzworträtsel
dangerous [ˈdeɪndʒərəs]	If you drive at 250 kmh, it can be ~.	gefährlich
(to) decide [dɪˈsaɪd]	~ which word you hear.	(sich) entscheiden
different [ˈdɪfrənt]	Euro coins are ~ in all the countries.	anders
dry [draɪ]	When there's no rain, the garden is ~.	trocken
easy [ˈiːzi]	10+10=20. That's ~!	einfach
energetic [ˌenəˈdʒetɪk]	You need energy to play football. It's ~.	energiegeladen, aktiv
engine [ˈendʒɪn]	His car has got a big ~.	Motor
equipment [ɪˈkwɪpmənt]	In the office there's a lot of ~.	Geräte, technische Ausstattung
exciting [ɪkˈsaɪtɪŋ]		aufregend, interessant
expensive [ɪkˈspensɪv]	The T-shirt costs 300 Euro. That's ~.	teuer
finish [ˈfɪnɪʃ]	They ~ school at 4 o'clock.	enden, beenden
free time [fri: ˈtaɪm]		Freizeit
friendly [ˈfrendli]		freundlich
game [geɪm]	Monopoly is a good ~.	Spiel
(to) get to work [wɜːk]	He gets to work by train.	zur Arbeit kommen
(to) get up early [ˈɜːli]	He gets up early at four o'clock.	früh aufstehen
guess [ges]	How many correct ~es have you got?	Vermutung
(to) guess [ges]		raten
hidden [ˈhɪdn]	You can't see the house. It's ~ by trees.	versteckt, hinter ... verborgen
hiking [ˈhaɪkɪŋ]	I go ~ in the mountains but not skiing.	wandern
hunting [ˈhʌntɪŋ]	He goes ~ in the forest.	jagen
indoor (pool) [ˈɪndɔː puːl]	An ~ swimming pool is in a big hall.	innen, (Hallenbad)
inside [ɪnˈsaɪd]	When it rains, the children play ~.	drinnen
it's more fun [fʌn]		es macht mehr Spaß
lorry driver [ˈlɒri draɪvə]		LKW-Fahrer
marbles [ˈmɑːblz]	Children often play with glass ~.	Murmeln
(to) match [mætʃ]	~ the questions with the answers.	zuordnen
missing [ˈmɪsɪŋ]	Karl isn't in class today. He's ~.	fehlen
(to) need [niːd]		benötigen
(to) operate [ˈɒpəreɪt]	How do you ~ this machine?	bedienen, benutzen
(to) order [ˈɔːdə]	He ~ed a beer in a pub.	bestellen
outside [aʊtˈsaɪd]	When the weather is good we play ~.	draußen
painting [ˈpeɪntɪŋ]	She likes ~ in oils and in watercolours.	malen
piano [piˈænəʊ]	She plays the ~ and the organ in church.	Klavier
platform [ˈplætfɔːm]	The train leaves from ~ six.	Gleis
pool [puːl]	~ is an American game like billiards.	Pool
pottery [ˈpɒtəri]	She does ~ and makes beautiful vases.	Töpfern
(to) practise [ˈpræktɪs]	You can only learn vocabulary if you ~.	üben
questionnaire [ˌkwestʃəˈneə]		Fragebogen
relaxing [rɪˈlæksɪŋ]	Reading is a ~ hobby.	entspannend
season [ˈsiːzn]		Jahreszeit
silk [sɪlk]	Her blouse is made of ~.	Seide
skating [ˈskeɪtɪŋ]	They go ~ on the lake in winter.	Schlittschuhlaufen
sound [saʊnd]		Laut
stone [stəʊn]	You can play "Kudoda" with small ~s.	Stein
summer [ˈsʌmə]	August is in the ~.	Sommer
(to) take [teɪk]	When you go to the UK, don't forget to ~ your passport.	mitnehmen
team [tiːm]	"Manchester United" is a football ~.	Mannschaft
text message [ˈtekst mesɪdʒ]		SMS Nachricht
tractor [ˈtræktə]	He drives the ~ on the farm.	Trecker
(to) type [taɪp]	You ~ with a keyboard.	tippen
underlined [ˌʌndəˈlaɪnd]	The words in the book are ~ in pencil.	unterstrichen
(to) understand [ˌʌndəˈstænd]	I can ~ Italian but I can't speak it.	verstehen

unusual [ˌʌnˈjuːʒʊəl]	He has an ~ hobby. He collects keys.	ungewöhnlich
vowels [ˈvaʊəlz]	a, e, i, o and u are ~s.	Vokale
(to) watch [wɒtʃ]	He ~es TV every evening.	(an)schauen
wet [wet]	When it rains, the garden is ~.	nass
winner [ˈwɪnə]	Number 1 in the race is the ~.	Gewinner

Unit 3

airport [ˈeəpɔːt]	Heathrow is a big ~ in London.	Flughafen
alarm clock [əˈlɑːm klɒk]	I get up when the ~ rings.	Wecker
area code [ˈeəriə kəʊd]	The area code for Berlin is 030.	Vorwahl
because [bɪˈkɒz]	She's cold ~ it's December.	weil
birthday [ˈbɜːθdeɪ]	My ~ is on 2 July.	Geburtstag
bottom row [ˌbɒtm ˈrəʊ]		untere Reihe
business trip [ˈbɪznɪs trɪp]	The Marketing Manager is on a ~.	Geschäftsreise
car registration number [ˌkɑː redʒɪˈstreɪʃn nʌmbə]	My ~ is M-TS 456.	Autokennzeichen
careful [ˈkeəfʊl]	Be ~ when you ride your bicycle.	vorsichtig
(to) catch the train [kætʃ ...ˈtreɪn]	I ~ from the main railway station.	den Zug nehmen
(to) celebrate [ˈselɪbreɪt]	Muslims don't ~ Christmas. They ~ Id.	feiern
cheap [tʃiːp]	It costs 5 Euro. It's not expensive, it's ~.	billig
clock [klɒk]		Uhr
colleague [ˈkɒliːg]	He's a ~. He works with me.	Kollege
company [ˈkʌmpəni]	Vodafone is a big ~.	Firma
(to) compare [kəmˈpeə]	When you buy a car do you ~ prices?	vergleichen
(to) decide [dɪˈsaɪd]	I can't ~ which car to buy.	sich entscheiden
details [ˈdiːteɪlz]		Angaben, Einzelheiten
(to) dictate [dɪkˈteɪt]	The boss ~s a letter to his assistant.	diktieren
(to) draw [drɔː]	She ~s beautiful pictures of animals.	zeichnen
(to) drive [draɪv]		fahren
(to) finish [ˈfɪnɪʃ]	The children ~ school at 2 o'clock.	beenden
flight [flaɪt]	My ~ number is LH 456.	Flug
freelance [ˈfriːlɑːns]	She works ~ for different companies.	freiberuflich
(to) get to work [get ...ˈwɜːk]	He ~s by car.	zur Arbeit fahren
(to) get up [get ˈʌp]	I ~ at six o'clock.	aufstehen
(to) give back [gɪv ˈbæk]	I want to ~ the car at 9 o'clock.	zurückbringen
Have you got the time? [gɒt ...ˈtaɪm]		Wie spät ist es?
how long? [haʊ ˈlɒŋ]	~ is a football match? – 90 minutes.	wie lange
how? [haʊ]	~ are you? – Fine thanks. And you?	wie
identity card [aɪˈdentəti kɑːd]	You must carry your ~ with you.	Ausweis
international dialling code [ɪntəˌnæʃnl ˈdaɪəlɪŋ kəʊd]	The ~ for America is 001.	Landesvorwahl
Internet access [ˈɪntənet ækses]		Internetzugang
leap year [ˈliːp jɪə]		Schaltjahr
(to) leave [liːv]	The train ~s at six o'clock.	abfahren
(to) look at [lʊk æt]	He ~s sports pages in a newspaper.	anschauen
luggage [ˈlʌgɪdʒ]		Gepäck
(to) make up [meɪk ˈʌp]	~ some sentences with these words.	bilden
meeting [ˈmiːtɪŋ]	My manager is in a ~.	Besprechung
mobile [ˈməʊbaɪl]	You can phone with your ~ on the train.	Handy
necessary [ˈnesəsri]	If you go to the UK, it is ~ to change money.	nötig, notwendig
newspaper [ˈnjuːspeɪpə]	The Times is a daily ~.	Zeitung
numbers [ˈnʌmbəz]		Zahlen
parents [ˈpeərənts]	My mother and my father are my ~.	Eltern
(to) pay [peɪ]	Do you want to pay in dollars?	bezahlen
phone number [ˈfəʊn nʌmbə]		Telefonnummer
(to) pick up [ˈpɪk ʌp]	You can ~ your tickets at 7 o'clock.	abholen
plane [pleɪn]	"Plane" is short for "aeroplane".	Flugzeug
possible [ˈpɒsəbl]		möglich
present [ˈpreznt]	When it's your birthday, you get ~s.	Geschenke
prompts [prɒmts]		Stichworte
quote [kwəʊt]	How much is the rental car? I need a ~.	Kostenangebot

(to) rent [rent]	I want to fly to the USA and ~ a car.	mieten
rental requirements [ˌrentl rɪˈkwaɪəmənts]		Bedarf, Erfordernis an Mietwagen
school [skuːl]	In UK children start ~ when they are 5.	Schule
(to) sort out [sɔːt aʊt]	He has to ~ all the problems.	sich kümmern um, sortieren
(to) start [stɑːt]	He ~s work at half past seven.	beginnen
suitcase [ˈsuːtkeɪs]	You pack your clothes in a ~ when you go on holiday.	Koffer
top row [tɒp rəʊ]		obere Reihe
tram [træm]	You can travel by ~ in San Francisco.	Straßenbahn
(to) visit [ˈvɪzɪt]		besuchen
watch [wɒtʃ]	What time is it? – Sorry, I haven't got a ~.	Armbanduhr
what? [wɒt]		was?
what sort of? [sɔːt]	~ music do you like? – Rock and Roll.	welche? was für?
where? [weə]	~ does he live? – In Tokyo.	wo?
why? [waɪ]		warum?

Unit 4

abuse [əˈbjuːs]		Beschimpfungen, Missbrauch
advice [ədˈvaɪs]	Take my ~ and stop smoking.	Rat(schlag)
affect [əˈfekt]		Wirkung
after [ˈɑːftə]	At 8.30 ~ breakfast.	nach
alone [əˈləʊn]	He lives ~ in the flat. He's not married.	allein
always [ˈɔːlweɪz]	You must ~ wear a seat belt in the car.	immer
any [ˈeni]		irgendein(e), irgendwelche
ashtray [ˈæʃtreɪ]	If you smoke, you use an ~.	Aschenbecher
available [əˈveɪləbl]		verfügbar
band [bænd]		(Musik)gruppe
(to) be keen on sth. [kiːn]		etwas gern mögen
before [bɪˈfɔː]	He gets up and goes jogging ~ breakfast.	vor
behind [bɪˈhaɪnd]	He's a fast runner. He leaves me ~.	zurück
bend [bend]		Biegung, Kurve
brain [breɪn]	He's intelligent. He has a very good ~.	Gehirn
by clicking on [ˈklɪkɪŋ]	Find the answer ~ the symbol.	indem Sie auf ... klicken
century [ˈsentʃəri]	100 years is one ~.	Jahrhundert
certainly [ˈsɜːtənli]	Do you love your wife? – I ~ do!	sicherlich
coffee break [ˈkɒfi breɪk]		Kaffeepause
column [ˈkɒləm]		Spalte
(to) count [kaʊnt]	She's only two but she can ~ from 1-20.	zählen
cupboard [ˈkʌbəd]		Schrank
darkness [ˈdɑːknəs]	There's no moon. There's only ~.	Dunkelheit
difficult [ˈdɪfɪklt]	Chinese is a ~ language to learn.	schwierig
drunk [drʌŋk]	After ten whiskies he's ~.	betrunken
eggs [egz]	Chickens give us ~s.	Eier
either ... or [ˈeɪðə ... ɔː]	You can get ~ bus number 6 ~ number 7.	entweder ... oder
every [ˈevri]	Monday to Sunday: ~ day.	jeden
everyone [ˈevrɪwʌn]	All people: ~.	alle, jeder
factory [ˈfæktəri]	They make cars in the ~.	Fabrik
FAQ [ef eɪ ˈkjuː]	Frequently asked questions.	häufig gestellte Fragen
(to) fall asleep [fɔːl əˈsliːp]	When I'm tired, I ~ in front of the TV.	einschlafen
food [fuːd]		Lebensmittel
fridge [frɪdʒ]		Kühlschrank
front door [frʌnt ˈdɔː]	We live at number 10. The ~ is red.	Haustür
full [fʊl]	There are no seats. The bus is ~.	voll
headache [ˈhedeɪk]		Kopfschmerzen
healthy [ˈhelθi]		gesund
herbal tea [ˌhɜːbl ˈtiː]		Kräutertee
How many ...? [haʊ ˈmeni]		Wie viele ...?
How much ...? [haʊ ˈmʌtʃ]		Wie viel ...?

I'd rather ... ['rɑ:ðə]		Ich würde eher / lieber ...
important [ɪm'pɔ:tnt]	He's taking a very ~ examination today.	wichtig
(to) improve [ɪm'pru:v]	He ~d his mark from a four to a three.	verbessern
just the same [dʒʌst ðə seɪm]	Her hair isn't grey. It's ~ as when she was 40.	genau so
late [leɪt]	He goes to bed ~, at 2 a.m.	spät
(to) leave (home) [li:v]		verlassen (aus dem Haus gehen)
(to) lend [lend]		(aus)leihen
light [laɪt]	At night you have ~s on the car.	Licht
like [laɪk]	I am ~ my mother. We are both tall.	wie
listener ['lɪsnə]	When you listen to the radio, you are a ~.	Zuhörer
(to) look up [lʊk 'ʌp]	~ the word in a dictionary.	nachschlagen, nachschauen
making a booking ['bʊkɪŋ]		eine Reservierung vornehmen
maybe [meɪ'bi:]	Yes or no? I'm not sure, ~.	vielleicht
meat [mi:t]	We eat ~ from animals.	Fleisch
memory ['meməri]	If you have a good ~, you don't forget.	Gedächtnis
(to) need [ni:d]	I ~ eight hours sleep a night.	brauchen
never ['nevə]	I don't like tea. I ~ drink it.	nie
nut [nʌt]	Some people are allergic to ~s.	Nüsse
often ['ɒfn]	He gets up late and he's ~ late for work.	oft
once [wʌns]		einmal
ordinary ['ɔ:dnri]	Not stars: ~ people like you and me.	gewöhnlich, normal
pet [pet]	Cats and dogs make good ~s.	Haustier
piece [pi:s]	Can I have a ~ of cake, please?	Stück
poor cow [pʊə 'kaʊ]		blöde Kuh
(to) prefer [prɪ'fɜ:]		bevorzugen
(to) pronounce [prə'naʊns]		aussprechen
(to) queue [kju:]	At a bus stop you stand in a ~.	in einer Schlange stehen
(to) reduce [rɪ'dju:s]	It's a good idea to ~ stress.	reduzieren
(to) repeat [rɪ'pi:t]		wiederholen
rush hour ['rʌʃ aʊə]	He gets to work at 6.30 before the ~.	Hauptverkehrszeit
(to) save [seɪv]		sparen
seldom ['seldm]		selten
sensibly ['sensəbli]	If you eat ~, you don't eat chocolate.	vernünftig
shame [ʃeɪm]	It's a ~ you can't come to my party.	schade
What a shame! [ʃeɪm]		Wie schade!
smell [smel]		Geruch
(to) smile [smaɪl]	I want a good photo. Say cheese! Smile!	lächeln
some [sʌm]		einige, ein paar ("some" wird zum Teil nicht übersetzt)
sometimes ['sʌmtaɪmz]	Not often but ~.	manchmal
square [skweə]		Quadrat
stamina ['stæmɪnə]	If you swim 5,000 metres, you need ~.	Ausdauer
still [stɪl]	They are ~ in love after 60 years!	immer noch
suburbia [sə'bɜ:biə]	I don't live in the city centre I live in ~.	Vororte, Stadtrandbereich
successful [sək'sesfʊl]	He's good at his job. He's very ~.	erfolgreich
suggestion [sə'dʒestʃn]		Vorschlag
surgery ['sɜ:dʒəri]	You talk to a doctor in his ~.	Sprechzimmer
tan [tæn]		(Sonnen)bräune
the same [seɪm]		der, die, das gleiche
there is ... [ðeər'ɪz]		es gibt ... / da ist ...
there are (not) ... [ðeər'a:]		es gibt ... / da sind ... (nicht)
trade journals ['treɪd dʒɜ:nlz]		Handelsmagazine
three times a day [θri: 'taɪmz]		dreimal pro Tag
too [tu:]	I like chocolate. She likes chocolate ~.	auch, ebenfalls
tower block ['taʊə blɒk]	There are a lot of flats in the ~.	Hochhaus
trapped [træpt]	Tom ~ the mouse Jerry.	fangen, eingeschlossen sein
tube [tju:b]	The underground in London is the ~.	U-Bahn

(to) turn on [tɜːn]	~ the TV, I want to watch the football match.	einschalten
twice [twaɪs]	Two times: twice.	zweimal
(to) use [juːz]	I ~ compuserve for my e-mails.	gebrauchen, verwenden
usually ['juːʒʊəli]	I ~ get up at six, but not on Saturdays.	normalerweise
(to) wear [weə]	The nurse ~s a uniform.	tragen
what for? [wɒt 'fɔː]	I go to the fitness club on Tuesdays. – What for?	weshalb?, warum?
wholemeal ['həʊlmiːl]	~ bread is brown not white.	Vollkorn
work overtime [wɜːk 'əʊvətaɪm]	She works 2 hours overtime a week.	Überstunden machen
world [wɜːld]	We live in a dangerous ~.	Welt
worries ['wʌrɪz]	I'm happy. I haven't got any ~.	Sorgen

Unit 5

according to [ə'kɔːdɪŋ]	~ the guidebook this is a good hotel.	nach, zufolge, laut
accident ['æksɪdənt]	He had an ~ in his car on the motorway.	Unfall
aerials ['eəriəlz]		Antennen
angry ['æŋgri]		wütend
(to) attend [ə'tend]		teilnehmen an
(to) believe [bɪ'liːv]	He says he's 30 but I don't ~ him.	glauben
building ['bɪldɪŋ]	Houses, hotels, schools are all ~s.	Gebäude
business and economy ['bɪznɪs … ɪ'kɒnəmi]		Handel und Wirtschaft
case [keɪs]	It was a very difficult ~.	Fall
(to) cheer [tʃɪə]	When the football team wins, the fans ~.	jubeln
cherry ['tʃeri]	"Mon chéri" has a ~ in the middle.	Kirsche
chest [tʃest]		Brust
chill [tʃɪl]	It was very cold and she got a ~.	Erkältung
chin [tʃɪn]		Kinn
(to) choke [tʃəʊk]		ersticken
(to) communicate [kə'mjuːnɪkeɪt]	Young people ~ by e-mail or mobile.	kommunizieren
(to) compete [kəm'piːt]		konkurrieren
(to) complain [kəm'pleɪn]	We often ~ about the wet weather!	sich beschweren
compensation [ˌkɒmpən'seɪʃn]	The worker got ~ after the accident.	Entschädigung
crowd [kraʊd]	A lot of people at a football match is the ~.	Zuschauermenge
customer ['kʌstəmə]	A person who buys things in a shop is a ~.	Kunde
dangerous ['deɪndʒərəs]	At night in a big city it can be ~.	gefährlich
decision [dɪ'sɪʒn]		Entscheidung
developments [dɪ'veləpmənts]	What are the new ~ in technology?	Entwicklungen
dressed up [dresd 'ʌp]	She's ~ because she's going to a party.	festlich gekleidet
(to) drive [draɪv]	He can't ~. He's learning to ~ a car.	fahren
emergency [ɪ'mɜːdʒənsi]	If there is an ~, you can call the police.	Notfall
(to) employ [ɪm'plɔɪ]	He works for me. I ~ him.	beschäftigen
entertainment [ˌentə'teɪnmənt]	The cinema is a popular form of ~.	Unterhaltung
enthusiastic(ally) [ɪnˌθjuːzi'æstɪk]		begeistert
event [ɪ'vent]	The birth of a baby is an important ~.	Ereignis
examination [ɪgˌzæmɪ'neɪʃn]		Prüfung
exciting [ɪk'saɪtɪŋ]	Not boring, but ~.	aufregend
fashion accessory ['fæʃn əksesəri]		modisches Accessoire
famous ['feɪməs]	Footballers and film stars are ~ people.	berühmt
feathers ['feðəz]	Birds don't have hair, they have ~.	Federn
(to) fight [faɪt]	Boxers ~. It's their job.	kämpfen
fit [fɪt]	The pullover is too big, it doesn't ~.	passen
fitting room ['fɪtɪŋ ruːm]	You can try a pullover on in the ~.	Anprobe, Kabine
fortnight ['fɔːtnaɪt]		14 Tage
(to) get used to it [get 'juːst]		sich daran gewöhnen
guide book ['gaɪd bʊk]	Tourists read a ~ about the city they visit.	(Reise-) Führer
(to) happen ['hæpn]	I can't see what is ~ing.	geschehen
heat [hiːt]		Hitze
hill [hɪl]		Hügel
home news ['həʊm njuːz]		Inlandsnachrichten
householders ['haʊshəʊldəz]	People who live in a house are the ~.	Hausbesitzer
however [haʊ'evə]		jedoch

human interest stories [ˌhjuːmən 'ɪntrəst stɔːrɪz]		ergreifende Geschichten über Menschen
humid ['hjuːmɪd]	Hot and wet weather is ~.	schwül
I'll leave it. [liːv]		Ich lasse es bleiben/sein.
injured ['ɪndʒəd]	He is OK. He wasn't ~ in the accident.	verletzt
(to) insure [ɪn'ʃʊə]		versichern
is about to [ə'baʊt]	Quick! The train ~ leave.	ist gerade dabei ...
jeep [dʒiːp]	In the army you drive a ~ not a car.	Jeep, Geländewagen
(to) jeer [dʒɪə]	The football hooligans ~ed.	johlen, buhen
(to) jest [dʒest]	To make a joke is to ~.	scherzen
jewellery ['dʒuːəlri]	Rings and earrings are ~.	Schmuck
leaflet ['liːflət]		Flugblatt
legal fees ['liːgl fɪːz]	Money that you pay a lawyer are ~.	Gebühren
letterbox ['letəbɒks]	The postman puts letters in the ~.	Briefkasten
lift [lɪft]	Can you give me a ~?	Kannst du mich mitnehmen?
(to) lose weight [luːz weɪt]	He's on a diet. He wants to ~.	abnehmen
loud [laʊd]	The disco music was ~.	laut
mainly ['meɪnli]		hauptsächlich
neighbourhood ['neɪbəhʊd]	"Chelsea" is an expensive ~ in London.	Gegend, Viertel
nervous ['nɜːvəs]	Before an examination I'm always ~.	nervös
no connection [ˌnəʊ kə'nekʃn]		keine Verbindung
noisy ['nɔɪzi]	In the big city it's often ~.	laut
nothing ['nʌθɪŋ]		nichts
nurse ['nɜːs]	A ~ works with doctors in a hospital.	Krankenschwester
ordinary ['ɔːdənri]	We're not famous, we're ~.	gewöhnlich
outrageous [aʊt'reɪdʒəs]		unglaublich, unmöglich, unerhört
particular [pə'tɪkjʊlə]		besonders
pick-pocket ['pɪkpɒkɪt]	Be careful of ~s in crowds.	Taschendieb
polite [pə'laɪt]		höflich
popular ['pɒpjələ]		beliebt, bekannt
(to) prove [pruːv]	I think he's the murderer, but I can't ~ it.	beweisen
(in) public ['pʌblɪk]		(in der) Öffentlichkeit
reaction [ri'ækʃn]	What do you think? What's your ~?	Reaktion
(to) replace [rɪ'pleɪs]		ersetzen
result [rɪ'zʌlt]	Can I have the ~ of my test?	Ergebnis
satellites ['sætəlaɪts]		Satelliten
science and technology ['saɪəns … tek'nɒlədʒi]		Wissenschaft und Technik
(to) scream [skriːm]	She was very frightened so she ~ed.	schreien
(to) send [send]	I ~ e-mails, I don't ~ postcards.	schicken
screw [skruː]		Schraube
shirt [ʃɜːt]	The man was wearing a white ~.	Hemd
shop assistant ['ʃɒp əˌsɪstnt]	Someone who works in a shop is a ~.	Verkäufer/in
shoulder ['ʃəʊldə]	Her hair was long, on her ~.	Schulter
(to) shout [ʃaʊt]	He can't hear very well. Shout!	rufen
size [saɪz]	What shoe ~ are you? – 39.	Größe
space [speɪs]		Weltraum
(to) subscribe [səb'skraɪb]	I ~ to Time magazine. I get it every week.	abonnieren
(to) sue [suː]	He ~d the restaurant because he was ill.	klagen, verklagen
survey ['sɜːveɪ]	We asked a lot of questions in the ~.	Umfrage
(to) take place [teɪk 'pleɪs]	The Olympic Games ~ every four years.	stattfinden
tennis court ['tenɪs kɔːt]		Tennisplatz
tie [taɪ]		Krawatte
tights [taɪts]		Strumpfhose
tournament ['tʊənəmənt]		Turnier
(to) transfer [træns'fɜː]	Banks can ~ money.	überweisen
trouser suit ['traʊzə suːt]		Hosenanzug
(to) try it on [traɪ]	Before you buy a new pullover, ~.	anprobieren
unfortunate [ʌn'fɔːtʃənət]	It was ~ that they missed the train.	bedauerlich
unbelievable [ʌnbə'liːvəbl]	It's ~ that she's forty. She looks thirty.	unglaublich
urgent ['ɜːdʒnt]		dringend

(to) wait [weɪt]	You ~ for a train at the station.	warten
wig [wɪg]	It's not her hair. She's wearing a ~.	Perücke
wildly ['waɪldli]		wild

Unit 6

acrostic [ə'krɒstɪk]		hintereinander zu lesende (Anfangs-) Buchstaben, die ein Wort ergeben
(in) advance [əd'vɑːns]	In summer it's a good idea to book ~.	im Voraus
advice [əd'vaɪs]	I have a problem. Can you give me some ~?	Rat(schlag)
after ['ɑːftə]	Do you get dressed before or ~ breakfast?	nach
arrival [ə'raɪvl]	The train arrives at 6.00. ~ time is 6 o'clock.	Ankunft
available [ə'veɪləbl]	The hotel is full. No rooms are ~.	verfügbar
beach [biːtʃ]	The children played in the sand on the ~.	Strand
but [bʌt]	The hotel was expensive ~ good.	aber
(to) cancel ['kænsl]	Lufthansa ~ed the flight because of fog.	annullieren, stornieren
clean [kliːn]	The air in the Alps isn't dirty, it's ~.	sauber
comfortable ['kʌmftəbl]	The sofa is very ~. I like to sit on it.	bequem, gemütlich
(to) compare [kəm'peə]	Before you book a hotel you ~ prices.	vergleichen
comparison [kəm'pærɪsn]		Vergleich
courtesy bus ['kɜːtəsi bʌs]	We didn't pay for the bus. It was a ~.	gebührenfreier Hotelbus
cruise [kruːz]	A holiday or a trip on a ship is a ~.	Kreuzfahrt
departure [dɪ'pɑːtʃə]	The plane leaves at 11.00. ~ time is 11 o'clock.	Abflug
destination [ˌdestɪ'neɪʃn]	Majorca is a popular holiday ~.	Ziel
dirty ['dɜːti]	Air in cities is ~.	schmutzig
either ['aɪðə]	I don't like tea. I don't like coffee ~.	auch nicht
entertainment [ˌentə'teɪnmənt]	The ~ was good. Films, talks, concerts.	Unterhaltung
expert ['ekspɜːt]	He knows a lot about art. He's an ~.	Experte
famous ['feɪməs]	Footballers and film stars are ~.	berühmt
far [fɑː]	Is it ~ to the hotel? – No, 2 kilometres.	weit
features ['fiːtʃəz]	What are the ~ of a good hotel?	Merkmale
guest [gest]	People in hotels are the ~s.	Gäste
harbour ['hɑːbə]	You can see a lot of boats in the ~.	Hafen
helicopter ['helɪkɒptə]	She had a skiing accident and went to hospital by ~.	Hubschrauber
helpful ['helpfʊl]	The man at the information desk was ~.	hilfsbereit
holiday destination ['hɒlədei destɪneɪʃn]		Urlaubsziel
honeymoon ['hʌnimuːn]	After the wedding the couple will go away on ~.	Flitterwochen
humid ['hjuːmɪd]	The weather was hot and wet. It was ~.	schwül
(to) inherit [ɪn'herɪt]		erben
ill [ɪl]	He's ~ in hospital.	krank
jade [dʒeɪd]	~ is a green stone. It is expensive.	Jade
laser beams ['leɪzə biːmz]		Laserstrahlen
leading ['liːdɪŋ]	Hilton hotels are ~ hotels of the world.	führend(e)
local ['ləʊkl]	The ~ shops are 100 metres from my house.	vor Ort, örtlich
market research [ˌmɑːkɪt ri'sɜːtʃ]		Marktforschung
much [mʌtʃ]	It's ~ hotter in Rome than in London.	viel
of course [əv 'kɔːs]	Can you help me, please? – Of course.	sicher, natürlich
per [pɜː]	It costs 100 Euro ~ night.	pro
(to) pick up [pɪk 'ʌp]	Can you pick me up from the station?	abholen
quick [kwɪk]		schnell
quiet ['kwaɪət]	The opposite of "loud" is ~.	ruhig
(to) recommend [ˌrekə'mend]	Can you ~ a good restaurant?	empfehlen
recreation facilities [ˌrekri'eɪʃn fəˌsɪlətiz]	A swimming pool, a tennis court and a cinema are ~.	Freizeiteinrichtungen
(to) regret [rɪ'gret]	We're sorry, we ~ that there are no rooms available in August.	bedauern
(to) remember [rɪ'membə]	She didn't ~ his birthday.	sich erinnern
(to) reserve [rɪ'zɜːv]	It's a good idea to ~ a seat on a train.	reservieren
safely ['seɪfli]	The plane landed ~. There were no problems.	sicher
sand castle ['sænd kɑːsl]	Children make ~ on the beach.	Sandburg

sandy ['sændi]	The children liked the ~ beach.	sandig, Sand-
seat [si:t]	You sit on a ~ in a train or plane.	Sitzplatz
(to) select [sə'lekt]	You can ~ what to buy in a supermarket.	aussuchen, auswählen
spa [spɑː]		(Heil-/Mineral-)Bad
spectacular [spek'tækjələ]	The photos of the mountains were ~.	atemberaubend, sensationell
spicy ['spaɪsi]	In India food is often hot and ~.	scharf, gut gewürzt
(to) stay [steɪ]	You can ~ in a hotel or a guest house.	übernachten, bleiben
suggestion [sə'dʒestʃn]		Vorschlag
sympathetic [ˌsɪmpə'θetɪk]		mitfühlend, verständnisvoll
tall [tɔːl]	He's 2 metres ~.	groß
terrible ['terəbl]	very bad	schrecklich
value for money [ˌvælju: … 'mʌni]	The holiday was expensive but good ~.	gutes Preis-/ Leistungsverhältnis
view [vjuː]	I have a good ~ from my window.	Aussicht
windy ['wɪndi]	In autumn the weather is often ~.	windig
worth it ['wɜːθ ɪt]	I was happy we visited China. It was ~.	es hat sich gelohnt

Unit 7

advertisement [əd'vɜːtɪsmənt]	There was an ~ for a job in the paper.	Inserat, Anzeige
annual ['ænjʊəl]		jährlich
apartment [ə'pɑːtmənt]	He lives in an ~, not in a house.	Wohnung
(to) become [bɪ'kʌm]	He wants to ~ a soccer player.	werden
bill (UK) / check (US) [bɪl/tʃek]	She paid the gas, water and electricity ~s.	Rechnung
boot (UK) / trunk (US) [buːt/trʌŋk]	Put your suitcases in the ~ of the car.	Kofferraum
(to) care about [keə]	We should all ~ our health.	sich um … kümmern
careful ['keəfʊl]	Be ~ when you ride your bike on the road.	vorsichtig sein
charity ['tʃærəti]	"Caritas" is a ~.	Wohltätigkeitsorganisation
(to) check [tʃek]	I think his number is 030 456023. I'll ~.	nachschauen, prüfen
children's home ['tʃɪldrənz həʊm]	He doesn't have parents, he lives in a ~.	Kinderheim
(to) climb [klaɪm]	Don't ~ over a fence.	klettern
clothes [kləʊðz]		Kleidung
(to) complete [kəm'pliːt]	Fill in the missing words. ~ the sentence.	vervollständigen
compost heap ['kɒmpəst hiːp]		Komposthaufen
container [kən'teɪnə]		Behälter, Kontainer
cop [kɒp]		(umgangssprachlich für) Polizist
(to) cry [kraɪ]	Babies often ~ at night.	weinen
dealer ['diːlə]	You can buy a car from a car ~.	Händler
details ['diːteɪlz]	Please give me ~ of the accident.	Einzelheiten
diver ['daɪvə]		Taucher
(to) donate [dəʊ'neɪt]	She ~s money to "Caritas".	spenden
donation [dəʊ'neɪʃn]	Bill Gates gives big ~s of money to charity.	Spende
dumpster ['dʌmstə]		Müllkontainer
electricity [ˌelɪk'trɪsəti]	We have no ~ so we can't watch TV.	Strom
environment [ɪn'vaɪrənmənt]		Umwelt
(to) fail [feɪl]	He ~ed his exam. He was unhappy.	durchfallen, nicht bestehen
faucet/tap ['fɔːsɪt/tæp]	You can drink water out of the ~.	Wasserhahn
favourite ['feɪvrɪt]	What's your ~ colour? – Blue.	Lieblings-
fence [fens]	There is a big ~ round the garden.	Zaun
film (UK) / movie (US) [fɪlm/'muːvi]		Kinofilm
first aid kit [ˌfɜːst 'eɪd kɪt]	In your car you must have a ~.	Erste-Hilfe-Kasten
for the first time [fɜːst 'taɪm]	I was in America ~ in 2002.	zum ersten Mal
(to) forget [fə'get]	I often ~ his birthday.	vergessen
furniture ['fɜːnətʃə]	Chairs, tables, beds are all pieces of ~.	Möbel
garbage ['gɑːbɪdʒ]	We throw ~ in the bin.	Abfall
(to) grow [grəʊ]	Rice ~s in China.	wachsen, wird angebaut
gloves [glʌvz]	In winter I wear ~ on my hands.	Handschuhe

handbag ['hændbæg]	A woman keeps make-up in her ~.	Handtasche
(to) happen ['hæpn]	There was an accident. What ~ed?	geschehen
(to) have fun [hæv 'fʌn]	Bye. ~ at the party.	Spaß haben
heavy ['hevi]		schwer
homeless ['həʊmləs]	He lives in the park. He's ~.	obdachlos
item ['aɪtəm]	There are ten ~s on the list.	Ding, Gegenstand
journey ['dʒɜːni]	He has a long ~ to work every morning.	Fahrt
key [kiː]	You can open and lock a door with a ~.	Schlüssel
legal ['liːgl]	It's not ~ to smoke cannabis.	legal
library ['laɪbrəri]	You can read a book in a ~.	Bibliothek
lift (UK) / elevator (US) [lɪft/'eləveɪtə]	I take the ~ to the tenth floor.	Fahrstuhl
(to) mention ['menʃn]	You ~ed a problem in your e-mail.	erwähnen
motorway (UK) / highway (US) ['məʊtəweɪ/'haɪweɪ]		Autobahn
neighbour ['neɪbə]	I live at house number 2. My ~ lives at number 4.	Nachbar
overhead projector [,əʊvəhed prə'jektə]		Tageslichtprojektor
paragraph ['pærəgrɑːf]	The article has five ~s.	Abschnitte
(to) pass [pɑːs]	He ~ed his exam. He was very happy.	bestehen
petrol (UK) / gas (US) ['petrəl/gæs]	How much ~ does your car use?	Benzin
mobile phone (UK) / cell phone (US) ['məʊbaɪl fəʊn/'sel fəʊn]		Mobiltelefon, Handy
plastic ['plæstɪk]	His shoes are not leather they are ~.	Kunststoff
pocket ['pɒkɪt]	Men often have money in their ~s.	Tasche
possible ['pɒsəbl]	It's not ~ to run 100 metres in five seconds.	möglich
purse (UK) [pɜːs]		Geldbörse, Portemonnaie
purse (US) [pɜːs]		Handtasche
(to) raise [reɪz]	She ~d a lot of money for charity.	aufbringen, auftreiben
(to) reach [riːtʃ]	I walked across the road to ~ my house.	erreichen
receipt [rɪ'siːt]	When you pay in a shop you get a ~.	Quittung
(to) recycle [riːˈsaɪkl]		wiederverwenden
(to) reduce [rɪ'djuːs]	Use recycled paper to ~ waste.	verringern, reduzieren
reduction [rɪ'dʌkʃn]	I didn't pay 30 Euro, I paid 20. I got a ~.	Ermäßigung
reply [rɪ'plaɪ]		Erwiderung, Antwort
request [rɪ'kwest]		Anfrage, Wunsch
rubber (UK) / eraser (US) ['rʌbə/ɪ'reɪzə]		Radiergummi
rules [ruːlz]		Regeln
rust [rʌst]	An old car often has a lot of ~ on it.	Rost
salary check ['sæləri tʃek]	The company pays me my ~ every month.	Gehalt
sales [seɪlz]	Shops have ~ at the end of summer.	Schlussverkauf
(to) save money [,seɪv 'mʌni]		(ein)sparen
(to) save [seɪv]		erhalten, retten
(to) sell [sel]		verkaufen
shop (UK) / store (US) [ʃɒp/stɔː]	You buy things in a ~.	Geschäft
(to) shout [ʃaʊt]	Careful! Danger! He ~ed.	schreien
simple ['sɪmpl]	It's not complicated, it's ~.	einfach
so that [ðæt]	You work ~ you can earn money.	damit
soft toys [sɒft 'tɔɪz]	Steiff makes a lot of ~.	Plüschtiere
(to) sound [saʊnd]	That ~s interesting.	klingen
spare parts [,speə 'pɑːts]	I need some ~ for my car.	Ersatzteile
speeding ticket ['spiːdɪŋ ,tɪkɪt]	If you drive at 80 in a town, you get a ~.	Strafzettel wegen überhöhter Geschwindigkeit
stapler ['steɪplə]		Heftgerät
statement ['steɪtmənt]	The minister made a ~.	Erklärung, Stellungnahme
(to) stress [stres]		betonen
strongly ['strɒŋli]	I feel ~ that war is wrong.	stark, energisch, zutiefst
suddenly ['sʌdnli]		plötzlich
(to) support [sə'pɔːt]	He ~s his village football team.	unterstützen
(to) switch off [,swɪtʃ 'ɒf]	When you go out of a room, ~ the light.	ausschalten
tap (UK) / faucet (US) [tæp/'fɔːsɪt]		Wasserhahn
tax [tæks]	We pay a lot of ~ to the government.	Steuer
taxi (UK) / cab (US) ['tæksi/kæb]		Taxi
(to) throw away [,θrəʊ ə'weɪ]		wegwerfen

tidy ['taɪdi]	A teenager's room is never ~.	ordentlich
torch (UK) / flashlight (US) [tɔːtʃ/'flæʃlaɪt]		Taschenlampe
toy [tɔɪ]	Children play with ~s.	Spielzeug
treasure hunt ['treʒə hʌnt]		Schatzsuche
underground (UK) / subway (US) ['ʌndəɡraʊnd/'sʌbweɪ]		U-Bahn
wallet ['wɒlɪt]	You have paper money, receipts etc. in your ~.	Brieftasche
waste [weɪst]		Abfall, Müll
welcome ['welkəm]	~ to Germany. How was the flight?	willkommen
what else? [wɒt 'els]	We need more wine and beer. What else?	Was noch?

Unit 8

accompanied [ə'kʌmpənɪd]	Served with or ~ by.	serviert mit
activists ['æktɪvɪsts]	Greenpeace ~ were at the demonstration.	Aktivisten
(to be) addictive [ə'dɪktɪv]		süchtig machen, zu einer Sucht werden
angry ['æŋgri]	There was a problem and the boss was ~.	wütend, böse
ankle ['æŋkl]	He fell and hurt his ~ so he couldn't walk.	Fußknöchel
annoying [ə'nɔɪŋ]	It's ~, I can't speak to him.	ärgerlich
another time [ə,nʌðə 'taɪm]	I can't come to the party. I'll see you ~.	ein anderes Mal
appointment [ə'pɔɪntmənt]	I have an ~ at the doctor's at ten.	Termin
(to) apologise [ə'pɒlədʒaɪz]		sich entschuldigen
apology [ə'pɒlədʒi]		Entschuldigung
(to) argue ['ɑːgjuː]	The pupil ~d he should get a good mark.	argumentieren
(to) arrest [ə'rest]	The police ~ed the robber.	verhaften
bacon ['beɪkn]	In hotels you usually get a full English breakfast with ~ and eggs.	Speck
beverages ['bevrɪdʒɪz]		Getränke
(to) blow the car horn [bləʊ]	You ~ if there's danger.	hupen
(to) borrow ['bɒrəʊ]		borgen, sich leihen
(to) bother ['bɒðə]	I'm sorry to ~ you, but can you help me?	stören
break-down ['breɪkdaʊn]	His car had a ~ on the motorway.	Panne
carved [kɑːvd]		tranchiert
chain [tʃeɪn]	"Aldi" is a supermarket ~.	Kette
(to) chew [tʃuː]	He has no teeth, he can't ~ his food.	kauen
chicken ['tʃɪkn]		Hähnchen
chop [tʃɒp]	A pork ~, please.	Kotelett
coat [kəʊt]	In winter I wear a ~ outside.	Mantel
(to) cough [kɒf]	He had a cold and a ~.	Husten
crutches ['krʌtʃɪz]	If you break a leg, you walk with ~.	Krücken
dentist ['dentɪst]	A doctor for your teeth is a ~.	Zahnarzt
dog owner ['dɒg ,əʊnə]	People who have a dog are ~s.	Hundebesitzer
evidence ['evɪdəns]	I think he's the robber, but I have no ~.	Beweismaterial
(to) fall [fɔːl]	In summer the price of oil ~s.	fallen
favour ['feɪvə]	Can you do me a ~ and ring the doctor?	Gefallen
flavoured ['fleɪvəd]		mit ...-Geschmack
fruit [fruːt]		Obst
garlic ['gɑːlɪk]	~ smells!	Knoblauch
get well soon [get 'wel 'suːn]	I'm sick. – Oh, I'm sorry. ~	gute Besserung
glasses ['glɑːsɪz]	I can't read the book. I haven't got my ~.	Brille
glazed [gleɪzd]		glasiert
go to court [kɔːt]		vor Gericht gehen
gravy ['greɪvi]	Sauce from meat is ~.	Soße
have to (don't have to) ['hæv tʊ]		(nicht) müssen, verpflichtet sein
hay fever [heɪ 'fiːvə]	If you are allergic to pollen, you have ~.	Heuschnupfen
headline ['hedlaɪn]		Überschrift
health risk ['helθ rɪsk]	Smoking is a ~.	Gesundheitsrisiko
healthy diet [,helθi 'daɪət]		gesunde Ernährungsweise
help yourself [help 'jʊəself]	Please ~ to food and drink.	bedienen Sie sich

(to) hold a conversation [həʊld ə ˌkɒnvəˈseɪʃn]	The music was very loud. We couldn't ~ in the disco.	ein Gespräch führen
I'd rather you didn't [ˈrɑːðə]	Can I open the window? – It's cold. I'd rather you didn't.	lieber nicht
(to) ignore [ɪgˈnɔː]	He didn't speak or help, he ~d me.	ignorieren
ill [ɪl]	He's ~ in hospital.	krank
illegally [ɪˈliːgəli]	He parked his car ~.	illegal
(to) imagine [ɪˈmædʒɪn]	Can you ~ life without a mobile phone?	sich vorstellen
impatient [ɪmˈpeɪʃnt]	You don't like waiting. You are ~.	ungeduldig
(to) improve [ɪmˈpruːv]	With good food his health ~d.	sich verbessern
(to) keep off [kiːp]	He mustn't drink alcohol. He must ~ it.	vermeiden
lawyer [ˈlɔːjə]	He has legal problems. He needs a ~.	Rechtsanwalt
lead [liːd]	The dog is not free. He's on the ~.	Leine
lettuce [ˈletɪs]	~ is green salad.	Kopfsalat
litter [ˈlɪtə]	Empty tins, paper, cigarettes are all ~.	Abfall
(to) lock [lɒk]	I ~ed the door with a key.	abschließen
(to) lose your voice [luːz ... vɔɪs]	When you ~, you can't speak.	Stimme verlieren
main courses [ˌmeɪn ˈkɔːsɪz]		Hauptgerichte
marks [mɑːks]	Did you get good or bad ~ in school?	Noten
meat [miːt]		Fleisch
menu [ˈmenjuː]	What is there to eat? – Look at the ~.	Speisekarte
mess [mes]	The dog made a ~ in the park.	Dreck hinterlassen
(in) moderation [ˌmɒdəˈreɪʃn]		in Maßen
mustn't [ˈmʌsnt]		nicht dürfen
not much [mʌtʃ]	Do you like this? – No, ~.	nicht so sehr
loaf [ləʊf]	You can buy a ~ of bread.	Laib
(to) offer [ˈɒfə]	Can I ~ you something to drink?	anbieten
once [wʌns]	She goes swimming ~ a week.	einmal
pavement [ˈpeɪvmənt]	Cars drive on the road, you walk on the ~.	Bürgersteig
pedestrian [pəˈdestriən]	People who walk and don't drive are ~s.	Fußgänger
physical activity [ˌfɪzəkl ækˈtɪvəti]		körperliche Bewegung
(to) place your order [ˌpleɪs ˈɔːdə]	You ~ for food at the bar.	bestellen
poultry [ˈpəʊltri]		Geflügel
printer ink cartridges [ˌprɪntə ɪŋk ˈkɑːtrɪdʒɪz]		Patronen für Drucker
(to) rely on [rɪˈlaɪ]	I always ~ him to help me.	sich auf jmd. verlassen
reply [rɪˈplaɪ]	I sent the e-mail, but there was no ~.	Antwort
roasts [rəʊsts]		Braten
sad [sæd]	She was ~ because her dog was sick.	traurig
seasoned [ˈsiːznd]	Food with salt and pepper is ~.	gewürzt
serious [ˈsɪəriəs]	He never smiles. He's very ~.	ernst
should (shouldn't) [ʃʊd, ʃʊdnt]		(nicht) sollen
sling [slɪŋ]	If you break an arm, you have it in a ~.	Schlinge
(to) slow down [sləʊ ˈdaʊn]	Car drivers should ~ near a school.	langsamer fahren
smell [smel]	There's a ~ of onions in the kitchen.	Geruch, Duft
(to) spill [spɪl]	Be careful. Don't ~ wine on your skirt.	(ver-)schütten
starters [ˈstɑːtəz]		Vorspeisen
(to) steal [stiːl]	Thieves ~ a lot of cars in big cities.	stehlen
steamed [stiːmd]		gedünstet
(to) take exercise [teɪk ˈeksəsaɪz]	She goes jogging and swimming. She takes exercises.	sich körperlich bewegen
tender [ˈtendə]	Good meat is ~.	zart
treatment [ˈtriːtmənt]	After the accident he had hospital ~s.	Behandlung
truth [truːθ]	He didn't tell the ~. He lied.	Wahrheit
urgently [ˈɜːdʒntli]	There's an accident. We need help ~.	dringend
valid [ˈvælɪd]	You must have a ~ ticket on the bus.	gültig
vegetables [ˈvedʒtəblz]		Gemüse
wedge [wedʒ]	A ~ of bread.	dicke Scheibe Brot
well done [ˌwel ˈdʌn]		gut durchgebraten
whole [həʊl]	The ~ family was there, every member of the family.	ganze
whole grains [həʊl ˈgreɪnz]		Vollkornprodukte
without [wɪˈðaʊt]	You can't live ~ water.	ohne
worry [ˈwʌri]	Don't ~, be happy.	sich Sorgen machen
wrapped [ˈræpt]		eingewickelt

Unit 9

(to) accept [ək'sept]	To say "yes" to an invitation.	annehmen
advantage [əd'vɑ:ntɪdʒ]	One ~ of flying is that it is fast.	Vorteil
afterwards ['ɑ:ftəwədz]	We watched a film and ~ we had a pizza	danach
again [ə'gen]	For one more time. – Again!	noch einmal
(to) agree [ə'gri:]	She ~d to help.	zustimmen
answering machine ['ɑ:nsərɪŋ məʃi:n]	If you phone when we are not in, you can leave a message on our ~.	Anrufbeantworter
appendicitis [ə,pendɪ'saɪtɪs]	He's got a pain in his stomach. It's ~.	Blinddarm-entzündung
(to) attend [ə'tend]	Two hundred people ~ed the wedding.	beiwohnen, besu-chen
beads [bi:dz]		Perlen
(to) be delighted [dɪ'laɪtɪd]	be very happy to	sich freuen
(to) bless [bles]	The priest in church ~ed the couple.	segnen
bride [braɪd]	A woman on her wedding day is the ~.	Braut
by ... -ing [baɪ]	He passed his exam by working hard.	indem
cathedral [kə'θi:drəl]	"Notre Dame" in Paris is a famous ~.	Dom
ceiling ['si:lɪŋ]	The lamp is hanging from the ~.	Decke
(to) celebrate ['seləbreɪt]	We ~d his birthday in a restaurant.	feiern
ceremony ['serəməni]		Zeremonie, Feier
coat [kəʊt]	It's cold. Wear a ~.	Mantel
coconut ['kəʊkənʌt]	You can find ~s on a beach in Hawaii.	Kokosnuss
coin [kɔɪn]	This is a one Euro ~.	Münze
cold [kəʊld]	He is ill. He's got a ~.	Erkältung
(to) collect [kə'lekt]	Can you ~ me from the station?	abholen
congratulations [kən,grætjʊ'leɪʃnz]	~ on winning the race!	Herzlichen Glückwunsch!
(to) connect [kə'nekt]	Can you ~ me to the Marketing Manager?	durchstellen, ver-binden mit
couple ['kʌpl]	Two people who live together.	Paar
customs ['kʌstəmz]		Bräuche
(to) dig [dɪg]	He ~s the garden in spring before he plants the potatoes.	graben, umgraben
disadvantage [,dɪsəd'vɑ:ntɪdʒ]	One ~ of flying is that it is expensive.	Nachteil
disaster [dɪ'zɑ:stə]	It rained and the flower show was a ~.	Unglück, Katastrophe
(to) enjoy [ɪn'dʒɔɪ]	I like playing golf. I ~ this sport.	genießen, gern machen
ever ['evə]	Have you ~ ridden a camel?	jemals
evil ['i:vl]	The opposite of good is ~.	böse
exactly [ɪg'zæktli]	He is ~ two metres tall.	genau
fingers crossed [,fɪŋgəz 'krɒst]	You have your ~ for good luck.	Daumen drücken
floor [flɔ:]	The building has 25 ~s.	Stockwerke
(to) get drunk [get 'drʌŋk]	If you drink ten beers, you will ~.	betrunken werden, sich betrinken
grandchildren ['græntʃɪldrən]	Your children's children are your ~.	Enkelkinder
groom [gru:m]	A man on his wedding day is the ~.	Bräutigam
(to) hold [həʊld]	I'm frightened. – OK, hold my hand.	halten
hospital ['hɒspɪtl]	If you have a car accident, you go to ~.	Krankenhaus
invitation [,ɪnvɪ'teɪʃn]	I have an ~ to his wedding.	Einladung
jewellery ['dʒʊəlri]	Rings and earrings are ~.	Schmuck
lake [leɪk]	He goes fishing in the river and in the ~.	See
lasso [læs'u:]	You catch cows with a ~.	Lasso, Wurfschlinge
(to) let someone know [let ... 'nəʊ]	Please ~ when your train arrives.	informieren, Bescheid geben
(to) look after [lʊk 'ɑ:ftə]	You have to ~ your children.	aufpassen
(to) make a note [meɪk ...'nəʊt]	Write it down. ~ of it.	notieren
(to) mark [mɑ:k]	We had a party to ~ the special day.	markieren, kenn-zeichnen
message ['mesɪdʒ]	Can you give him a ~?	Mitteilung, Nachricht

(to) move [muːv]	He got a new job and ~d to Vienna.	umziehen
necklace ['nekləs]	She's wearing a pearl ~.	Halsband, Halskette
never mind ['nevə ˌmaɪnd]	I'm sorry, I can't come. Never mind!	macht nichts
occasion [ə'keɪʒn]	His birthday was a special ~.	Anlass
pattern ['pætn]		Muster
petals ['petlz]	The flower has red ~s.	Blütenblätter
pretty ['prɪti]	The little girl has beautiful eyes. She's ~.	hübsch
(to) promise ['prɒmɪs]	The children ~d to help in the garden.	versprechen
protection [prə'tekʃn]	A sun hat gives you ~ from the sun.	Schutz
reason ['riːzn]	Why? What's the ~?	Grund
(to) refuse [rɪ'fjuːz]	To say "no" to an invitation.	ablehnen
relatives ['relətɪvz]	Members of your family are your ~.	Verwandte
(to) reply [rɪ'plaɪ]	To answer a letter is "to reply" to it.	antworten
request the pleasure [rɪˌkwest 'pleʒə]	We invite you to the party. We ~ of your company at the party.	... geben sich die Ehre, Sie einzuladen
ribbons ['rɪbnz]	She had coloured ~ in her hair.	Bänder
rosary ['rəʊzəri]	A Catholic will pray in church with a ~.	Rosenkranz
sari ['sɑːri]	A traditional dress in India.	Gewand indischer Frauen
sensible ['sensəbl]	It is ~ to have health insurance on holiday.	vernünftig
separate ['seprət]	The children have ~ rooms. One each.	getrennt
shape [ʃeɪp]	The box is in the ~ of a heart.	Form
(to) share [ʃeə]	Don't eat all the sweets yourself. ~ them.	teilen
ship [ʃɪp]	You can fly to America or go by ~.	Schiff
something soft (a soft drink) ['sʌmθɪŋ sɒft]	I don't drink alcohol. Can I have ~?	ein Getränk ohne Alkohol
(to) sound [saʊnd]	The job ~s good when he talks about it.	klingen
special ['speʃl]	Her fiftieth birthday was a ~ day.	besonderer
speech [spiːtʃ]	The politician is giving a ~ on TV.	Rede
spirits ['spɪrɪts]		Geister
(to) spoil [spɔɪl]	A motorway will ~ the beautiful village.	zerstören, verderben
stain [steɪn]	If you have coffee on your blouse, it ~s.	einen Fleck hinterlassen
suits you ['suːts jʊ]	Blue is a good colour for you. It ~.	steht dir
throughout [θruː'aʊt]	There was silence ~ the concert.	durch, hindurch
(to) tie [taɪ]	She ~d the ribbons.	binden
unfortunately [ʌn'fɔːtʃnətli]	~, he can't come because he's ill.	leider
wealthy ['welθi]	If you have a lot of money, you are ~.	wohlhabend
while [waɪl]	I'll look after the cat ~ he's on holiday.	während

Unit 10

a lot of [lɒt]	A thousand Euros is ~ money.	viel
above [ə'bʌv]	The picture is ~ the table on the wall.	über, oberhalb
advantage [əd'vɑːntɪdʒ]	One ~ of the new flat is that it is big.	Vorteil
(to) afford [ə'fɔːd]	I can't ~ a Ferrari. It's too expensive.	sich leisten
against [ə'genst]	The ladder is ~ the tree.	gegen, direkt am
alarm clock [ə'lɑːmklɒk]	My ~ rings at 5.30 in the morning.	Wecker
already [ɔːl'redi]	It was 6 o'clock and ~ dark.	schon, bereits
armchair ['ɑːmtʃeə]	A comfortable chair is an ~.	Sessel
audience ['ɔːdɪəns]	People who listen to a concert are the ~.	Zuschauer, Zuhörer
average ['ævrɪdʒ]	The ~ age in our group is 30.	Durchschnitts-
(to) be able to ['eɪbl]	He's not ~ speak Russian, he can't speak Russian.	können
(to) behave [bɪ'heɪv]	He was polite. He knew how to ~.	sich benehmen
behind [bɪ'haɪnd]	She stood a few steps ~ her husband.	hinter
between [bɪ'twiːn]	House 6 is ~ 4 an 8.	zwischen
bookcase ['bʊkkeɪs]	I have all my books in a ~.	Bücherschrank
bookshelves ['bʊkʃelvz]	In the book shop there are a lot of ~.	Bücherregale
buffoon [bə'fuːn]	He laughs and jokes a lot. He is a ~.	Clown

calm [kɑːm]	Don't panic. Keep ~!	ruhig
carpet ['kɑːpɪt]	Most people like to have ~s on the floor.	Teppich
championship ['tʃæmpjənʃɪp]	Greece won the football ~ in 2004.	Meisterschaft
(to) choose [tʃuːz]	Cinema, theatre or a disco? You ~.	aussuchen, wählen
comfort ['kʌmfət]	When you are sick you need ~.	Trost
(to) command [kə'mɑːnd]	The general ~ed his troops.	kommandieren
corner ['kɔːnə]	The table has four legs and four ~s.	Ecke
curl [kɜːl]		Locke
curtains ['kɜːtnz]	The ~ at the window are red.	Vorhänge
(to) describe [dɪ'skraɪb]	Can you ~ the robber? Was he tall?	beschreiben
(to) design [dɪ'zaɪn]	Lagerfeld ~s clothes.	entwerfen
desk [desk]	I work at my ~ in the office.	Schreibtisch
destination [ˌdestɪ'neɪʃn]	Majorca is a popular holiday ~.	Ziel
(to) dim [dɪm]	If you ~ the lights, it's romantic.	dämpfen
disadvantage [ˌdɪsəd'vɑːntɪdʒ]	A ~ of the new flat is that it is noisy.	Nachteil
(to) discover [dɪ'skʌvə]	Columbus ~ed America.	entdecken
emptiness ['emptɪnəs]	You feel empty. There is ~ inside you.	Leere
endless stream [ˌendləs 'striːm]	I smoke and never stop. I smoke in an ~.	ununterbrochen
(to) escape [ɪ'skeɪp]	I want to ~ from the stress of work.	entkommen, flie- hen
ever ['evə]	I am ~ open to new ideas.	immer
expert ['ekspɜːt]	He knows a lot about art. He's an ~.	Experte
face [feɪs]	She has big eyes in an oval ~.	Gesicht
fare [feə]	Money you pay on a train or bus is the ~.	Fahrgeld
(to) feel [fiːl]	I ~ ill, I'm going to bed.	sich fühlen
founder ['faʊndə]	Bill Gates is the ~ of Microsoft.	Gründer
freezer ['friːzə]	You keep ice-cream in the ~.	Tiefkühlfach, Kühltruhe
fridge [frɪdʒ]	You keep cheese in the ~.	Kühlschrank
frock [frɒk]	She was wearing a pretty summer ~.	Kleid
(to) frown [fraʊn]	He didn't smile for the photo, he ~ed.	Stirn runzeln
grapes [greɪps]	You make wine from ~.	Weintrauben
(to) grow [grəʊ]	Rice is ~n in China.	anbauen, wachsen
(to) hang around [hæŋ ə'raʊnd]	The homeless men ~ the railway station.	sich aufhalten, (umgangssprach- lich: herum- hängen)
hardly ['hɑːdli]	He spoke quietly. I could ~ hear him.	kaum
however [haʊ'evə]	He ran fast. ~, he didn't win.	jedoch, aber
human beings [hjuːmən 'biːɪŋz]	~ and animals must live together.	Menschen
in front of ['frʌnt]	She stands ~ the mirror every morning.	vor
influence ['ɪnfluəns]	Parents have a lot of ~ on their children.	Einfluss
instead of [ɪn'sted əv]	They gave him money ~ a present.	(an)statt
(to) invent [ɪn'vent]	Edison ~ed electricity.	erfinden
layout ['leɪaʊt]	Is the ~ of your flat good?	(Raum-)Aufteilung, Anordnung
loon [luːn]	He often plays the fool. He's a ~.	(umgangssprach- lich) Blödmann
microwave ['maɪkrəweɪv]	You can cook a quick meal in a ~.	Mikrowelle
mistake [mɪ'steɪk]	He made a lot of ~s in the examination.	Fehler
(to) misunderstand [ˌmɪsʌndə'stænd]	In a foreign language it is easy to ~ people and what they are saying.	missverstehen
moon [muːn]	The ~ shines at night.	Mond
(to) move [muːv]	The family ~d from Geneva to Berne.	umziehen
movies ['muːvɪz]	The American word for "films".	Kinofilm
necessary ['nesəsri]	On a bus it is ~ to have a ticket.	notwendig
object ['ɒbdʒɪkt]	Pens, handbags, guitars are all ~s.	Gegenstände
on the contrary ['kɒntrəri]	He's not stupid. ~, he's very intelligent.	im Gegenteil
on the bum [bʌm]		schnorren
opposite ['ɒpəzɪt]	House 2 is ~ house 1.	gegenüber
on the make [meɪk]		auf Abenteuer aus sein
peaceful ['piːsfʊl]	It was ~ by the lake.	ruhig, friedvoll

pen knife ['pen naɪf]	A knife in your pocket is a ~.	Taschenmesser
(to) predict [prɪ'dɪkt]	It's difficult to ~ the weather in the UK.	vorhersagen
(to) prefer [prɪ'fɜ:]	Tea or coffee? I would ~ tea, please.	vorziehen, lieber mögen
(to) pretend [prɪ'tend]	He's not happy, but he ~s to be.	so tun als ob
(to) produce [prə'dju:s]	Whisky is ~d in Scotland.	produzieren
(to) protect [prə'tekt]	The sun hat ~s you from the sun.	schützen
rectangular [rek'tæŋgjʊlə]	A lot of tables are ~.	viereckig
(to) remind [rɪ'maɪnd]	to make me remember	jmd. an etwas erinnern
rent [rent]	Money you pay for your flat is ~.	Miete
round [raʊnd]	He travelled ~ the world.	um (herum)
same [seɪm]	All the houses were red and white, the ~.	gleich
(to) scream [skri:m]	She was frightened and so she ~ed.	schreien
shape [ʃeɪp]		Form
(to) share [ʃeə]	The girls ~d the sweets between them.	teilen
simple ['sɪmpl]	Fish and chips is a ~ meal.	einfach
so that [səʊ ðət]	I wore my glasses ~ I could read.	damit, so dass
sofa ['səʊfə]	You can sit on a chair or a ~.	Sofa
someone ['sʌmwʌn]	~ knocked at the door. I don't know who.	irgendjemand
(to) spoil [spɔɪl]	The bad weather didn't ~ the holiday.	verderben
square [skweə]	Ritter Sport chocolate is ~.	quadratisch
standard lamp ['stændəd læmp]	A lamp that stands on the floor is a ~.	Stehlampe
(to) stare [steə]	Don't ~ at people like that. It's not polite.	anstarren
storage space ['stɔːrɪdʒ speɪs]	I need a lot of ~ for all my clothes.	Aufbewahrungs- raum
(to) suit [su:t]	When I'm sad I wear blue. It ~s my mood.	passen zu, entspre- chen
suitable ['su:təbl]	A bikini is not ~ for the office.	passend
therefore ['ðeəfɔ:]	He saw an accident. ~ he phoned the police.	daher, deshalb
to the left of [left]		links (davon)
to the right of [raɪt]		rechts (davon)
too [tu:]	He arrived ~ late and missed the train.	zu
(to) turn on [tɜ:n]	He ~ed on the TV.	einschalten
unusual [ʌn'ju:ʒl]	Green is an ~ colour for hair.	ungewöhnlich

Acknowledgements

The authors and publishers are grateful to the following copyright owners for permission to reproduce artwork, photographs, illustrations and texts. It has not been possible to identify the sources of all the material used and in such cases the publishers would welcome information from copyright owners.

Illustrations on pages 24, 44, 56, 76, 93, 105, 106, 110: Martin Guhl, Duillier, Schweiz

Cover: *top:* © gettyimages/Ghislain & Marie David de Lossy; *bottom:* MHV/image100

page 5: *unit 1:* © dpa-Fotoreport/picture-alliance; *unit 2:* MHV/EyeWire; *unit 3:* Sue Morris, Schwindegg; *unit 4:* © Look/Jan Greune

page 6: *unit 5:* © Apple Computer; *unit 6:* © The Madison; *unit 7:* © Photonica/Robert Discalfani; *unit 8:* MHV/PhotoDisc

page 7: *unit 9:* MHV/Stockbyte; *unit 10:* © Softroom

page 8: *Nicole Kidman and Paul Hogan:* © dpa-Fotoreport/picture-alliance; *Cathy Freeman:* © picture-alliance/ASA; *Mel Gibson:* © Picture Press/picture-alliance/Everett Collection/Walt Disney Co.

page 9: see page 8

page 11: zefa/masterfile/Matt Brasier

page 12: *top:* Mauritius/age; *bottom:* Ropi/Mark Henley

page 13: Look/Boris Potschka

page 15: Mauritius/Sammy

page 18: *from left to right:* MHV/EyeWire; MHV/© irisblende.de; MHV/MEV; © bayerische drachen & gleitschirmschule; *bottom:* MHV/EyeWire

page 19: © The Mangum Group

page 20: Ropi/Di Nonno/tamtam

page 21: MHV/MEV (2)

page 22: Alexander Keller, München

page 23: laif/Kirchner

page 25: MHV/PhotoDisc

page 28: Sue Morris, Schwindegg

page 30/31: MHV-Archiv

page 36: © Corbis/Tim Thompson

page 38: *top:* © Look/Jan Greune; *bottom:* MHV/© irisblende.de

page 39: MHV/PhotoDisc (2)

page 40: © "Out of the Darkness" Musik und Text: Todd/Sprackling/Dorney/Male © by BMG Music Publishing LTD* (50%) SVL: Music-Edition Discoton GmbH (BMG Music Publishing Germany) München für Deutschland, Österreich, Schweiz, ehem. Ostblockstaaten, ex. Litauen, Lettland, Estland / Notting Hill Music* (3,5%) / Momentum Music LTD-Universal Music Publishing GmbH* (25%) / WB Music Corp.* (21,50%) *Für Deutschland, Österreich, Schweiz, GUS, osteurop. Staaten (ohne Baltikum), Türkei und Länder des ehem. Jugoslawien: NEUE WELT MUSIKVERLAG GMBH & CO. KG / Tim Dorney Publ.

page 41: *left:* MHV/MEV; *right:* MHV/EyeWire

page 42: © United Features Syndicate Inc./distr. kipka-komiks.de

page 43: *left:* © Du darfst/www.rezept-und-bild.de; *right:* © Ketchum GmbH

page 45: MHV/© irisblende.de

page 46: MHV/MEV

page 48: © Apple Computer

page 49: Cornelia Dietz, Ingolstadt

page 50: *top:* © dpa-Fotoreport/picture-alliance; *bottom:* Mauritius/Stock Image

page 52: MHV/PhotoDisc

page 53: MHV-Archiv

page 54: © www.britainonview.com

page 58: *left:* © The Madison; *middle:* Rambagh Palace Hotel; *right:* Banyan Tree Maldives

page 59: © The Peninsula Hotel Hong Kong

page 60: MHV/MEV

page 61: © Hong Kong Tourism Board

page 62: MHV/MEV (2)

page 66: *top:* © Photonica/Robert Discalfani; *bottom:* MHV-Archiv

page 67: MHV-Archiv

page 69: MHV-Archiv

page 70: MHV/Dynamic Graphics

page 71: © Steiff GmbH

page 78: *1:* MHV/superjuli; *2:* © Mauritius/age fotostock; *3:* MHV/PhotoDisc; *4:* MHV/© irisblende.de; *5:* © f1online/Diaphor/Schuster; *6:* © f1online/Stassen/Schuster; *bottom:* MHV/PhotoDisc

page 79: © f1online/Explorer/Schuster

page 81: © 2000 Oldways Preservation & Exchange Trust

page 82: *top:* MHV-Archiv; *bottom:* MHV/MEV

page 85: © f1online/Alex Bartel

page 88: *left:* Rita Anneser; *middle:* MHV-Archiv; *right:* MHV/Stockbyte

page 89: laif/Piepenburg

page 91: *top:* laif/Celentano

page 96: *top:* © Softroom, London; *bottom:* www.londonperfect.com

page 97/98: © Softroom, London

page 99: Anna Bennett-Long, Puchheim

page 100: "Run for Home" © by Alan Hull Productions LTD. SVL: Musik-Edition Discoton GmbH (BMG Music Publishing Germany) München für Deutschland, Österreich, Schweiz

page 101: © United Features Syndicate Inc./distr. kipka-komiks.de

page 108: MHV/EyeWire

page 111: Rambagh Palace Hotel

page 112: © The Madison

page 116: Banyan Tree Maldives